Rin-Tin-Tin:
The Movie Star

Ann Elwood

Rin-Tin-Tin: The Movie Star. Copyright 2010 Ann Elwood. All rights reserved. Except for fair use, no part of this book may be used or reproduced in any manner whatsoever without written permission from the author.

Cover photograph courtesy Rin-Tin-Tin Collection, Riverside, California.

ISBN: 9-781-453-866658

For Louis

Table of Contents

Preface 1

1: The Legend of the Pilot and the War Puppy 6

2: Duncan the Not-so-Obscure 37

3: The Right Dog at the Right Time 65

4: The Dog of War, the Dog of the West 93

5: Overcoming the Limitations of a Dog Star 107

6: Rin-Tin-Tin, the Magic Actor 125

7: Rin-Tin-Tin Carries Fire 141

8: Rin-Tin-Tin's Last Years and the Career of His Son 163

Filmography 175

Timeline 233

Appendices 245
   Appendix 1: Backgrounds of the Men of the 135th Aero Squadron 246
   Appendix 2: Lee Duncan's Family Trees 248

Sources 249

About the Author 267

Preface: The Wonder Dog

A Movietone News film of 1932 featured four scenes, relatively equal in length: 1) Herbert Hoover, in white pants, pledging reconstruction as he accepted the Republican nomination; 2) the canine star Rin-Tin-Tin performing at an orphanage as a voice-over announced his death; 3) Crown Prince Friedrich Wilhelm of Prussia looking dissolute, smoking a cigarette, and attributing world-wide unemployment to the Treaty of Versailles; 4) Franklin Delano Roosevelt conferring with his running mate, John Garner. It may seem odd to us now that the death of this dog, Rin-Tin-Tin, was considered to be just as important as the machinations of presidential candidates and the opinions of a crown prince. Then it was not viewed as odd. Rin-Tin-Tin was beloved by the millions, and his fame was phenomenal.

Famous people adored Rin-Tin-Tin. Russian director Sergei Eisenstein posed with him, writer Willa Cather was a fan of his, and poet Carl Sandburg reviewed his films. Millions of not-so-famous people adored him, too. When Rin-Tin-Tin died, B.F. Yard of Vandercook, Michigan, a 71-year-old door-to-door salesman who described himself as a plain old man and very poor, wrote a letter to Lee (Leland) Duncan, Rin-Tin-Tin's owner and trainer: "I can never forget the impression made upon me when I sat through his first picture, awed and wishing I had had the great privilege of seeing the picture in its making, patted him and praised him for his work and I believe he could have understood and appreciated my adoration. He was one of God's spiritual Ideas." Children sent him letters by the thousands and received in return his photograph signed with a pawprint. When he went on tour, crowds waited at train stops along the way to give him flowers and ice cream, one of his favorite foods.

Who was this dog to inspire such adoration from so many? Born in France, he was a relatively small German shepherd by modern standards. He ran very fast with a long straight stride, and he leaped effortlessly to great heights. His expressive dark eyes mesmerized audiences, making them even more willing to believe that he understood and was involved in the movie's human story.

A personality in his own right, he played himself in the vast majority of his movies. Long before Lassie, he helped to make animal pictures the rage.

When the North Begins (1923), his breakthrough movie, was a big hit from the beginning, even in big cities. "It caught on like wildfire," said *Variety*. At the

1500-seat Metropolitan theater in Baltimore, an estimated 32,000 people saw it the first week, so it was held over for a second. In San Francisco at the Warfield Theatre, it broke all box office and attendance records.

After *Where the North Begins*, Rin-Tin-Tin played the lead in almost all his movies. Critics commented on his ability to compete with human stars. For example, publicity for *The Lighthouse by the Sea* (1924) said that Rin-Tin-Tin was "the equal, if not the superior, of the human actors, because of his uncanny understanding and portrayal of human emotions." The word "uncanny," applied both to his intelligence and his acting, appeared over and over in movie reviews.

The dog's movie career lasted from 1921 to 1932, a mere eleven years, but that was the great majority, more than three-quarters, of his lifetime. During that time, he acted in twenty-eight full-length movies, several shorts, and two twelve-episode serials. From 1923 to 1930, when he was with Warner Brothers, the studio managed to provide enough diverse roles, star turns in acting and stunts, and character transformations for Rin-Tin-Tin to keep audiences coming back for more. Warner supposedly did not go bankrupt because Rin-Tin-Tin's enormously popular pictures kept it from financial disaster. Yet in spite of all his fame, Rin-Tin-Tin remained humble (at least as publicity would have it). Unlike so many other headline-making Hollywood stars, he did not frequent gin-mills, divorce his wife, act like a prima donna, or demand a larger salary.

Rin-Tin-Tin was not only a movie star. He and Lee Duncan also appeared in acts on stage to promote his movies and as part of vaudeville shows. And he was a radio personality. For interviews on the radio, Duncan asked Rin-Tin-Tin not only to show off his barking repertoire but also to do tricks, relying on the audience's imagination to see them, much as ventriloquist Edgar Bergen relied on the listening audience to envision his dummy, Charlie McCarthy.

Toward the end of his life, Rin-Tin-Tin's career faltered but did not plummet. His movies showed some signs of fading popularity perhaps because of the coming of talkies (but maybe not), the presumed end of interest in Westerns, the inability of movie-makers to introduce anything new into dog pictures, or Rin-Tin-Tin's old age. Or maybe it was just because executives at Warner Brothers thought Rin-Tin-Tin was through. Or maybe it was because what Rin-Tin-Tin represented was no longer as interesting as something else – the powerful child as exemplified by Shirley Temple, for instance.

Preface: The Wonder Dog

We can find intellectual reasons for why it was that Rin-Tin-Tin, a particular dog, achieved such fame at this time in history, the dynamic decade that begins with the World War I and ends with the beginning of the Great Depression. Putting his popularity into historical context demands taking into account the American reaction to the war and the great economic and social change of the 1920s, along with the concomitant desire for law and order; the politics and culture of California and Los Angeles, the increasing popularity of silent movies, and the changes that took place within the movie industry. It demands examining the special ability of a German shepherd to play the role of a melodramatic hero in movies, the reasons why movie-makers wanted to put a dog in that role, and how movie-makers surmounted the limitations of dog-as-hero.

Yet though we can make logical arguments to address the implied questions above, they are never completely satisfying. When we watch Rin-Tin-Tin's old silents, with their corny subtitles and grainy film, the dog captures us in a way that goes beyond intellectual analysis. We find ourselves connecting with him. We cheer him on, empathizing as he strains his whole body prodigiously on his third try to gain access to a second-story window. He can bring tears to our eyes as he pleads for love and acceptance. When we see him slinking on his belly, an obvious dog trick, we still believe what it conveys about his sense of betrayal at being wrongly accused; it brings back those times in our childhood when we too were misjudged. The dog has magic. If it is legerdemain, we don't care.

Most of Rin-Tin-Tin's movies reside in the original cans, in places like the library at the University of California, Los Angeles, locked away from viewers into order to preserve them, even though by now they have perhaps been reduced to dust. Only nine of them (transferred to DVD or VCR format) are available now, but luckily they span the length of his career. They are: *Where the North Begins* (1923), *The Lighthouse by the Sea* (1924), *Clash of the Wolves* (1925), *The Night Cry* (1926), *Hills of Kentucky* (1927), *Tracked by the Police* (1927), *The Show of Shows* (1929, in which he had only a bit part), *The Lone Defender* (1930), and *The Lightning Warrior* (1931).

While we can know Rin-Tin-Tin the actor as we ourselves can see him in his still extant films, the primary story of his life has come from Lee Duncan, and much of it is of questionable veracity. Like the Wizard of Oz, Duncan was a man who hid behind a projection of himself. He created the story of his and Rin-Tin-Tin's life and recorded it in interviews and in a typewritten unpublished manuscript, *Mr Duncan's Notes* (1933). James W. English's book, *The Rin Tin Tin Story* (1949) repeats the *Notes* almost word for word. Neither source is entirely accurate or complete. Moreover, Warner Brothers hype also contributed to the falsehoods about Duncan and Rin-Tin-Tin.

Luckily sources exist from which a more complete and accurate narrative of Rin-Tin-Tin's life and career can be at least partially resurrected. Some of the evidence lies in the voluminous Rin-Tin-Tin Collection at the Riverside (California) Metropolitan Museum and in the production files of Rin-Tin-Tin's movies at the Margaret Herrick Library in Los Angeles. More exists in *Variety*, industry newspapers, and big city and small town newspapers from the 1920s and early 1930s, some of which are available in print form, others electronically on Proquest and Newspaper Archive. With these sources, I have been able to recreate the arc of Rin-Tin-Tin's career and to determine some of the reasons for his enormous success.

To correct the story of Duncan's life, I have used contemporary primary sources, census records, and histories of the places he and his parents and grandparents lived. For instance, the Fallbrook Historical Society in Southern California contains papers concerning his maternal relatives, and from those I was able to trace part of his genealogy. I have unearthed from the federal census a living father (Duncan implied he died) and a stepfather and half-sister Duncan never mentioned. Newspaper stories reveal a marriage and divorce that were expunged from all his own records. For Duncan's military career, I consulted histories of the 135th Aero Squadron, general histories of World War I, and Duncan's enlistment and discharge papers.

Once having collected all the material, I was in a quandary about how to present Rin-Tin-Tin's biography in an interesting and relevant way. I did not want to try to cover all details. Certainly, writing the story of Rin-Tin-Tin's career movie by movie would have involved too much tedious repetition. I finally decided to tell the story of Rin-Tin-Tin's birth and life up to his breakthrough movie, *Where the North Begins*, in two analytical but narrative chapters; then to cover his movie career in five thematic chapters addressing why the time was right in the 1920s for a German shepherd movie star, the meaning of his roles in Westerns, the significance of a male *canine* hero, the extent of Rin-Tin-Tin's acting and athletic abilities, and the realities of his training and temperament. A chapter on his death and the career of his son, Rin-Tin-Tin Jr., ends the story. For these chapters, I also consulted books and magazines of the time, as well as historical monographs. Synopses, cast lists, and reviews of Rin-Tin-Tin's movies have been relegated to a filmography at the end of the book.

I cannot begin to express adequately my gratitude to all the people who helped me with this book: Kevin Hallaran, archivist at the Rin-Tin-Tin Collection in Riverside, who gave me invaluable help; George Ellison, Special Collections, Glendale Public Library; the staff at the Margaret Herrick Library, Academy of Motion Picture Arts and Sciences; expert dog trainer Jt Clough (she uses initials for her first name and middle name), who analyzed *The Night Cry* with me; the history department at University of California, San Diego, where I am a visiting scholar; my colleagues in the history department at California State University, San Marcos, especially Jeff Charles, Anne Lombard, Patty Seleski, Kim Quinney, and Jill Watts; California State University, San Marcos's Faculty Center; Lezlie Lee-French; the members of my writers' group, Mary Lou Locke, Abigail Padgett, and Janice Steinberg, who read the manuscript and gave me invaluable advice; Daphne Hereford, who provided me with information about Rin-Tin-Tin; Susan Orlean, who has graciously communicated with me about our mutual interest in Rin-Tin-Tin; videographer Tahna Edwards; the friends who listened to me talk at such great length about the project and who critiqued chapters: Neil Brooks, Rahul Deshpande, Bill Gaupsas, Aline Hornaday, Carol Orsag Madigan, Robin and Mike Pratt, Nigel Quinney, Hillel Schwartz, Joe Selig, Diane Shepard, and Linda Wood.

My deep emotional commitment to this book arises, I am aware, from the world in which I live, which is to say that I am not the only one with interest in the subject of dogs as they have been affected by human culture. But I have a more personal inspiration: my beloved dog, Louis, a German shepherd.

I hope to do honor to Rin-Tin-Tin by telling his story as truly as I can, by putting him in the context of his time, and by trying to get at some answers to the questions: Why did this particular dog become such a beloved celebrity, and what was he really like? We start with his birth during World War I.

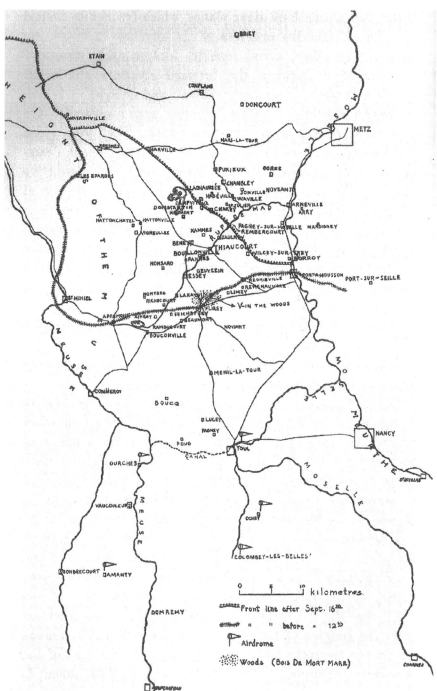

The Battle of St. Mihiel (from Percival Gray Hart, *History of the 135th Aero Squadron*).

1
The Legend of the Pilot and the War Puppy

Here follows the predominant story, repeated up until now as true, that Lee Duncan told about Rin-Tin-Tin's puppyhood in his manuscript Mr Duncan's Notes. *It includes some detail from other sources. I question its truth later in the chapter.*

The scene is the battle of St. Mihiel, a precursor of the Meuse-Argonne offensive. It is mid-September 1918, roughly two months before the Armistice. The officers (pilots and observers) and enlisted men of the 135th Aero Squadron are stationed at Ourches, about twenty kilometers from the front lines. Set in rolling hills and fronting on the Meuse River, Ourches is home to about fifteen families and their cows. The airfield there, active since the beginning of the war, once housed the famous Lafayette Escadrille.

Rain comes the night before the battle, bringing with it high winds and low clouds. It is not good flying weather – or trench-warfare weather, either, for that matter. By the end of the first day of the battle, September 12, 1918, the contested space between American and German lines has become a muddy hell. In the empty air above the mass carnage, Lawrence Smart, a pilot of the 135th, looks down on the scene with amazement:

> The land looked like some of the pictures I remembered seeing in *Dante's Inferno*: splintered trees, men moving out of trenches, walking, running, and crawling, behind a well-placed barrage; towns and villages knocked out and burning; roads on our sides of the lines choked up with men and artillery. There didn't seem to be a level spot left on the ground – it was either pockmarked with shell holes by the thousands, or cut by trenches in a crazy, zigzag fashion. There was no sign of vegetation or life, except for the men and their war machines.

That same day, Henry Sheets, a squadron observer, takes a walk into the trenches from Flirey, a town on the font line's edge, and writes in his diary:

Never have I seen a more gruesome sight. Never have I felt such absolute solitude as I felt out there in the drenching rain, in that slimy mud, miles, it seemed, from any living human being, but completely surrounded by many, many dead with their mud stained gray-black faces, with their hair and clothing streaked with mud and blood, with their glassy eyes staring straight forward into space, with their bodies in all sorts of grotesque poses – partly supported in a semi-sitting posture by barbed wire or lying in the mud, face up, staring ahead, with that horrible vacant stare, at the rain soaked sky. The sound of hand-to-hand fighting, which finally seemed only a short distance away, was even a relief, a relief to know that there were actually living people within earshot. [He starts back to Flirey, wanting to run, but not doing so.] There were too many dead, too much mud, too many shell holes, too much wire, too much desolation.

Three days later, the battle over, Lee Duncan goes to this silent, cratered No-Man's Land with a patrol led by Captain George Bryant of the 90th Aero Squadron. The patrol's official mission is to check on an abandoned and largely destroyed German airfield at Flirey, but the men also hope to find souvenirs. Later, officer Percival Hart noted that they found clothing, letters, reports, and books and that he himself scored "a large gilded eagle from an officer's helmet." In a ruined dugout that Duncan thinks "might have been a headquarters" for trained war dogs, Duncan finds two *live* souvenirs – carrier pigeons trapped in a wicker basket strapped to the back of a dead dog. Then he hears whimpering. He searches for and finds the source: five puppies with their mother, a German shepherd, lying in a burrow that, "very much like a wolf," she has crawled into. Duncan is only twenty-four. If he has anything like the same sensibility as Harry Sheets, he is shocked by his first experience of full-on war, so to find innocent living things in such a place is probably a consolation and delight. Weak and hungry, the mother greets Duncan with defiance and bars him from her young. Perhaps it is her training as a war dog that makes her react this way, or perhaps it is the experience of giving birth terrified by screaming shells and earsplitting explosions. But Duncan is not concerned with her, except as a hindrance. He wants to get at the huddled puppies, so young their eyes are still closed, so after a "hard struggle," he subdues her and picks up the puppies.

He has met Rin-Tin-Tin.

Back at headquarters, Captain Bryant pulls some strings so that Duncan can keep two of the puppies as his own. Duncan chooses a male and a female who have similar markings. Bryant keeps the mother, whom he names Betty, and gives the other three puppies, all males, to his friends; none of those dogs reaches the United States.

Duncan names the puppies Rin-Tin-Tin and Nanette, after the small yarn dolls French girls give their soldier boyfriends to wear dangling from their caps or the shoulder straps of their guns. According to Duncan, the dolls stand for two young lovers, who were the only people to escape a shelter in Paris during a bombing. (Another version of this story, which appeared in a 1925 issue of *The Literary Digest*, puts the lovers, "sweethearts, who had clung together in the hope that their love would save them," in a village, not Paris.) That very day, Duncan buys a pair of the dolls from a little French girl, who tells him the story "in broken English." Later in life, he always wore a pair of gold-and-cloissonne charms of Rin-Tin-Tin and Nanette on his watch chain. Incidentally, the name "Rin-Tin-Tin," not a French name like Pierre or François, probably originated as a drummer boy's nickname, an imitation of a drumbeat, like "rat-a-tat-tat." It appears, for example, in the refrain for 1817 bawdy war song, "La Vivandière," by P. J. Béranger.

At the base, Duncan makes a den for the mother and puppies in a straw-filled oil drum and puts it in a corner of a hangar. Only after three days of going hungry does the mother come out of the den and eat some chopped horse meat. The puppies' eyes open six days after they were found.

Within the first three weeks after Duncan finds the puppies, the weather turns cold and it begins to snow, so he fashions a shelter made from a pup tent spread over poles that he scavenges from a farm where hops for making beer are grown. He also heats up stones with a blowtorch, puts them in tin cans, and wraps the cans in sacks to create makeshift heaters for the puppies. He moves from his barracks into the hangar so that he can reheat the stones at night and pays an aviation mechanic to keep the stones and puppies warm while he is flying "over the lines." An enlisted man, he has been recently (before the battle) elevated to flying status and given a fifty percent pay raise after removing a dead observer from the rear cockpit of a downed plane.

While Duncan is rigging up tents and heaters for the puppies, the pilots and observers of the squadron are creating their own story – of flying dangerous missions to take pictures of the Hindenburg Line, of relaxing at headquarters by reciting literature and playing the piano, of drinking and pursuing nurses. Traveling around in a Cadillac driven by a chauffeur, narrowly missed by German shells, the officers court those nurses and dine at the city of Nancy's Stanislaus (probably the historic Hotel Stanislaus). At least one night they stay out until two a.m. They say little else about the elegant city, once the headquarters of a duke, but in 1918 famous for Art Nouveau (School of Nancy). If they see the rabbit-warren medieval quarter, the square with its fancy gold gates, the barges on the tranquil river, the green parks – or the results of German shelling – they don't mention them. It's all about booze and conquest.

The enlisted men, too, carouse with enthusiasm. *Their* short history in *A Brief History of the 135th Aero Squadron* is a spoof in which war provides the metaphor for drinking alcohol and seducing women: "As to the rest of us . . . we have learned to fly as well by night as by day and no few of us prefer the night flying. . . . One man alone and single handed has been known to capture as high as fourteen Mademoiselles and still return with a belt full of ammunition, and always have shown a high degree of courage and skill in outwitting them."

On September 29, the squadron moves to their new headquarters at Gengoult Field in Toul, a medieval city, protected by hills to the east, that lies between the Moselle River and a canal. The officers occupy the city's stone houses, eat and drink in its cafes, and go to dances. They continue to fly over enemy lines.

Even though Bryant says Duncan can leave the puppies with their mother, who stays with Bryant back at Columbey-les-Belles, an airfield 15 kilometers (between nine and ten miles) from Toul, Duncan takes the two puppies with him. He doesn't think anyone else will care for them as he does, and he is already so attached to them that he can't tolerate the idea of being separated from them. From a mess sergeant, he buys eight cans of milk, worth about 40 cents, at the exorbitant price of 100 francs (about twenty dollars), and he dips the puppies' noses into a pie pan of the milk to try to teach them to drink it. They are only about three weeks old and not adept enough at lapping to get enough nourishment, so, until October 3rd (four days after the move), they are flown back to be nursed by their mother at Columbey-les-Belles. After that, Duncan feeds them with canned milk and water mixed with hardtack biscuits he grinds by rolling a wine bottle over them -- and oatmeal (if he can get it).

Some of the men object to the noise the puppies make, so Duncan objects to *them*, saying they can come in "any hour in the morning" and think they can make noise with impunity, but if one of his puppies makes noise he is "threatened with his life." He is vigilant about their welfare, making sure that no one hurts them. When he has to fly a plane, he leaves them with the few "boys" he can trust.

In his time on the ground, when he doesn't go "over the lines," he often plays with his puppies, using a rubber doll that has a squeaker in it. When he hangs the doll on a string over their heads, the puppies approach it "very much the same as a baby with a rattle." He teaches them commands like "come" and "heel." Finding his puppies more and more interesting (and he always calls them "his"), he spends more and more time with them. It takes his mind off what's happening – men dying from bullets, plane crashes, or the Spanish influenza epidemic, "every day . . . some close buddy taken away."

At one point during the six weeks or so before the Armistice on November 11, 1918, Duncan meets with an English-speaking German prisoner who tells him that his father raised and trained German shepherds for police and war work (outpost night guard duty) at the kennel near Flirey where Duncan found Rin-Tin-Tin and Nanette. The German thinks he knows Rin-Tin-Tin's mother from Duncan's description.

It is about this time that Duncan becomes interested in the wartime work of dogs, especially Red Cross dogs. He compares dogs' strength and versatility to those of horses – how much they can haul, how fast they can move, how well they can swim.

His interest in wartime life extends to the French people he comes in contact with, but he is more observer than participant. He sees that women are replacing the labor of men gone to war. In the fields, they sing while they work. They go to church dressed in "gay colored dresses and sunbonnets." Some of them are skilled in needlework and make handkerchiefs for soldiers. One of the passages in his *Notes* (1933), hazed with sentimentality after fifteen years, reads: "It was often that we saw the old grandmother sitting in the shade of her little stone house busy working with her needle while all around her would be the old family rooster and half-dozen hens. Just a sweet picture hard to forget."

Sometime after September 29, William Collier, an enlisted man from Fresno, California, is put on flying status – he and Duncan are now "the only two enlisted men of our squadron to have this good break." They are "going over the lines every day now."

Later, on November 3, a formation of eleven planes leaves the base to bomb Chambley, a German airbase near Metz. One plane is piloted by Collier with Duncan as his observer/gunner. During this mission, Duncan, "while engaged in aerial combat," is wounded in the elbow joint. His arm goes numb, and he is at risk of blood poisoning.

Duncan is sent to the hospital at Menil la Tour, a few miles from the base. While he is in his hospital bed, some friends watch out for the puppies, who stay in a box in the hospital's tool shed until after he is able to walk outside. The loud sounds of big guns and plane engines don't bother them – it's something they grew up with. Twice a day they entertain the wounded by doing "cute little things" like pulling the finger out of a glove, which "cause the boys to forget their pain."

Duncan is at the hospital on November 11, when the armistice is signed. Otto E. Sandman takes over as commanding officer around December 1st. It will be almost six months before the squadron is sent back to the United States. After Duncan leaves the hospital, he starts spending nights in old barns in order to follow orders to keep the puppies away from the rest of the squadron. They are at the age where they can be irritating. Alone with them, he studies their behavior and teaches them. Nanette is the smarter of the two, first to "sit up for her doll and to speak."

Sometimes when Duncan is walking the puppies, they come upon the men having a football game. The puppies see the ball and take off after it, ending up in the middle of a scrum before Duncan can catch them. They keep on playing, even if they are limping. He complains that it is fun for the puppies but hard on him; often he is told to keep them away.

His attachment to the puppies is paramount. When he is awarded nine days leave for Paris, he goes only for nine hours. He is saving his money to pay for the puppies' passage to the United States. He spends some time in nearby Nancy, but says little about it.

However, it's not as if Duncan is cut off entirely from humankind, but it is as if he is at an emotional remove. He sympathizes with the French who have come home to find a pile of stones where their house had been – and even the old public drinking fountain gone. He says the soldiers, although themselves on short rations, give the French people, especially the little children, whatever food they can. He takes the puppies to say good-bye to his laundress, who, her husband having died, continues to live in an abandoned chateau with most of its walls destroyed. (The chateau's glass conservatory still stands even though one end has been blown away.) He has watched the laundress put the soldiers' clothes in a wheelbarrow and take them to the river to wash them with a wooden paddle. The Americans admire her for staying put in the middle of a war. She gives Duncan two flintlock dueling pistols more than 100 years old, and an egg laid by one of her chickens. He pays his last laundry bill with all the money he has ($3.50). She has tears in her eyes when she says farewell to the puppies "with the hope that they would go safely through the war and reach America some day."

The men of the squadron leave Toul for the west coast of France about February 1. By spring of 1919, they are in Bordeaux enduring final physical examinations and delousing. On April 25, the day their ship, the *Huron*, is to depart, Duncan discovers that he cannot take the puppies with him unless he can get official permission. When he goes to see Major Kneass, the officer in charge of the remount station, an orderly tells him the major is too busy selling the Army's mules and horses to deal with Duncan's problem. He suggests that Duncan try to arrange for a sailor to smuggle the puppies on board in his duffle bag, but he says that if the puppies are found, the ship's captain can order them thrown overboard. Duncan is unwilling to risk that. In the end Otto Sandman, Duncan's commanding officer, persuades Kneass to allow the pups on board.

The ship's carpenter builds a kennel for the puppies, and every day of their fifteen-day journey, Duncan takes them on deck for exercise, even though the deck is sometimes sloshing with sea water. Nanette becomes ill with "a bad one

[cold]," which may be the first signs of the distemper that will kill her shortly after their arrival in the United States. Duncan treats her with castor oil the ship's doctor gives him. On the day they are to land, Duncan leaves the puppies below in their kennel and goes to join the troops celebrating their homecoming on deck. When he goes back down to check on the puppies, he sees that the door to the kennel is open and Rin-Tin-Tin is gone. Panicked, he envisions Rin-Tin-Tin's feelings: "what he must be thinking of me for leaving him." He fears that Rin-Tin-Tin might have been thrown overboard and asks himself why "they" didn't "put him out of [his] misery" before doing that. He is "just about mad and half sick" when one of the sailors brings the puppy back after finding him three decks below inside a ventilator pipe.

The *Huron* arrives in New York on May 6, 1919. When Duncan brings the puppies from the ship to the shore, he feels them "straining at the end of their new leads." He interprets their anxiety as arising from differences they perceive between the sound of big guns and the sound of crowds and music, and between the sight of "red flashes across the sky" (from being "born under fire") and strange faces and strange dress – "things happening so fast they could not grasp it." He talks to them, which seems to calm them down. His identification with them is so strong that he thinks he knows what they are feeling, and one suspects it is as much about his own emotions as it is about theirs.

That is the second – and lasting – legend of Rin-Tin-Tin's puppyhood. It is the story that Duncan told in the manuscript he wrote, dated June 21, 1933, and that is retold with some additions in James W. English's *The Rin-Tin-Tin Story* (1949). It is also the story repeated in studio publicity throughout Rin-Tin-Tin's career. I question its truth.

How much do we know to be absolutely true about Duncan and Rin-Tin-Tin? We know from Duncan's discharge papers that from November 1, 1917 to May 26, 1919 he served in World War I as a gunnery corporal with the 135th Aero Squadron; we know that he was wounded (Purple Heart) and was involved in the battle of St. Mihiel (World War I Victory Medal with St. Mihiel battle clasp). His name is in the list of the wounded in *A Brief History of the 135th Aero Squadron* and in that of the squadron's enlisted personnel in other histories.

The Legend of the Pilot and the War Puppy

We know that Rin-Tin-Tin was born in France. Yet evidence suggests that he was born much later than mid-September 1918.

Both Percival Hart and Lawrence Smart, officers in the 135th Aero Squadron, remembered Rin-Tin-Tin, admittedly after the fact (Hart in a book published in 1939, Smart in one published in 1968). Their stories differ significantly from the legend concocted by Duncan. Hart says: "About this time [September 16, 1918] an incident occurred which later led to a certain amount of vicarious fame for the Squadron. Corporal Lee Duncan found on the old battlefield a black German shepherd dog grieving by the grave of his dead master and brought him back to the field. He was bred to a French shepherd dog, and one of the puppies was the famous Rin-Tin-Tin." Smart tells approximately the same story. In Hart's squadron history, Frederic Lovenberg adds more detail about the puppies' time in France after the Armistice: "While we marked time at Tresses [a town close to Bordeaux] our two little German police puppies grew apace. Their father had been a souvenir of the St. Mihiel drive, being picked up at Thiaucourt [about 10 kilometers deeper into former German territory than Flirey] about September 15."

The officers also remember Duncan flying as observer with Collier on November 3, but that's all they have to say about him.

On September 21, 1960, Otto Sandman, Duncan's commanding officer, wrote a letter of condolence to the newly widowed Eva Duncan, in which he first expressed his admiration for Duncan, then reminisced about the puppies:

> I first met him [Duncan] when I took command of the 135th Aero Squadron in France in 1918 and well remember the German police dog which he brought back to the Squadron area.
>
> Then when the pups were born in Toul how he cared for them in a cold hangar that snowy winter, the difficulties he had in getting them proper nourishment, the train trip in the 40 & 8 box cars to Bordeaux, the resistance he met from the men in the Squadron due to the disturbances created nightly by the pups, how he moved them and himself to a cow barn away from the men during our three month stay at Tresses, the impasse at the

>Port of Embarkation toward Army personnel bringing animals home to the states and the fortunate situation in that an old friend of mine happened to be Port Executive, the trip home, the arrival at Roosevelt Field on Long Island, the sickness and passing of Nanette, and then the eventual developments at Lankershim [where Duncan lived for a while] and Hollywood.

Of course, there is at least one problem with Sandman's recollection as revealed in this letter. How could Sandman remember that Rin-Tin-Tin's father was a dog found on the battlefield after the Battle of St. Mihiel in mid-September 1918? Official records show that he did not take over the command until December.

That's all any of the officers has to say about Rin-Tin-Tin. According to them, Rin-Tin-Tin was not born on the battlefield, but was the result of a mating between a grown dog found on the battlefield with a female shepherd dog.

Though the story the officers tell of Rin-Tin-Tin's birth differs from Duncan's legend of finding puppies in an abandoned kennel in mid-September, it follows, in its broad outlines, the *first* recorded story I can find that Duncan himself told about the origins of Rin-Tin-Tin, in a *Los Angeles Times* article published in October 1919, only about six months after Duncan and Rin-Tin-Tin arrived back in the United States and just a few years before Rin-Tin-Tin began his movie career. Evidently, by that time, Duncan had trained Rin-Tin-Tin so well in "war and police work" that he was able to exhibit him at a dog show held in connection with the Los Angeles Live-Stock Show at Exposition Park from October 18 to 26. The article describes Rin-Tin-Tin as "a German military dog that was brought to Los Angeles from France by Lieut. L. Duncan." It goes on to say that at Thiaucourt Duncan and six other men found Fritz, a wounded war dog (named later?), lying next to the bodies of eleven other dogs "killed by an exploding shell and that they took the live dog to camp, made him a mascot; and mated him with "a war prisoner" female that Captain Bryant (of the Second Army Air Service) captured in Belgium. Rin-Tin-Tin was the result – a war orphan with a "heroic ancestry" and "thrilling puppyhood."

The Legend of the Pilot and the War Puppy

In August 1922, the *Oakland Tribune* ran essentially the same story – that Duncan captured the father, now a "famed police dog" in the trenches along the Hindenburg Line at the battle of St. Mihiel and that Rin-Tin-Tin was his son. Another from October of that year says that Rin-Tin-Tin himself was the adult dog found on the battlefield: "This clever dog was found wounded on a battlefield, during the war, by Mr. Duncan, who treated the animal's wounds and brought him back to America as a 'souvenir.'" Still another, probably a studio release, which ran from September 1923 through December 1924, identifies two adult dogs, captured from the Germans, as Rin-Tin-Tin's parents.

In the most fanciful of Duncan's 1920s stories, he was an officer and an aviator, and Rin-Tin-Tin flew with him. For example, a 1926 article in *Collier's* had it that Rin-Tin-Tin, born as "shells whistled and spat red death over the western front," went with Duncan on thirty-six flying missions, "one for a record duration of more than four hours under fire."

For Duncan, the story of a grown dog found on the battlefield as father of Rin-Tin-Tin must have presented a time problem that he became aware of only after the fact. Gestation in dogs is fifty-eight to sixty-five days. Even if Fritz had been mated to a female as early as mid-September (which is very unlikely, given his wounds and his probable sorrow over the death of his master), the puppies could not have been born until mid-November, shortly before the Armistice. Rin-Tin-Tin could hardly have had a "thrilling puppyhood" in wartime, let alone have been a "military dog."

It is not until summer of 1923, the year that Rin-Tin-Tin's first hit movie, *Where the North Begins,* came out, that the story of the puppies found on the battlefield (or No Man's Land) right after the battle of St. Mihiel begins to appear in publicity. Sometimes the stories say Rin-Tin-Tin was alone, other times with the rest of his litter (ranging in number from four to six), and with or without their mother. For a while that story ran parallel with the earlier one(s).

The story has variations, some of them far-fetched: e.g., that a German soldier had probably taken the puppies, "pure-blooded Belgian police dogs with skinny ratlike bodies and long black noses," from an Alsatian farm, then left them in a dugout, where Americans found them, "whimpering with hunger." But how could a soldier on the move carry a litter of puppies with him and how could the Allied troops know that the puppies were pure-blooded?

In his 1933 manuscript, Duncan bolstered the credibility of his story by saying that he knew precisely when the puppies were born and that it was in the midst of the battle of St. Mihiel. His evidence rested on when he said they opened their eyes, six days after he found them on September 15 or 16, which would mean that they were born three days before. He was wrong – puppies open their eyes when they are twelve to thirteen days old, not nine days, which would mean, given that they opened their eyes when he said they did, that they were born *before* the battle, not in the thick of it. On the other hand, by that time, he had stopped saying that Rin-Tin-Tin flew with him on missions.

Why else do I think Duncan's legend of finding Rin-Tin-Tin as a puppy is false, besides the facts that the officers of the 135th told a different one and that his first tale is close to theirs? It has to do with weather and with Duncan's motives, both conscious and unconscious.

In Duncan's manuscript and in English's book, right after finding the puppies in mid-September, Duncan went to great lengths to keep them warm in very bad weather. According to him it was snowing, something that would have been extremely unusual at that time in that part of Europe. Officers Hart and Smart made no mention of snow in September, though the subject of weather came up often: It rained, sometimes poured; it was foggy. Hart said of September 27, "Summer was departing, and Fall was in the air, bringing in its train cold nights and raw cloudy days." One imagines that if there had been snow, the officers who contributed to Hart's squadron history, particularly Lieutenant Roy L. Peck, who kept a diary, would have remarked on it. No mention was made of snow during October and November in Smart's book either, though plenty was said about fog and rain. And other servicemen, not of the 135th, but who served in nearby places and wrote frequent letters or kept diaries, mention no snow in September and October of 1918. For example, William Schira, who was stationed in Langres, north of St. Mihiel, wrote in his diary on November 19, "It snowed today. The first snow I've seen this year." On November 18, Paul B. Hendrickson, a bugler in the Army's 33rd Division, who had been stationed that fall and winter at various places within 100 miles northwest of Nancy, wrote, "First snow fell this evening." Snoden L. Vance, who had been in St. Mihiel, wrote on December 3, when he was in Germany, "[I]t is pretty cold here but there has been no snow at all."

The Legend of the Pilot and the War Puppy

Further evidence rests in a fragment of a photograph, probably from an official squadron photograph, that shows two puppies with a group of soldiers. (The fragment is reproduced at http://www.rintintin.com/story.htm). In it, Duncan, a handsome man with close-set eyes and a wide smile, sits with a flop-eared puppy, the darker of the two, between his ankles. The puppy leans against one of his legs, his paws hanging over it. He must want to be there – Duncan is not holding him. Next to Duncan is a soldier with another, lighter-colored puppy, whose ears are erect. Who are the puppies? I see no reason not to believe that the darker-colored one with Duncan is Rin-Tin-Tin and the other is Nanette. German shepherd puppies' ears start standing up when they are five to six months old, so they are probably around that age. And that is why the photograph is significant.

I have been unable to locate the entire photograph. A smaller fragment, reproduced below, unfortunately does not include Nanette.

Fragment of a 135th Aero Squadron photograph (*Life*, October 20, 1958, 69, uncredited).

While I cannot prove it definitively, I think the the photograph was taken after the squadron returned to the United States, in May, 1919. My evidence is anecdotal. In a search for dates of World War I squadron photographs, I found two references that indicate it was the practice to take squadron photographs after coming back to the United States: one by John Frye who says he has a "photo of [his father's] squadron on return from France," and the other by Arnie Reischl about a squadron photograph with a notation on the back: "493d Aero squadron left America Nov 22, 1917. Arrived France Dec 13, 1917. Left France Dec 13, 1918, Arrived America Jan 21, 1919." Both are from the Aerodrome Forum website. If I am right, the puppies were about five or six months old when the photo was taken in May, and therefore had been born in December or January.)

This brings us to more important questions: Why did Duncan play with the truth? Why does the legend of finding Rin-Tin-Tin as a puppy abandoned by his human caretakers in September of 1918 better suit his purposes than the story that Rin-Tin-Tin was the son of a dog found in the trenches at that same time? I think Duncan moved the date of Rin-Tin-Tin's birth back three months and changed its circumstances in order to make assertions about Rin-Tin-Tin's breeding and to present him as a survivor of the war, whose experience of it paralleled Duncan's story about his own. More, his story of finding the puppies, abandoned by German soldiers, nurtured only by their mother, resonates with the truth of Duncan's own abandonment as a child

The legend of finding Rin-Tin-Tin in a bombed-out kennel gave Duncan a better chance of presenting Rin-Tin-Tin as a pedigreed German shepherd than did the one of finding an adult dog on the blank expanse of a battlefield. The detail of the kennel lent credence to his claim that he tracked down a German prisoner who knew something about the kennel and therefore Rin-Tin-Tin's parentage. How could he establish anything about the past of a lone adult dog with no connection to a place or person? Also Rin-Tin-Tin's mother in the first story is either a dog "captured" by Bryant or a "French shepherd dog" – in either case, a known pedigree appears to be unlikely.

Duncan could have played up the mysteries of Rin-Tin-Tin's origins, but instead tried hard, after the dog became famous, to unearth his parentage to prove that he was a canine aristocrat. That was not true at first. When he exhibited Rin-Tin-Tin at the Los Angeles dog show in 1919 and against three years later at the German Shepherd Club show in 1922, it was mainly as a competitor in jumping and other skills. The 1922 show was "unsanctioned," according to the Rin-Tin-Tin web page. A *Los Angeles Times* story about the Shepherd Dog Club show in February 1924 noted that "any shepherd dog may be entered. It is not necessary that the dog be registered [with the American Kennel Club] in order to compete . . . . Many people own dogs which would point up high in a contest but which have not been registered, according to officials of the club." Duncan said Rin-Tin-Tin made up in the field for any lack of "ring technique." Rin-Tin-Tin didn't look like a show dog, said "Fred," in a 1925 *Variety* review: "He isn't a dog that would ever get a thing in the show-ring, being short in body and a little low. . ."

After describing the puppy's supposed discovery in a dug out, a 1924 *Los Angeles Times* story says: "Screaming shells were music to his [Rin-Tin-Tin's] ears . . . He never thought of danger. His job was to go through and carry aid to the wounded men out there in their hell-holes. Hops through the clouds in a roaring plane became an everyday occurrence." In three sentences, this sums up a good deal of what Duncan wanted the world to believe early on: both that Rin-Tin-Tin was a war dog hero and that he had flown with Duncan in wartime. Even in the October 1919 story, before Rin-Tin-Tin became a movie actor, Duncan was presenting him as a "military dog," who had experienced the war. Though by 1933 Duncan no longer claimed that Rin-Tin-Tin had been a war dog or had flown missions with him, Rin-Tin-Tin was often featured in his movies as a Red Cross dog. (See "4: The Dog of War, the Dog of the West.")

I think there is an even deeper reason for the fabrication of the puppy-on-the-battlefield story: finding Rin-Tin-Tin and his sister as puppies abandoned by all but their mother resonated with his own life. Instead of bonding with his mates, Duncan focused on the puppies. The puppies were his alone. They were the center of his life, and he created an invisible barrier around them. He fed them, played with them, trained them. When he talked about other men in the 135th and their relationship to Rin-Tin-Tin, it was mainly about their complaints – having puppies around, getting in the way of a football game, and making noise – or it is about his enlisting their help in caring for them while he has to be away. And even if he does entrust the puppies to a fellow enlisted man when necessary, he gives up a trip to Paris after the war because he can't trust his dogs "for such a long time with anyone else." Above all, I think that Duncan saw himself as a parent figure and that he threw himself into this role because of his loneliness. He cared for his puppies like a mother.

In a paragraph about the trip home, Duncan called the puppies his "little war orphans" and said, "You see, besides having two very smart, interesting puppies, they meant more to me than that. I felt there was something about their lives that reminded me of my own life. They had crept right into a lonesome place in my life and had become part of me."

With Rin-Tin-Tin and Nanette he was in control. He could mold them.

Had Duncan not been an alienated outsider, abandoned as a child, he might not have become so attached to the puppies (seeing them as also abandoned) or so good at promoting Rin-Tin-Tin later. Loss helped turn him into someone who attached more readily to animals than people, and like many loners he had an instinct for what would become popular and figured out how to become part of it.

As Duncan remembered being told, his mother "married at the early age of sixteen." I think it is significant that he did not mention his father in this sentence – it would have been just as easy to say, "My parents married when she was sixteen and he was twenty-six." The marriage is on record in Tulare County (California): Lizzie N. Ellis, 18, of Poplar, married G.G. (George Grant) Duncan, 26, of Porterville, at 11:30 in the morning on January 1, 1891 in Visalia. (Duncan was wrong about how old she was.) Witnesses were T.L. Doss, Lizzie's uncle on her mother's side, and Mrs. Jane Garrett, about 37 years old. (I can find Garretts who lived in Tule River and Garretts who lived in Poplar, but no Jane Garrett shows up in federal census records.) Unless Jane Garrett was related to him, none of G.G.'s family was present at the wedding, .

Though difficult to prove, it seems logical that the Duncans were not in favor of the marriage. Lizzie's father, John Ellis, certainly did not have the prestige of G.W. (George Washington) Duncan, G.G.'s father. In 1870, G.W. was raising stock, with real estate valued at $800 and a personal worth of $6,000.

G.G. was the only boy; he had three sisters, all younger. A 14-year-old boy named George Fasset, born in Texas, lived with them "at home"; he was probably G.G.'s cousin on his mother's side. According to the 1892 *Memorial and Biographical History of the Counties of Fresno, Tulare and Kern, California*, G.W. Duncan was by then a prosperous farmer in Tule River (now Springville): "In the immediate vicinity [of the junction of middle Tule River with the north branch] are some fine homes with profitable orchards and vineyards; among them may be mentioned the places of G. W. Duncan, J. R. Hubbs, and Louis Weber." In 1900, still in Tule River, G.W. was living with his wife, Laurinda; a daughter, Laura, a schoolteacher, age 23; and a son, Hopeton, aged 14. He owned his own farm free and clear.

One suspects that G.G. was the black sheep son. G.G. had six sisters by the time he was grown. He was the only boy and the oldest until, when he was about 21, that other boy, Hopeton, a wishful name, was born. Perhaps the hope was that he would turn out better than his brother.

Lizzie Ellis, Duncan's mother, was born in Bear Creek, Missouri in 1873, one of five children. Her father, John Green Ellis, a farmer, and her mother, Malissa Doss, were married in 1870. In 1884, when Lizzie was ten or eleven, the family, along with John's brother William S. Ellis and his children, moved to Fallbrook, about 55 miles north of the city of San Diego. John and William each claimed 160 acres as homesteads south of the town. Richard O'Neal, of the Santa Margarita Rancho, sued both brothers, saying that the land belonged to an old Spanish land grant, Santa Margarita, which stretched from San Juan Capistrano to Oceanside, where Camp Pendleton now sits, on the coast highway between Los Angeles and San Diego. William fought and won his case on the basis that it was government land, but John gave up. His land went to O'Neal.

John's family moved north and settled in Tulare County, along with two of Malissa's brothers: Minor Linn and Thomas Lawrence Doss. Thomas Doss and John Green Ellis ended up living in Poplar, while Minor Doss lived in Porterville, east of Poplar. On February 22, 1886, Malissa, John's wife and Lizzie's mother, died in Tulare.

Poplar was a small town in the center of farming country, where farmers raised grain and livestock. The land around Poplar was so dry that residents formed a cooperative to dig a ditch to bring in water from the Tule River.

Leland was born October 1, 1893, in Hanford, California. In his *Notes*, he said he was born before his mother was eighteen; in fact she was closer to twenty. Duncan's sister, Marjorie, was born three years later, in October 1896.

In his *Notes*, Duncan said they "lost" his father, and his use of the word "lost" is significant. Actually, on January 8, 1897, Leland's father deserted the family. Leland was three years old. Perhaps he was never told that his father left the family, though he must at some time have read the microfilmed orphanage record that is among the papers he left to the City of Riverside. That is the first and last time he mentions his father. G.G. might not have gone far away. In 1898, a George Grant Duncan, age thirty-two, was listed in the Tulare County Great Register as living in Pleasant Valley (Springville), quite close to Poplar.

In February 1898, a little more than a year after his father deserted the family, Leland's mother "thought it best" to put Leland and his sister in a Methodist orphanage, Fred Finch, in Oakland, a suburb of San Francisco. It is significant that none of Duncan's relatives who lived in the region took the children in. Perhaps they were affected by the depression of 1893-1897 and the decline in the price index of farm products in the 1890s. However, G.W. Duncan kept his land, and it could have been at the expense of the children. Some deep family rancor among the adults might have been responsible.

Duncan remembered vividly the rides he and his mother and sister took to get to the orphanage – his first ride on a train (his mother called it the iron horse), the ride on the ferry to Oakland, and the ride on the street car to Piedmont Hills. But at the end of the trip was "the private home for just such unfortunates as we were." On the document admitting Leland to the orphanage, in which Lizzie listed their home as Poplar (her father's town), she wrote "I do not know" in answer to the question "Is the father dead?" In answer to the question: "If either or both parents have deserted the child, state when," she wrote, "Father deserted" and gave the date; she agreed to give $2.50 a month for Lee's keep. The application was approved on February 21, 1898; Lee was examined by a doctor on March 21 and admitted on March 22.

He wrote in his *Notes*: "And how she kissed us, left us on the porch and walked down that long lane to the carline will be a picture I will never forget." Leland had suffered his second loss – of his mother – even though it was temporary. His remembrance of the orphanage reveals how bereft he felt:

The days that followed were very lonely and sad and when night came, it seemed as though my bed was falling into some dark well or canyon. For years I could not eat oatmeal mush and cod-liver oil made me deathly ill. . . . this was all forgotten on Sunday when Mother came to see us and we could all be together for a long walk in the hills among the wild flowers. Christmas soon came and all I wanted was a ball of colored yarn to make a mat for my grandfather's [probably John G. Ellis's] coal-oil lamp. This is I did by the aid of the spool and four pins.

Timothy A. Hacsi, in *Second Home: Orphan Asylums and Poor Families in America*, ranks 19th century orphanages that gave children contact with the outside world higher than those that isolated children behind closed walls. In that way, Fred Finch was better than many orphanages in that the children did have contact with outside society. They went to public school at Fruitvale (a neighborhood of Oakland), though there was a kindergarten on the premises for the little ones. All the children, Methodist or not, attended the "Higgins" church.

Sending children to orphanages for a short time was not an uncommon practice in the late 1800s. However, according to Hacsi, orphan asylums often were last resorts for children who had no friend or family to take care of them, though "for many children . . . a year or two in an asylum while their families struggled to overcome some sort of disaster may have been a better fate than being with their families." At least children received an education in orphanages, so some working-class families used them not only as caretakers but schools. In tracing the nineteenth century history of orphanages, Hacsi finds that most were "more homelike" than other institutions and unlike other institutions, had become more so after the Civil War, yet in his judgment they were still too harsh in meting out discipline and lacked warmth and the opportunity for emotional and psychological development. In short, though they were called "homes," they were not "home."

It seems that Duncan did not know how long he would be in the orphanage or if he would ever be reunited with his mother. He remembered lining up for people coming to the orphanage looking for a child to adopt and being passed up because he had big ears, but "Mother would not part with either of us and she thought I was the best looking boy of the lot." It isn't clear that Lizzie thought of putting the children up for adoption, but if they were not eligible, why were they put on display?

The children did go back with their mother: "It was a grand and glorious day for us when Grandpa and Mother came to take us back to the ranch with him." He does not say which ranch – the Ellis ranch in Poplar or the Duncan ranch in Tule River Township (now Springville) – but since he later identifies it as a sheep ranch and mentions that the nearest neighbor was nine miles away, it was most likely the Ellis ranch. He could not have been in the orphanage more than two years and four months, probably less, though he wrote that he had been there three years.

Duncan never forgot the Fred Finch orphanage and never hid the fact that he was – at least metaphorically – an orphan:

> The three years spent in the orphanage did many things for me, mostly making me understand the many thousands of orphans I was to visit with Rin-Tin-Tin in years to come and to give them a better, happier outlook on life and to be able to help teach them that the home they were in was a Godsend and the means of obtaining an education to go out into the world on their own and to be better men and women for having lived that life.

In the Rin-Tin-Tin Collection, many letters and documents from Fred Finch and other children's homes testify to Duncan's avowed fondness for the place where he felt his bed fall into a black hole, where he developed an aversion for oatmeal and cod-liver oil so intense that they made him ill. His attachment to that small part of his life could be because orphans appealed to the sentimental in the early part of the 20th century. However, I think there was more to it, that he found a stability at Fred Finch that he did not find elsewhere and that, as a famous man, bringing Rin Tin to visit orphanages helped him reconcile his feelings of abandonment. Rin-Tin-Tin was his entree, his vindication, his connection. It is doubtful that without Rin-Tin-Tin he would have made those visits.

Duncan's visits to orphanages did not always appear in the press, but letters in the Rin-Tin-Tin Collection archives support his contention that he often made them. For instance, in 1928 a widow who had put her son in the Fred Finch Orphanage thanked him for visiting the orphanage with Rin-Tin-Tin and Nanette. (Rin-Tin-Tin's mate was named Nanette after the first Nanette.) The widow had, after the death of her husband, gone to California, but the "success" she wished for did not come and she had to put her boy in "The Home." Her son was "more than delighted, with the 'antics' of the dogs" and gave her a picture of Rin-Tin-Tin he had somehow gotten, which she had framed and was going to keep for him until "he grows to be a man." In 1930, a letter from someone named Stannard confirmed Duncan's appointment to visit the Kansas City Boys' Orphan Home with Rin-Tin-Tin after a performance: "I know you will be amply repaid for the time spent at this home by the beaming smiles and cheers of 135 real boy's [sic]; After all a dog is the Boy's Pal." The director of Fred Finch hit Duncan up for money, using flattery as a ploy: "I find that you and Rin-Tin-Tin paid a visit to the Home way back in 1927 and that a 'play was given in the Social Hall on November 3, 1934, which was the life story of Lee Duncan, owner of Rin-Tin-Tin.'" Duncan did contribute money to Fred Finch, and when he died, in 1960, the orphanage flew the flag at half-staff in his honor.

Back at the ranch after leaving the orphanage, Leland suffered another loss. Now five or six, he would ride down and watch Shep, his grandfather's best sheep dog, as he rounded up the flock when it was time to water them. When Leland asked to play with Shep, his grandfather explained that it took years to make a good sheep dog and he could only "admire him from a distance." Duncan says it was "then I felt my first longing for a good dog." His grandfather gave him a lamb instead. At first the boy's masculinity was insulted: "only a little girl should have a lamb because in my storybook, <u>Mary</u> had a little lamb." He named the lamb Johnnie, and the lamb pulled his sled and played games with him and Marjorie. He tried to take the lamb to bed with him, but his mother would catch him at it and send the lamb back to the pen. When Johnnie ate a favorite rose bush, Duncan's grandfather, furious, had him killed. Duncan wrote: "It was then that he killed something inside of me and it took many years to outgrow that hurt." Duncan had suffered the assassination – a cruel and horrific one – of his first pet.

He was given a second pet, a dog, after the family moved from the ranch to Visalia the "next winter" – probably 1899. Duncan was told the move was because the school in Visalia was better and some relatives lived in the town. We know that by July 5, 1900, the day the census taker recorded it, Lizzie and her children were living in Visalia with William Duncan, the children's great-uncle; William's daughter, Kate; Kate's husband, William Nickerson, the son of a wealthy farmer; and the Nickerson children. Lizzie was the housekeeper.

Lizzie and her children must have left the Nickersons and gone off on their own – at least for a little while. Duncan wrote: "With Mother renting a room to a [railroad] engineer [Walters] that was on a pension with a short run helping pull trains over the high Tehapic [Tehachapi Pass] Mountains, we managed to get on quite well in our new little cottage." Walters gave him a stray smooth-haired fox terrier, named Jack, who had climbed up in the cab of the train to get warm in cold weather.

On February 6, 1902, when Leland was eight, Lizzie married twenty-nine-year-old day laborer Oscar Sherman Sampson, in Visalia. The marriage certificate tells us that this was Lizzie's second marriage and that she did not know if her first husband was alive or dead.

In his *Notes*, Duncan never once mentions Sampson or his stepsister, Shirley (once referred to as Charlotte in census records), born in 1906, though he often talks of his mother and Marjorie. The Rin-Tin-Tin Collection (which holds Duncan's papers) is clean of any sign of Sampson. Duncan had "lost" his biological father when he was so young that he probably didn't remember him. He had a stepfather he may never have acknowledged. Maybe by the time Sampson came along, Lee, in his own mind, had become man of the house. In his *Notes*, his mother figures large, and he is the one who supports her and his sister. The addition of Sampson to the household may have looked to him like a betrayal. There was no father figure in his childhood who meant anything positive to him except the Grandpa for whom he made the lamp mat (but who was probably the same one who killed the pet lamb).

Census and voter registration records give Duncan's Sampson-less story the lie. Lizzie was married to Sampson until at least 1920. We find her living with

Oscar Sampson in Burbank, a suburb of Los Angeles, in the census records for 1910 and in the voter registration records for 1916 (at 512 Angeleno Avenue); she was living with him in Lankershim (now North Hollywood) in census records for 1920. And the clincher: in 1930, when Duncan was a rich man, thanks to Rin-Tin-Tin, the census taker found his mother, a widow going by the name Sampson, and his half-sister living with him in Beverly Hills. (Since Sampson died in 1940, she was probably divorced or separated, not widowed.)

In his *Notes*, Duncan says the family moved to Los Angeles and left his dog Jack behind, though he doesn't specify exactly when. His mother said the dog would be sent along later, but that did not happen. Supposedly she found a home for the dog with a neighbor, a "home" which might have been the proverbial farm to which so many unwanted dogs are consigned by the parents of the children who love them. Because his mother "thought it best," Leland never saw Jack again. "For ten days I was sick of heart and body and had to go to bed. Nothing mattered but my dog." After being inconsolable, he finally came to terms with his loss: "It was one of the big moments in my life when I promised Mother I would not bother her anymore about Jack and from that time on, Jack was just a memory." His excuse for his mother's action was that "dogs and children in a big city do not always work out."

His story of having to leave Jack behind because the family was moving to a "big city" doesn't fit well with the facts. Perhaps the family went to Los Angeles for a short time before they moved to rural Fallbrook, where they were living, not far from his mother's Ellis relatives, in 1905, three years after Lizzie married Sampson in Visalia. (The evidence: An Oscar S. Sampson, age 32, appears in the Great Register of Voters for San Diego County on the same page as Lizzie's Ellis relatives – Duncan's great-uncle William, age 52, and his two cousins who were of voting age.) If the family made a move to Los Angeles, it is likely that Sampson, a farmer, found work on a farm on its outskirts.

Duncan's early life contained more than this: his experiences on ranches and camping in the Sierras gave him solace. But I believe the losses in his early life influenced how Duncan treated the puppies. They represented his childhood innocence and vulnerability. He lavished on them all his affection and all the attention he could muster. He gave them what he never had. They were as connected to him as most children are to their parents.

Like many people with troubled childhoods, Duncan re-invented himself. From a man who was in reality a gunnery corporal during World War I, he became, in his post-war stories, an officer and aviator accompanied on dangerous missions by his brave war dog mascot. That this story worked well as studio publicity for Rin-Tin-Tin's movies may be coincidental – or not. No matter what story is "true" about Rin-Tin-Tin's birth, it is impossible that he was a war dog. Even if he had been found as a puppy in mid-September, he would have been alive during the war, yes, but he would hardly have been able, as publicity later claimed, to bring aid to wounded men in hell-holes, act as a sentry, or carry dispatches. No two-month-old puppy, even a very talented one, is capable of those tasks. By 1933, Duncan stopped talking about it.

Perhaps Rin-Tin-Tin originally had to be a war dog in order to bolster Duncan's claims that he was a lieutenant and a pilot, which began as early as 1919. Obviously this later served as excellent publicity for his canine movie star, but Rin-Tin-Tin was still a nobody in 1919 when the article about the Los Angeles dog show mentioned his "thrilling puppyhood." Even after Duncan abandoned the story of Rin-Tin-Tin as war dog who flew in planes, he clung to his own assumed rank as an officer. And even after he dropped his officer status, he clung to his story that he was an aviator.

As Hart and Lovenberg both make clear, Lovenberg somewhat testily – "Corporal (not Lieutenant) Duncan" – Duncan was not an officer. And he was not an aviator. His war record verifies this. In the squadron history, he was officially listed as a gunner, probably one who fixed and maintained guns or fired from the ground. The aviators of 135th Aero Squadron acted as part of an observation team, not as fighters. Their two-seater plane (De Haviland 4 with American-made Liberty engines) did not have room to carry an enlisted man whose only function was to be a gunner. The pilot and observer were each supplied with a machine gun to be used for defense. While the pilot flew the plane, the observer took pictures, dropped pamphlets, made note of the terrain and of enemy emplacements and movements. If they were attacked by an enemy plane, one or both dropped whatever they were doing and used their guns on it.

In writing the 1933 manuscript (remember that it was unpublished), Duncan gave up the pretense of being a commissioned officer and described himself as an enlisted man. Perhaps it fitted the idea he had of himself then – a plain fellow who yearns for the wilderness and is tender-hearted toward those less fortunate than he. Or perhaps someone blew the whistle on him. However, he kept up the pretense of being an officer in his public life. In 1954, in a story about movie dogs, Duncan was still a lieutenant. It could be that he needed to present himself as an officer because studio publicity demanded it or that he was more comfortable with that role when on stage. Sometimes, too, masquerading as an officer gained him privilege. For instance, a letter to a George Morris on May 1, 1930, from the General Publicity Department (of Warner Brothers) orders that a Cord-Auburn car is to "call for *Capt.* [italics mine] Lee Duncan and Rin-Tin-Tin at 2440 Amsterdam Ave., N.Y.C." on May 3 to take them to Roosevelt Field.

While Duncan could sometimes drop the status of being an officer, he could not so easily give up that of being an aviator. In writing his *Notes* in 1933, long after the war, to explain how he could be an aviator while still an enlisted man, he made up a special circumstance – an act of semi-heroism – that does not correspond with the records. He claimed to have been given flying status shortly before the battle of St. Mihiel (September 12-15, 1918) because he helped extricate a dead observer, whose body had fallen on the stick, from the rear cockpit of a downed plane. His story cannot be true. It does not gibe with the dates of crashes that killed members of the 135th. Nor does it gibe with the dates of crashes for the 90th Aero Squadron, which was stationed at the same air base. With one exception, the accident that killed Lieutenant Blair Thaw, the first commander of the 135th, on August 18 (which did not kill the observer), Hart mentions no deaths before the battle of St. Mihiel, nor are any listed in the histories of the squadron. Four men crashed on September 12, the first day of the battle, but their planes, and bodies, were not found until afterwards – one plane on September 18, the other plane on September 21.

Indeed, Duncan fabricated a great deal of his military experience. It began with his assertion that he joined the Air Service on April 7, 1917, the day after war was declared. This is not true: Duncan's discharge papers show that his military service ran from November 1, 1917 to May 26, 1919. Why would he say he enlisted so early? It might be failed memory, but it also might have been a desire to appear patriotic.

Maybe he did try to join up in April and was rejected: The U.S. Air Service called for volunteers, and so many young men showed up eager to be aviators that at least one of two was rejected "because of age, marital status, physical defect, or intelligence." The government promoted the idea of commissions in the Air Services to colleges, and the myth was that its pilots were college boys. Certainly the pilots and observers of the 135th Aero Squadron, while many were college-educated and came from the professional classes, knew that while the ideal was an elite force, the reality was something different. Lawrence L. Smart, who had been a student at the University of Delaware, tells how, in 1917, fifteen men at Fort Myer (Virginia) Officers' Training Camp were chosen from 100 others for training with the Royal Canadian Air Force. "I got by the first question all right: 'had I ever attended college?' But most of the boys had. More sixteen and seventeen-year-olds had gone to Yale and Harvard than the deans of those universities knew about. One alert youth had even attended Fordham – which he had never seen!" (See "Appendix 1: Backgrounds of the Men of the 135th Aero Squadron, page 245- 246)

The Air Force wanted college men. Duncan wasn't one. It is doubtful that he even finished high school because, according to the 1910 census, he had not attended school since he was fifteen.

Learning to fly was one of Duncan's motives for joining up: "I noticed in the paper where men knowing anything about a machine gun could report at Berkley [sic], California, and might be given a chance to go into the Air Service. That is what I wanted to do. I thought, it would be great to learn to fly." But his description of the enlistment process points up his feelings about his social class. He was going through his physical when he saw a sign that said "smile," so he obeyed, and then:

> . . . within the next five minutes, a chap sitting at his desk with his typewriter before him looked up and asked me to take that smile off my face. I didn't let on like I heard him at first because when I can't smile, you know I am ill. Anyway, he called me the second time and I hadn't been in the army long enough to be talked to in that tone of voice so I reached over the desk and caught him by his coat lapel with my left hand and let him have a good stiff punch to the nose with my right. Now my

scout training should have taught me not to do such a thing but – it had also taught me not to take an insult.

Then, Duncan said, the "chap" wrote "unskilled laborer" in his "flying record" because, as he explained, such behavior wasn't acceptable in the army.

Duncan probably concocted the story of punching the recruiter in the nose to explain the designation of "unskilled laborer" that appears on his discharge papers. Certainly nowhere else in his manuscript or in the book by English is there any mention of violence on his part. Though he was a salesman for a sporting goods company, not an unskilled laborer, even that job could hardly have qualified him to become a lieutenant in the Air Service – the emphasis on recruiting college men and men of "breeding" ruled it out. Strangely, though he is still identified as an unskilled laborer in his discharge papers, on his draft registration card (June 5, 1917) his profession is listed as "salesman for B.H. Dyas."

I doubt that Duncan had much, if any, flying experience in the war. According to Duncan himself, he had no flight training in the United States – "The nearest plane I had at Kelly Field was a wheelbarrow" – but spent his time building roads and driving a truck. Overseas, in Scotland, he trained with the Royal Air Force, learning gunnery, photography, and the intricacies of the Liberty engine. In the 1933 manuscript, Duncan spends a whole page describing in technical detail the mechanics of the machine guns mounted on the planes, the difficulties in adapting guns used on the ground to air, and the problems of firing a gun through a propeller; he compares shooting down an enemy plane to shooting ducks. He adds some comments about target practice and learning, as an observer, to use a camera. To be fair he does say he received some aviator training: "He [his instructor] not only taught me to fly a plane but how to take advantage of the wind, sun and cloud." He claims that when he left for France he "was as much at home in the air as . . . on the ground. . . ." He also says, "I had been given a pretty good ground training and had been up in most of the British ships from the F.E.2.B pusher type to the biggest bomber." Though this is possible, it is not probable. Pilots needed intensive training in flying specific planes, not casual experience in flying many. Why would the Royal Air Force train a member of the 135th Aero Squadron, whose mission was observation, in flying bombers? Also, if this were true, where is the evidence that he put his training – any of it – to use once in France?

Unlike the officer pilots in their memoirs and squadron histories, in his manuscript Duncan talks of his supposed time in the air in the vaguest of terms: "That afternoon, I went over the lines and it was then that I learned the difference between flying for a joyride and flying with someone shooting at you." No stories of daring escapes from Fokkers by undertaking classy and dangerous maneuvers. No mention of what devastated battlefields looked like. No details about the failure of engines and forced landings. I think Duncan was more truthful when he said he was "working in the armory department in charge of guns and ammunition. I was testing and shooting every day."

Some of the enlisted men did *learn* to fly: Hart says, in his entry for September 1, "About this time some of the more fortunate of the enlisted men were being given instruction in flying and aerial gunnery." Yet Smart and Hart mention Duncan as being in the air on only one occasion – the flight on November 3 when the eleven planes left the base to bomb Chambley. Smart says (and this is similar to Hart's recounting): "One of our enlisted men, Sgt. Collier, a self-taught pilot, accompanied us that trip with Corporal Duncan going along as his observer. Collier was one of the original enlisted men who had joined the squadron at its inception in San Diego, California. He proved to be an excellent pilot and went on several missions before the war was over." This is supported by the enlisted men's history of the squadron: "This distinction [being allowed to fly a plane], however, does belong to *one* [italics mine] man of this organization, Sergt. William S. Collier, who has practically taught himself to fly and is now a seasoned pilot of no small degree and who performed a few missions over the lines before the signing of the Armistice." If Collier flew a "few" missions, it is unlikely that Duncan flew thirty-six (as the *Collier's* article reported) and no one noticed.

However flimsy the story of being an aviator was, Duncan could not give it up. He liked the idea of being an aviator and found opportunities to present himself as one. For instance, on May 22, 1927, Duncan attended an air meet called the great Air Carnival at Santa Monica's Clover Field. Billed as a "World-War flier," he came with Rin-Tin-Tin, who was dressed in a Red Cross vest and entertained the crowd with his "startling antics." However, though the article tells of how aviators flew more than sixty planes, one upside down, and how a stunt man walked the wings and swung from the landing gear of another, Duncan does not seem to have taken a plane up into the air at that event.

Why was it so important to Duncan's self-image (beyond the image of him and Rin-Tin-Tin as war heroes) to be an aviator? The sky was a frontier, and Duncan was a man of the frontier, both in the sense of the Western frontier where he lived as a child, which preserved the past while testing its inhabitants' mettle, and the more abstract frontier of modern technology (the movies). Moreover, he invented himself throughout his life. What better role for someone like him than a World War I aviator?

Being an aviator was glamorous. The planes, contraptions of wood and canvas, resembled fragile flying tents, open to the elements. That they were dangerous there is no doubt, and the war hero facing extreme danger was a romantic figure. The observer often stood up in the cockpit, half his body unprotected against wind – and gunfire. Neither pilot nor observer had a parachute. If a plane was hit by enemy bullets or anti-aircraft fire, the men were doomed to a terrifying fall to earth and certain death, often in searing flames.

Smart wrote: "It is not easy for men today to get a vivid or clear picture of what was happening when, in 1917, we were on fire with a determination to conquer our space above the earth. We were part of a rare phenomenon in life – the emergence of something new – a novelty of such magnitude that it could change our whole life." In October 1917, when the pilots of the 135th were stationed at Taliferro Field, Hicks, Texas, sometimes they would fly (without orders) to local towns:

> Before we could land and taxi up to a fence everyone in town would be driving or running toward the field. Such enthusiasm! They would crowd around, feel the fabric, shake the wings, ask all kinds of questions. The girls would write their names all over the wings and punch holes in the fabric with their heels. . . . You would have thought we were conquering heroes instead of just ordinary cadets AWOL from our field.

Duncan wanted to present himself as a hero, but not necessarily as a blue blood, and Rin-Tin-Tin gave him the opportunity to do that. He didn't see himself as a dashing officer living in a clubby, glamorous world, sometimes billeted in chateaux. In his *Notes* you read nothing of elite glamour – nurse-chasing in Cadillacs, frequenting the cafes of French cities, popping Champagne corks. He comes across instead as a rugged individualist, a self-made man who understood guns and nature. On the other hand, he was a showman who wanted to present himself to the world as an World War I aviator, and for that he needed an officer's title. But he was not exactly like Billy Bishop, who, after the war, bragged about his supposed lone attack on a German aerodrome, or Bert Hall, who became a vaudeville star wearing an assortment of medals, some of which he had won and some of which he had not won. Off stage, Duncan seemed somewhat self-effacing, and he didn't recount acts of his own heroism, except the one of pulling the observer out of the plane, which had a reason for being other than self-aggrandizement.

Something of a disjuncture exists between the World War I world we historians record and Duncan's reminiscences. He seems not to fit anywhere as an archetype. Perhaps it is not so unusual in writing a biography of someone who was really just a bit player in a spectacular historical event to find that the person does not fit in a big category.

In the end, because Duncan was a loner, and lonely, and because he had a deep-seated interest in animals, the puppies became the center of his life and, the way that loners do, he wove exaggerated tales about his life with them. It is no accident that Rin-Tin-Tin was the dog from the war who ended up as a movie star. Duncan raised him and his sister as his children. His attachment to them was extreme. He spent his hours (hours he might have spent with his mates or chasing girls) playing with and training them. He made up stories about how he had found them and what roles they had played in the war. Later it all dovetailed with 1920s moviegoers' desire for a hero who transcended human frailties and folly

2
Duncan the Not-So-Obscure

According to the story promoted by Duncan, Warner publicity, and the press, Warner plucked Rin-Tin-Tin out of obscurity and turned him into a star. It was in the tradition of the Hollywood genre of the drugstore waitress catapulted to fame after she catches the eye of a major producer who glimpses her over the edge of his Coke glass. The story goes like this: Duncan, a complete unknown, trudges with Rin-Tin-Tin in tow from studio to studio seeking to get his talented dog in the movies. Only by sheer luck is he able to catch the interest of Harry Warner and sell him on Rin-Tin-Tin's talents and his screenplay for *Where the North Begins* (1923). From then on their fortunes are made.

But the reality of Rin-Tin-Tin's rise is far more idiosyncratic, deliberately managed, and, in hindsight, predictable. To my mind, it is also more interesting. Yes, by 1923, Rin-Tin-Tin was a star. However, this was not a matter of luck, nor did it come about only because he was enormously gifted and Duncan a talented trainer. Early on, Duncan, though without obvious privilege or connections, positioned himself as a player – an authentic outdoors man, rancher, and son of pioneers – in a real-life Hollywood story. He was part of a coalition of Hollywood lovers of the idea of the West and of manly (and, actually, also womanly) pursuits like hunting and the outdoor life. That coalition included the hugely influential B.H. Dyas, in whose sporting goods store Duncan worked; government and automobile companies anxious to open up and exploit the California wilderness; and dog and horse afficionados who showed off their animals in dog and horse shows. It is ironic: in Duncan's *Notes*, where he spins the story of the unknown dog trainer and dog who finally get a lucky break from Warner, he is an inveterate dropper of names of influential people.

Duncan was a son of the West. He spent much of his childhood on his relatives' ranches in Tulare County and Fallbrook and in the wilderness close by.

Both his mother's and his father's parents were pioneers of a sort, and love of nature was in his genes. His *Notes* emphasize three things close to his heart: wilderness, especially the Sierras, ranch life, and animals – the ones he owned and the ones he hunted. Several years before Duncan enlisted in World War I, B.H. Dyas hired him as gun salesman and wilderness consultant because of his expert knowledge of guns, the woods, and hunting. According to his *Notes*, he sometimes took famous and influential clients on hunting trips into parts of California that were just becoming accessible. Among the important people he met were the wealthy Anita Baldwin, who bred dogs; hunting guide Jim Owens; and actor Eugene Pallette, who shared his love of dogs, hunting, and wilderness.

After the war, he went back to Dyas, continued his friendship with Pallette, met movie stars like Pauline Fredericks, and married a rich socialite, Charlotte Anderson, who owned blooded show horses. He never mentions his marriage in his *Notes*, nor does it appear in James English's book about Rin-Tin-Tin, nor is there a scrap of information about it in the Rin-Tin-Tin Collection at Riverside.

Duncan's families had much in common, and it is worth looking at them in more detail to see the origins of Duncan's deeply held feelings about rural and wild California. Both families were involved in frontier ranching and town building. They helped create the California that Hollywood glamorized in movies.

Sometimes Lee Duncan sounds remarkably like the Duncan grandfather he may not have known. George Washington Duncan (known as G.W.) tells in his "Memoirs" of how he left home in Illinois to go west when he was sixteen, stopped for a while in Mormon country near Salt Lake City, then, in 1851, traveled as a cook on a wagon train to Sacramento. He tried mining at Angels Camp, east of San Francisco, but was unsuccessful. In the mid-1850s, he filed on a piece of land in Tulare County close to the Eastern Sierras. The trip there was rough; he was often thrown off a bucking horse. Nonetheless he wrote glowingly of antelope bounding over uninhabited land, of acorn-hunting grizzlies (one of which one of his companions shot and left wounded), and of "the deep hush of grand and solemn forest – God's true temple." He called himself a "child of Nature." While he thought that the mountains should be exploited to supply fuel and water to make the desert bloom, he also thought that destruction of the forests was "vandalism" and that the government should protect them so that they would "continue to furnish material for our children's children to make beautiful their homes." He was something of a philosopher. When writing about his land, he said, "How blind is man! How little we know of the future. . . . I am not a fatalist, but still it often seems as though some men's destinies are written out in full on the scroll of time."

His property, a claim with a house, lay in what was then (and now) a prime spot. The 1892 *Memorial and Biographical History of the Counties of Fresno, Tulare and Kern, California* waxed rhapsodical about it:

> The climate is all that can be desired; the water of the river, aided by the magnificent oaks, keeps the air balmy, while only four miles to the east are the pine forests on Black mountain, which send down their cool, healthful breezes each evening at twilight. By a ride of two hours one can be landed amid the pines and meadows on the slopes of the Sierras. . . . The soil here is rich and easily tilled. Being in the thermal belt, the orange and lemon, as well as the banana, do exceedingly well. Almost anything can be produced in the line of fruits.

G.W. planted a peach orchard with pits from peaches he bought from a grower near Columbia (east of Stockton and Sacramento), and he grew potatoes – ten tons of them. As was so common in dry Tulare County, he worked with his neighbors to dig a ditch that brought water to the land. After he had settled in, he made a trip back to Angels Camp, partly to persuade his two brothers, Oliver and William, to leave the mines. Only Oliver came back with him at that time.

The nearest town (later named Springville) was on the trasnhumance route of shepherds, who often stayed the night there when taking sheep into mountain pastures in the summer. Jeff Edwards, in his *100 Year History of the Tule River Mountain Country*, mentions that the men who settled in and near Springville (Tule River Township) did so because "Here they could hunt, trap, and raise cattle. . . . Most of the customers were miners."

Duncan's grandfather on his father's side, then, was a relatively wealthy man, who had done well in life, but also thought deeply. No doubt he was tough, but he was also intelligent, and he, like his grandson Lee, loved the mountains and Nature. His brother William's son, William Tilden Duncan, had a similar sensibility. He wrote articles for the magazine *Los Tulares* about how his father hunted a grizzly bear in 1868 and about how he himself disapproved of the shameful treatment of local Yokut Indians "through white man's greed." He had a reverence for the past. It showed in his stories of Hunter Jim, the huge Indian (probably Piute) who smiled a "terrible smile" and hunted big game with flint-tipped arrows, and in his appreciative description of the old stones settlers used to build houses and Native Americans used to make mortars. His stories seem like tall tales, but perhaps they were not. He certainly knew how to tell them. The characters of these men were part of Duncan's inheritance. If he did not know his grandfather G.W., he certainly would have heard about him from his uncle William, with whom he, his mother, and his sister lived for a time.

That part of Tulare County was a beautiful little place during the time G.G., Duncan's father, was growing up and even when his son might have visited as a child in the early 1890s. It was isolated and rural, yet it had a tourist attraction – a spring, whose water had healthful properties, in the center of town. By 1892, the year before Lee was born, Tule River Township had a store, a post office, blacksmith shop, box factory, furniture shop, and hotel – all of which were the "result of a year's growth." According to Jeff Edwards, it eventually boasted a dance hall and a planing mill, powered by the water from the Tule River, which had been brought to town by a ditch; people went there to swim, dance, and have a good time.

Poplar, the nearest town to Duncan's maternal grandfather's ranch, consisted of just a store and blacksmith shop in 1892; it was in the center of farming country, where farmers raised grain and livestock. The land around Poplar was so dry that residents, like those in Tule River Township, formed a cooperative "in the early days" to dig a ditch to bring in water from the Tule River. The cooperative later formed a company that founded a general merchandising house, still doing business in 1913. (I have been unable to find the ranch where John Ellis lived on the *California Index Map of Tulare County 1892.)*

In Duncan's childhood world (the one he wrote about), it was nearly always summer; in his *Notes*, he mentions winter rarely. He worked doing odd jobs for neighbors and on the ranch in Tulare, which was probably his grandfather Ellis's because his Duncan grandfather and great-uncle had moved away by the time he was seven or eight, G.W. to San Jose and William to the town of Visalia. Duncan may have known the place on the fork of the river only when he was little, if at all. Yet he knew William Duncan well and went back to Tulare County to visit long after Rin-Tin-Tin became famous.

In 1898, according to the Great Register of Tulare County, John Ellis was still in Poplar. By 1900 he had moved. The 1900 Federal Census lists a John G. Ellis, a farm laborer, as living in Visalia, not far from the Nickersons (William Duncan's daughter's family), married to Martha, with four children, one of whom, Rhoda, was born in 1880 in California. This, of course, does not gibe with the census record of 1880, which places Lizzie's father in Missouri, married to Malissa. Still, I think this is Lizzie's father.

Lee and Jack, his fox terrier, "had many happy days" when he was a child in Tulare County. One summer (their first summer vacation, according to Duncan's *Notes*), the family went in a covered wagon to Deer Creek Hot Springs (now California Hot Springs) in the Sierras, "there to enjoy the cool streams and high mountains covered with pine, spruce and redwood trees." Duncan described the family's trip by horse and wagon over dangerous mountain curves as thrilling. They "chopped down lovely trees to use as drags and to be used on the curves so that the wagon and horses would not go tumbling down the mountain side into the river many hundred feet below." In the mountain camp, he had to put Jack on a lead so he made a chain of baling wire, fashioning links with pliers. He made several such leads for his friends (boys) in camp who also had dogs.

Deer Creek Hot Springs was a popular place. Every day, according to estimates, about 190,000 gallons of mineralized water, some hot, some cold, flowed into Deer Spring Creek. From one spring, water issued "from an orifice in the solid rock in intermittent jets and with a gurgling noise, resembling a wash-boiler full of clothes boiling very rapidly; but the water is ice-cold, and when mixed with lemon juice and sugar makes a beverage that defies competition from venders of so-called 'Arctic Soda.'" In addition to the springs' exciting special effects and soft-drink-making capacities, they were considered therapeutic for people with rheumatism, blood disorders, and other ills — better, even, than patent medicines.

Duncan said in his *Notes* that he spent all the summers that followed either on his grandfather's ranch or in the Sierras. His "trip of trips" came when he joined the Boy Scouts and went with the troop to Mt. Whitney. There he taught Jack, the mascot of the troop, to climb trees, swim, run and jump in his arms. "It was on this trip that I learned how every boy loved a dog and also this outdoor camp life was to be very valuable in years to come." (Since the Boy Scouts reached the United States only in 1910, when Duncan was sixteen or seventeen and long after he lost Jack, it is likely he belonged to one of the precursors of the organization, like Seton's Woodcraft Indians.)

When he requested a pony from Santa Claus, Duncan was given one. He named her Stormy "because it was so cold and stormy that I had to ride her in the barn at first." He rode her mending fence and said that he "loved to cross the river where I taught her to swim with me and Jack on her back" and that they were together two years, which two he does not say. The river he spoke of could have been the slough that ran through Poplar. But perhaps it was the Tule River, which flowed by the Duncan ranch.

After he was about eleven, Duncan probably spent part of his childhood in Southern California with his Ellis relatives in Fallbrook and his grandfather John Ellis, who moved to Bonsall, which is close to Fallbrook, sometime before 1903 or 1904, according to California Voter Registration records. In 1910, according to the federal census, he was still living in Bonsall with his second wife, Martha, and four children, one of whom was named Adell, the same name as William Ellis's wife. He was still a farmer, renting his land.

William Ellis, Duncan's great-uncle, failed in an attempt to raise horses in the Guadalupe Valley, in Baja California. Then, done in by grasshoppers and other plagues, he sold his ranch in Fallbrook but rented buildings on the Santa Margarita Rancho (one-and-a-half miles southwest of Fallbrook) and finally bought more land within a half mile of town, where he built a two-story house. This was sometime before 1910, when he is listed in the census as owning his own property free and clear. He switched to sharecropping about 3000 acres in grain, hay, and pasture on the Santa Margarita Rancho. His spread lay on the edge where of Fallbrook Air Park is now, two miles south of downtown Fallbrook. According to Duncan, the adobe ranch house sat high in the bend of the Santa Margarita River and had a patio and a porch surrounding it. Just above it was a lake. It was here that Leland learned to fish, shoot a shotgun, and hunt mountain lion, bear, and buffalo.

In his *Notes*, Duncan says that his cousin Lee Ellis was foreman on the 350,000-acre "San Margareto" [sic] Rancho, a job he obtained sometime between 1910, when the census listed him as a farm laborer with a wife and three-year-old daughter, and 1920, when it listed him as a ranch foreman with three children.

William Ellis's son Raymond, about Lee Duncan's age, remembered what it was like on the ranch:

> The wonder of it all is how the boys and young men ever lived to maturity on those large ranches where at 10 and 12 years of age they were riding half-broken horses and driving two-horse teams. Then at 14 and 15 they were driving six-horse teams, riding bucking horses and doing every different kind of job. Sometimes they were being attacked by mean bulls, trampled by runaway horses or even run over by wagon loads of hay. It was a rough life!

In Fallbrook there were two general stores selling groceries and dry goods, a hardware store, blacksmith shop, bank, livery stable, butcher shop, barber shop, pool hall, and drug store. There were three Protestant churches. There also was a family of Hatfields: a famous rainmaker, Charles Hatfield, "who shot chemicals in the air to make it rain"; his brother, "Steve, the hobo, who worked on the ranch in the summer and saved enough money to keep him in wine through the winter"; and the black sheep brother, Joe. The veterinarian was also a drinker. The town had its sophisticates: there were a British Colony and a van Rensselaer family, from New York, who lived on an inheritance.

Sometime before May 1910, when the 1910 Federal Census recorded their whereabouts, the Sampsons moved from Fallbrook to the city of Los Angeles, then later to "the beautiful Casa Verdugo hills between Glendale and Burbank" (both very close to Los Angeles), just 150 miles, Duncan said, to the ranch (probably the Ellis Ranch).

The 1910 Federal Census for Tulare County, also taken in May, shows a Leland Duncan in Porterville, living as a lodger and working as a clerk in what appears to be a gunnery store (the census-taker's handwriting is difficult to read). He had not attended school since September 1909 (a month short of his sixteenth birthday). The census-taker recorded his mother's birthplace as California (it was Missouri), and he is listed as seventeen, when he was really sixteen. However, since Porterville is so close to where his relatives lived, and for other reasons, I think this is the Leland Duncan we know.

It is unclear exactly when Duncan moved back to Los Angeles, but he did. In 1911-1912, he – at least one L. Duncan – was listed in the Glendale City Directory as living in Glendale and employed by Shaver's Grocery.

Duncan started working for Bernal H. Dyas, at his sporting goods store, sometime after 1912. In his *Notes* he said that his job was to sell guns as well as to contact people planning a vacation in the High Sierras and give them information they would need for their trip. This makes sense in that he had grown up near the High Sierras and was an outdoors man, thus was "able to be of service to the less fortunate who perhaps planned all year on their trip of two weeks and where to spend it."

It was at Dyas that Duncan met Los Angeles movers and shakers who came into the store looking for guns and information. One of them may have been financier and sportsman Motley Flint, at least according to Duncan's obituary in the *Los Angeles Times*, which said that Flint helped him launch Rin-Tin-Tin's movie career. Because the obituary contains several errors of fact – for instance, that Duncan "spent his childhood" in an orphanage and earned the Silver Star in World War I, I cannot guarantee that this statement is true. However, we do know that Flint loaned the Warners money for their incorporation as Warner Bros. in April, 1923.

In the 1910s and 1920s, it was not unusual for Hollywood theater and movie actors to be hunters. They could hunt in and close to Los Angeles, which was still a small town, with its ranches and dirt roads. Venice, next door to Los Angeles, was a duck-hunting paradise before being dredged to build homes in

1923. Movie actresses like Grace Valentine, photographed with her shotgun for an article in the *Los Angeles Times*, prided themselves on their hunting ability. Movie actors and Los Angeles businessmen formed shooting clubs to buy land to hunt on.

Along with automobile dealers and local government officials, Dyas sponsored hunting trips into wilderness that, because of new roads, had become accessible by automobile. The company also distributed maps of California showing where the best hunting and fishing places were. In 1916, the *Los Angeles Times* ran an article about hunting coyotes, whose "warm, tough pelt, formerly valueless, is now exported to Europe to protect the shivering soldiers" and sold for $8; it featured Bernal Dyas and Harold L. Arnold, a Hudson car distributor. In the Sierra Nevada, which Duncan knew well, hunters killed silver foxes, bears, and other animals for their pelts, which sold for between $8 and $100. "There is no better bear country than our lofty Sierra Nevada, so close to the city that our aqueduct gets its sparkling supply from their glacial hearts," said the *Los Angeles Times*.

Hollywood also was involved in opening up the wilderness. In December of 1916, for instance, "[f]our cameramen representing film companies which produce animated weekly pictures" went on a duck hunting and trout fishing excursion to Bear Valley in conjunction with a promotion by supervisors of San Bernardino and Los Angeles County. The film they made would show the world "that Southern California will have a resort where the wintry pastimes of a more northern clime may be enjoyed as well as those of a warmer one." The cameramen's services were obtained through Forrest Arnold, sales manager for the Pacific KisselKar Company. Meanwhile, about the same time, Dustin Farnum of the William Fox Feature Film Company and Edward Salisbury, a writer and explorer, went on a Dyas-sponsored trip to seek out new hunting grounds within 200 miles of Los Angeles so that Dyas could answer the questions sportsmen asked about where they could shoot ducks, geese, quail, and rabbits. One of the best places they found was in the San Joaquin Valley "from Bakersfield to the upper end of Tulare Lake [near Duncan's boyhood home]." The *Los Angeles Times* story about this enterprise was accompanied with a photograph of a Fox movie star, Miss Kingston, triumphantly holding "a few more victims [dead ducks] of the demon hunters."

Before going into the military in World War I, Duncan owned dogs for hunting. His dog of choice was the tough Airedale, capable of dealing with big game, a "man's dog." He says in his *Notes* that he was fascinated with the Airedale's "gameness" and bought two puppies from George Harker of Buck Horn Kennels in San Fernando, with whom he began to go on hunting trips, "not just to go and kill something but to be away enjoying Nature's playground and to have a chance to enjoy our dogs." He went with the dogs on their first hunting trip to Toluca Lake, in the San Fernando Valley between Burbank, North Hollywood, and Universal City, "where Charles Farrel [sic] and so many of the picture people later built their homes." Their mission was to tree a raccoon that was stealing apples and chickens from the Weddington ranch. Duncan climbed a tree and went out on a limb to get the raccoon while his young dogs went into the water with the old experienced ones. It is typical of Duncan's name-dropping that he mentions Farrell and Weddington. Boston born, Farrell played the role of the male human lead, Dave Weston, in the Rin-Tin-Tin movie *Clash of the Wolves* (1925). His major claims to fame were the pictures he made as a matinee idol with Janet Gaynor from 1927 to 1952 and his role as Gale Storm's father in the 1950s television series *My Little Margie*. The Weddingtons, a wealthy family, often appeared in the society columns of the *Los Angeles Times*.

From those puppies, Duncan went on to breed champion Airedales. He bought the Airedale Champion Coast Range Firefly and mated her with Anita Baldwin's Champion Tintern Tiptop, who had won five firsts at the San Francisco exposition. Baldwin was the daughter of an extremely wealthy real estate speculator, "Lucky" Baldwin, notorious for his philandering. She raised horses and dogs of other breeds besides Airedales.

Duncan was determined to prove that show dogs could be excellent hunting dogs and thought that was an idea original with him. Actually it wasn't. Airedale fanciers had long determined that the standards of the breed should emphasize hunting as well as looks. Others had noted that show and hunting dogs had the same ancestors. A hyperbolic article from *The Breeder and Sportsman* quoted in a 1912 *New York Times* article extolled the hunting, herding, and guarding capabilities of the Airedale, "Accordingly the American-bred Airedale is noted the world over as a showdog, and in no other country has [sic] the breed's sporting possibilities been tested under all conditions as in the United States."

In his *Notes*, Duncan said that he sent Firefly to a friend's ranch in the mountains to guard and herd turkeys. "She loved the life and the turkeys especially the little ones and more than once had to ward off a hungry coyote or bobcat." She had her puppies, which spent two years in the mountains. Duncan saw them as much as possible. He kept four male puppies and traded the two females for male Walker foxhound puppies, then shipped the foxhounds, the same age as his puppies, to the turkey ranch. Those six dogs went with him to hunt bears, lions, bobcats, lynx, and raccoons "for the next four years [probably 1913 to 1917] on some of the most wonderful trips a man could take."

In the Kaibab National Forest, then a 2500-square mile preserve for deer on the north rim of Grand Canyon, Duncan and his hunting dogs met Hades Church of Big Saddle Camp. They also met Jim Owens. The first employee of the federal government on the Kiabab Plateau, Owens, like Duncan, had learned to hunt on a ranch while protecting stock from predators, and, according to Duncan, had "the finest pack of game dogs as ever lived." In 1906, he was a guide for Teddy Roosevelt in his Arizona hunting trips. Dama Margaret Smith, in her book *I Married a Ranger* (1930), reported that Owens claimed to have killed more than 1100 cougars in twenty years, and as partial proof the walls of his cabin were covered with cougar skins and the ceiling was decorated with their claws.

It was through his interest in hunting and dogs that Duncan made friends with Eugene Pallette "of Motion picture fame who had been with me many times to the ranch." Born in Kansas to a theater family in July 1889, Pallette was a virile man with an outsize personality. Before breaking into movies in 1910, he had been a streetcar conductor and jockey, but he quickly became a star. (Overall, he was in 240 movies.) He played a Union soldier in *Birth of a Nation* (1915) and Prosper La Tour in *Intolerance* (1916). By 1917, according to his draft registration, he was married to actress Phyllis Gordon (the dates of their marriage are otherwise unknown); he was blue-eyed and stout; he was living at 1607 Harvard (Hollywood), about six miles from the Dyas store. In 1929, he built a hunting club in Oxnard, not far from the Navy base at Point Magu, "a place where politics and business make a great side dish." According to one internet biography, he was a right-winger, who, during the Cold War, bought 3500 acres in Oregon on which he built a bombproof compound with a stockpile of food, a sawmill, and power plant; his Hollywood friends visited him there, some to hunt and fish, others, perhaps, to hide out from The Bomb.

In his *Notes*, Duncan describes a hunting trip with Pallette in May 1916, the year Pallette starred as the villain, still "young and relatively slim," with Norma Talmadge in *Going Straight*. The hunting trip began when a Mrs. Gill, who raised milk goats in Pasadena, found one of her goats dead, killed by a mountain lion, and called the county office. Because the state hunter was away in the mountains and couldn't get back for four days, Dyas agreed to help and enlisted Duncan, to whom he said (according to Duncan):

> "Now, Lee, if your dogs are what you say they are, this will be a big thing for us both. If we can get those lions almost in the back yard of Pasadena, you might say, and hang them in our window you will be doing three things. Helping a poor widow, giving the store a big newspaper story, and causing a lot of people to come in and see the big cats and last but not least, you can have a full week with your dogs in the hills."

Duncan called Pallette. In his *Notes*, he mentions, peripherally, that Pallette then made $1000 a week while he himself earned only $30 plus 2% of sales, but they were equal when in the mountains. They arrived at the Gill ranch at 8 p.m., and while Pallette talked with Mrs. Gill, Duncan took two Airedales and one of the hounds and tied them to small trees by a stream. Then he arranged the camp, opened a can of beans, and made tea. Pallette usually cooked, while Duncan performed the more mundane camp tasks of finding the wood, carrying water, and washing dishes, all learned through his "early Scout training."

Duncan and Pallette tried to sleep but goats were close to camp and the goat was snorting, so Duncan turned Firefly loose. At one a.m., Firefly was barking in a tone that said "treed." Duncan arose, put on his clothes, and with shoes unlaced, took up his gun and flashlight ready to investigate. Pallette, not taking him seriously, said Firefly had probably gotten one of the goats trapped against a ledge. However, Duncan found Firefly had indeed treed a lion. He shot it between the eyes "which served as targets." He saw this incident as proving his idea about the ability of show dogs: "As I flashed my light on Firefly, mauling and pulling at that lion, I knew that I had proved my theory that a show dog could and would do things besides pose, if given the task." Three days after that, Firefly grappled with and vanquished two other mountain lions – one climbed a tree and the other fled. It was Duncan's last hunt before the war.

When Duncan, with Rin-Tin-Tin, returned to Los Angeles as a war veteran, he went back to work at Dyas. In October 1919, Dyas moved to a fancy new store in the Ville de Paris building at 7th and Olive Streets.

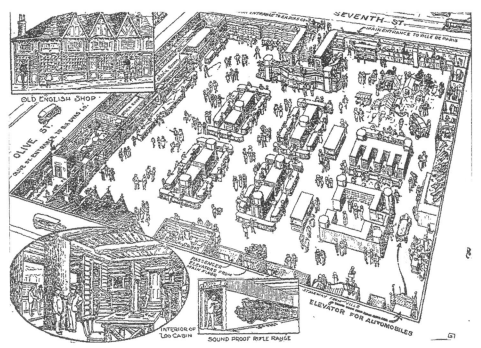

The Dyas Sporting Goods Store (sketch by Arthur B. Dodge for "Novel Way to Utilize Space,", *Los Angeles Times*, September 28, 1919, V1).

A *Los Angeles Times* story described the new store in great detail. The subheads to the headline "Many at Sport Shop's Opening" read "New Dyas

Store Breathes the Spirit of the West" and "Log Hunting Lodge Already has Won Wide Fame." An estimated 16,000 people came to the opening of the spectacular "downtown Mecca of thousands." A semicircle of glass aquariums flanked the marble entrance. After entering, customers descended to the basement. If they were planning a hunting or fishing trip and needed a lot of gear, they could drive their automobiles onto a huge elevator on the Olive Street side and be lowered to the basement, where the cars could be outfitted. The store featured goods for outdoors sports – "fishing, hunting, camping, tramping" – as well as equipment for more urban sports. Each section had friezes – scenes "painted by a famous artist," which brought "California before the eager eye." Whole stuffed animals – deer, elk, moose – stood on platforms, and animals' heads stared down from walls and pillars. But the "triumph," in the far-right corner, was the hunting lodge of bark-covered logs. In its center was a giant slice from a California tree. It had a fireplace and animal skins nailed to the walls. Above the door of the cabin were two deer heads with "mild and beautiful faces," their "horns in the death lock . . . secured just as they were breathing their last, after a battle extending over an area of nearly an acre of ground." Leading from the cabin was a soundproof cement rifle range, "real in every practical sense, and is in charge of one [unnamed, Duncan?] whose gun-wisdom is proverbial." The store also had a gun-repair shop and library. There was a department for bicycles and motor bikes.

We know that Duncan was working for Dyas at Christmas 1919. The Dyas Christmas card ad to its customers in the *Los Angeles Times* listed employees, more than 100 of them, one of which was L.L. Duncan. The 1920 Federal Census (taken January 6) lists him as a salesman for sporting goods.

Perhaps through his connection at Dyas, Duncan succeeded in hooking up with William Matern, a rich hotel man, collector of paintings, and owner of German shepherds. Duncan claimed that Matern and "a few of us" started the Shepherd Dog Club of California (also known as the Shepherd-Police Dog Club) and worked out their dogs "along the lines of war dogs and every weekend found us with our dogs, going through their paces and jumps." Matern had been showing German shepherds as far back as 1915, and in July 1921, posed for the *Los Angeles Times* with his dog Alrich Von Maternhof, who had "captured enough blue ribbons at various shows to fill a book," next to his

Chandler (a touring car) in an article touting the breed's talents as guard dogs – and also advertising W.P. Herbert Company, a Chandler dealer.

Duncan trained Rin-Tin-Tin in "war and police work" with the Club on weekends and probably also on his own. He succeeded so well that he was able to exhibit him at the dog show at Exposition Park in October 1919, less than six months after their return to the United States. He did not mention this in his *Notes*. However, he *did* say in his *Notes* that during this time before Rin-Tin-Tin's fame, he, his mother, and his sister Marjorie made up a little family living together. Records expose this as a fantasy. Both Duncan children were boarding elsewhere, and Lizzie was living with Sampson and their daughter.

In January 1920, the federal census taker found Lee, a sporting goods salesman, living as a lodger in a house owned by a widow and her brother, at 109 Hope Street, near the Dyas store, in the heart of Los Angeles. In the 1920 voter registration list (undated by month), he was a salesman living on McCormick Street in Lankershim, not far from the Sampsons.

Moreover, according to the same federal census, taken on February 6, Lizzie was still living with Oscar Sampson and their daughter, on a farm on Lankershim Boulevard in Lankershim, about twenty miles north of the heart of Los Angeles. Sampson had risen in status – he was now a ranch manager. Marjorie, who had become a music teacher, was rooming on 4th Street in Lankershim with Cecil Wilcox, who worked in a farm store, and his wife Johana; others in the surrounding area were ranchers.

Duncan said that, traumatized by his experiences in the war, he was restless and "couldn't get his feet on the ground" at work so he took a three-months leave of absence from Dyas in spring of 1920 and went to work for the California Highway Commission as a manual laborer doing pick-and-shovel work and painting guardrails. After that, he returned to work at Dyas.

Probably sometime in late 1921, Rin-Tin-Tin joined the cast of *The Man From Hell's River*, a "snow" movie, filmed at Yosemite National Park and released on January 29, 1922. Duncan does not mention this in his *Notes*. The film, set in a French-Canadian trading post, was based on James Oliver Curwood's novel *The God of Her People*. It is a classic melodrama in which Rin-Tin-Tin saves the heroine, played by Eva Novak, from the evil Gaspard (Wallace Beery). At a crucial moment, Rin Rin Tin jumps on Gaspard, who then falls off a cliff.

Rin-Tin-Tin: The Movie Star

On February 12, 1922, the *Los Angeles Times* ran a photograph of Rin-Tin-Tin with Eva Novak, noting that he acted very "brilliantly" in the film and was paid $300 for it. If any one event marked the genesis of Rin-Tin-Tin's movie career, *The Man From Hell's River* was it. Ads for the movie at first merely mentioned an "all-star cast," but, by July 1922, some were billing Rin-Tin-Tin as coequal with stars Novak and Beery. By August, according to *The Mansfield News* (Ohio), Rin-Tin-Tin was proving "to the satisfaction of all that a dog can also be a star."

Rin-Tin-Tin probably also had a part in *Where Romance Rides*, adapted from Zane Grey's *Wildfire*, released on April 2, 1922. Though his name does not appear on cast lists and the film is unavailable for viewing, the following appeared in the *Decatur Review* (Illinois): "'Wildfire'. . . has been completed. Rin-Tin-Tin, a police dog, makes his film debut in it." Rin-Tin-Tin may also have had a small role in *Kindred of the Dust* (released in February 1922).

Rin-Tin-Tin scales a very high wall. (Courtesy Rin-Tin-Tin Collection, Riverside, California)

Duncan the Not-So-Obscure

In early 1922, Duncan entered Rin-Tin-Tin, now three, in a Pasadena dog show for both ring and field. According to James English in *The Rin-Tin-Tin Story*, the show took place in February. In a May 1922 article, *The Mansfield News* (Ohio) said it occurred on March 4 and was sponsored by the Shepherd Dog Club of the West. It was "unsanctioned." Certainly Rin-Tin-Tin had no official canine papers, he or his father having been found on a battlefield, though later claims have been made that he was pedigreed. Duncan said that, while Rin-Tin-Tin may have lacked ring technique, he made up for in the field and "performed spectacularly, scaling an 11-foot barrier." I cannot find this story in the *Los Angeles Times*, but an old photograph shows Rin-Tin-Tin clearing the barrier. (See facing page.)

If Duncan's *Notes* are correct, the show at which Rin-Tin-Tin performed so brilliantly ended in disaster. After the show was over on Saturday, Duncan took Rin-Tin-Tin out for a run outside the hotel. He was "enjoying himself hugely, running about the park, happy to be just a dog," when a truck delivering Los Angeles Sunday papers came around the corner, and a boy riding on the top of the truck's load threw a bundle down. Rin-Tin-Tin, blinded by the headlights, was hit before Duncan, who was behind him, could save him. Rin-Tin-Tin's left front leg was broken in four places.

Duncan wrote, "In spite of the crushed and bleeding leg now hanging helplessly, he hardly whimpered as I picked him up in my arms and he kissed my face and hands as I carried him into the hotel." The hotel keepers let Duncan take Rin-Tin-Tin to his room and give him first aid. The next day, Marjorie drove them to the office of a dentist friend, who may have been Leach Cross, "The Fighting Dentist," with whom Duncan made a short film. There they x-rayed both front legs. On the fourth day after the accident, Duncan used the x-ray of the good leg as a model to put the broken leg in place. He does not say anything about how painful this must have been for Rin-Tin-Tin or why he chose to treat the dog himself rather than go to a veterinarian. He made a splint for the leg, wound gauze around it, then applied plaster of paris he'd mixed up in "a nice, new ten cent wash pan." A friend who rode to work with him on the Pacific Electric cars suggested a leather over-the-shoulder, harness-like apparatus to hold the cast in place. The suggestion came with an admonition to not remove it too soon – Duncan would know when to take it off by observing how Rin-Tin-Tin was trying to use the leg.

After Duncan went to work, Rin-Tin-Tin began crying for him "in a lonely mood" so that the neighbors ("some old people") thought there had been a death in the family. Duncan moved Rin-Tin-Tin from the house on "Sherman Boulevard" (he probably meant the Sampsons' place on Lankershim Boulevard) into east Los Angeles near his work to live with a Mrs. Ed Needhans. He could then see his dog each noon.

Duncan left the cast on for nine weeks – until sometime around the middle of May. It worked loose "though not enough to do any harm." Duncan took another x-ray and found that the leg had healed beautifully except that one of the four bones overlapped another slightly. It was only noticeable by touch. In his movies, Rin-Tin-Tin was often called upon to limp after having been injured, usually by a villain. Possibly, during his nine weeks in a cast, he learned to limp on cue. Or, according to dog trainer Jt Clough, Duncan may have used the trick of putting a piece of tape on his foot to make him limp.

Sometime in early 1922, Duncan married Charlotte Anderson, a socialite horsewoman from northern California at least six years older than he. The marriage was short-lived (Anderson filed for divorce in 1925), but is important to Rin-Tin-Tin's biography. Charlotte undoubtedly gave Duncan access to important people in the horse and dog show worlds, and Rin-Tin-Tin played a fundamental role in the marriage, variously as "orphan," divorce "correspondent," and source of contested income and alimony. Rin-Tin-Tin's opposite number was Charlotte's horse, aptly named Nobleman, a Kentucky thoroughbred. These animals were sources of identity (and in Rin-Tin-Tin's case, income) for their human owners and were substantially responsible for bringing them together and causing them to part. The divorce became final in 1928, though the interlocutory judgment was entered on June 1, 1927.

The couple had at least two things in common – they both liked horses and both were fibbers, though the main thing Charlotte lied about was her age.

She was born Charlotte Rickettson. A colony of Rickettsons lived in Aurora, New York, site of the Roycroft Community of the Arts and Crafts movement. She may have been the Charlotte Rickettson, then age 16, who, according to the 1900 Federal Census, was living in Aurora as a lodger in the household of Earleton H. Paine, his wife, and two children with three other Rickettson girls: Grace, 18; Belle, 13; and Hellen, 11. Charlotte and Grace were listed as artists, the two younger girls as being "at school." Only eleven

Rickettsons were recorded by the 1900 Federal Census, and all lived in Aurora, which adds some credence to the notion that this Charlotte Rickettson may have been the same one that married Duncan.

In any case, in 1907, Charlotte married Joseph S. Anderson, a forty-year-old mineral water agent and horse fancier, born in Canada. The marriage took place a few days before the divorce to his first wife was final – or not. Though the 1910 Federal Census lists this as his second marriage, it is possible there were more: one newspaper article claimed that Charlotte was his fourth wife. The census tells us that they lived in Oakland, California, and were parents of a two-and-a-half-year-old daughter, California Mercedes. On their place in Fruitvale (in Oakland), they kept horses, among them the famous Kentucky thoroughbred Red Delight, who was later killed by a street car while Charlotte was leading him.

Joseph met a tragic end. After falling from a horse, he died in on July 5, 1914, in the Acropolis Hospital (Oakland). According to a story in the July 24, 1914 issue of the *Oakland Tribune*, just before his demise he called Deputy County Clerk Paul Wuthe to his bedside to arrange to "remarry" Charlotte but died before it could happen. An article in the March 10, 1916 *Oakland Tribune* said he did go "through a marriage ceremony with his wife. The reason for the ceremony never was given out and remains a mystery."

Charlotte filed a petition for probate of his will – the estate was estimated to be worth $40,000 to $50,000, a considerable sum in those days. Joseph's sons by an earlier marriage – Reginald, twenty-two, and Stanley, twenty-one, both from Toronto – challenged the "will of the capitalist," which had left them $100 each, with the rest of the estate going in trust in equal shares to Charlotte and her daughter. However, they later settled for $575 each.

By 1918, Charlotte was living in Pleasanton, some twenty miles southeast of Oakland. In the 1920 Federal Census, having shaved three years off her age, she was listed as a thirty-three-year-old widow, with a daughter, Mercedes, age twelve. Her occupation: general farming with three hired hands. In fact, her occupation was not that plain: the "farming" included the raising of show horses, among them Nobleman.

I have been unable to find out when and how Duncan and Charlotte met or when and where they married. Nothing appears about their wedding in the newspapers I have been able to access, and Duncan never mentions the marriage in his *Notes*, nor does James English in his biography. They might have met through Pauline Fredericks or Anita Bryant at a combination horse and dog show – for instance at the Thousand-Dollars-a-Night Horse Show held in connection with the Los Angeles County Fair in San Fernando, September 19-24, 1921, where Charlotte showed Nobleman. In filing for divorce, on March 6, 1925, Charlotte said their marriage had lasted three years by then, which indicates that they married at least by early March 1922. In the 1930 Federal Census, Duncan says his age at first marriage was twenty-nine, which would place the marriage sometime after October 1922. Yet the marriage almost certainly took place *before* that: On April 29, 1922 an article ran in the *San Francisco Chronicle* about the police dog section of a Kennel Club exhibit listing Rin-Tin-Tin's and Nanette's owner as "Lee Duncan of the Charmeran Stock Farm." (Charmeran belonged to Charlotte.) When they married, Charlotte was either thirty-five or thirty-eight.

Except for their love of horses, they were mismatched. Though Rin-Tin-Tin was no longer a nobody, Duncan's future was unsure, while Charlotte was a rich widow, who raised blooded horses. Duncan was a California ranch boy, she an emigre from New York to San Francisco. One of the issues in their divorce was Duncan's treatment of the horses. When she filed for divorce, she claimed cruelty that began soon after they married. The *Los Angeles Times* reported:

> Mrs. Duncan charges that her husband said he owned the place and had bought the blooded steeds from Kentucky, embarrassing her immensely. But that wouldn't have been so bad, the wife avers, if Duncan had not mistreated her horses. He overrode them, abused them, and returned them to the stable without proper care, the wife alleges.

Charlotte also said that Duncan neglected her: "she charges that he rarely took her to places of amusement, and even failed to put in an appearance after inviting her to dinner on several occasions. Twice he took her to dinner, and then couldn't pay the check." When a woman came to their stables and, claiming permission from Duncan, asked to ride one of their horses, it was the last straw.

(A later story says the woman came up to Charlotte when she was riding Nobleman at a horse show and said Duncan said she could ride the horse whenever she wanted to.) Charlotte must have seen Duncan as a crass, though up-and-coming user, interested more in her horses and his dog than in her. His missteps, inviting people to ride her horses and acting as if he owned her ranch, seem typical him – of his self-aggrandizement, of his ability to take on a role.

In early May 1922, after Rin-Tin-Tin's leg was healed, Duncan brought him home. He doesn't specify what home he means, probably his mother's place? Or where he lived with his new wife? (His 1922 voter registration lists him, a "motion pic," as still living on McCormick Street.)

Duncan continued working with Rin-Tin-Tin to perfect his jumping and other skills. In the meantime, the dog had a part in *My Dad* (released July 23, 1922). The movie, produced by F.B.O, takes place at a north woods trading post and contains many of the elements of Rin-Tin-Tin's later successful movies: a frontier setting, an innocent man accused of a murder he didn't commit, a girlfriend attached unwillingly to the villain, and a happy ending in which the dog is instrumental.

By late August 1922, Charlotte was "Mrs. Charlotte Anderson Duncan of Pleasanton" (the first mention of her marital status I can find) in an article in the *Woodland Daily Democrat* (California), which announced she would show "the famous Nobleman, winner last year of the blue ribbon in the five-gaited stallion class" at the California State Fair in Sacramento (September 2-10).

In early September 1922, *My Dad* played on Broadway in a two-week run. *Variety*'s reviewer panned the picture as "just a snow picture . . . about on a par with the run of snow stuff the U was turning out a few years ago." He did, however, praise the "hunt for the evidence . . . [that] really gives the picture its punches" and said that part of that redeeming action was the scene in which Rin-Tin-Tin and the hero fight the villain. At the "right price," he said, "it could be successful as part of a double feature for two or three days." A September 1922 *Lima News* (Ohio) review stated: "The real hero of 'My Dad' is that splendid dog actor, Rin-Tin-Tin. Never afraid, never self-conscious, always interesting, this famous canine provides several of the film's big thrills."

When *My Dad* opened at the Pantages Theater in Los Angeles in early October 1922, Duncan went on stage with Rin-Tin-Tin in a vaudeville act to show off the dog's "cleverness as a police dog." This presages the promotional tours that Duncan and Rin-Tin-Tin took throughout his career and contributed a great deal to the dog's success. The *Los Angeles Times* review made full, admiring mention of Rin-Tin-Tin as having an "important part" in the movie. The ad the following day identified Duncan as "of Pleasanton" and touted "RIN-TIN-TIN (Himself), The Famous Police Dog Hero Salvaged from the War Zone." The two shared the bill with "'20 Minutes in Chinatown,' An Episode of Tong Warfare in San Francisco's Chinatown," a singer, opera singers, and "Sargent & Marvin, Vaudeville Favorites with Their Little Saws."

It seems that Charlotte, Lee, and Rin-Tin-Tin lived together – at least sometimes – at her place. An *Oakland Tribune* article in late August 1922 implied it: "Pleasanton['s] . . . latest honor has come from the metropolis where Rintintin, the greatest of police dogs . . . is being featured in 'The Man from Hell's River,' as the 'dog hero.' Rintintin is the pet of Lee Duncan of Chameron Farm of this valley."

In November, Rin-Tin-Tin and Duncan appeared in an American Legion minstrel show in Van Nuys (in the San Fernando Valley), in which Duncan put Rin-Tin-Tin through his tricks and he himself appeared in a black-face number. They were one act in a roster of former professional vaudevillians, among them Harry Boulanger and W.H. Tracy. Duncan was now listed as living in Lankershim whereas he had been "of Pleasanton" in October when he appeared at the Pantages.

In spite of the fact that Rin-Tin-Tin had had roles in at least two full-length movies in 1921 and 1922, Duncan claimed that Rin-Tin-Tin made his "first movie" at the Ambassador dog show in December 1922. Yet *Los Angeles Times* reporter Maurice Stephens intimated that there was an earlier show, in 1921, when, in his review of *Where the North Begins* in early September 1923, he said: "Two years ago, at the Ambassador in Los Angeles, he made a record jump of twelve feet. This jump is used as a slow-motion subject and marked Rintintin's debut before the camera."

Whenever the show took place and the movie was made (and I cannot locate evidence to verify either date), it was a short movie. Cameraman Charlie

Jones, who knew Duncan because his two little girls took music lessons from Duncan's sister Marjorie, asked if he could film Rin-Tin-Tin in competition to try out a new slow-motion camera that according to Duncan, he had invented. (Actually, a slow-motion camera that took 700 frames a second was invented in 1894 by Etienne-Jules Marey.) Duncan agreed, and Jones filmed Rin-Tin-Tin scaling a high wall. After clearing the top at 11 feet 9 inches, Rin-Tin-Tin leapt over the head of actress Mary Miles Minter and several other people. His main competition, a beautiful imported Shepherd named Marie, who also was an actor, lost by three inches. Rin-Tin-Tin was judged the best working shepherd. Duncan said, "If I couldn't win with him on the bench, I had at least reached the top with him as a working dog. Everyone complimented me on the manner in which he did his work, showing such a happy mental attitude, never demanding a trace of force." Rin-Tin-Tin was, according to Duncan, in all the Los Angeles papers; however, in a search of the 1920s *Los Angeles Times*, I was unable to find any stories about the event.

While Rin-Tin-Tin was an exceptionally talented jumper, other German shepherds could perform as well. For instance, Hans Tossutti, in *Companion Dog Training* (1942), claimed, "I am quite proud of the fact that, in 1928, I had in one of my classes a student who set the world's record for German Shepherd Dogs in jumping and scaling a height of twelve feet four inches."

Duncan started a scrapbook of clippings about Rin-Tin-Tin, "never dreaming that some day he [Rin-Tin-Tin] would be in all the newspapers all over the world." He "was so excited over the motion picture idea that I found myself thinking of it night and day. I wanted to talk pictures instead of guns."

Jones sent Duncan a $350 check from the Novagraph Picture Company along with a letter telling him that his film of Rin-Tin-Tin jumping was a best seller and would open at Grauman's Million Dollar Theater in Los Angeles. (I can find no mention of this short film, nor much else except for music programs, in 1922-1923 advertisements in the *Los Angeles Times* for Grauman's Million Dollar Theatre, but it is possible that the theater advertised it elsewhere.) Ever cautious, Duncan thought Jones might have made a mistake, so he wrote Jones a letter asking for confirmation before he cashed it.

During this time, Duncan says, he was working on a film story for Rin-Tin-Tin. He had gotten the idea for doing this from an article in a physical culture magazine on how to turn a hobby into a moneymaker; the magazine offered a prize for the best story. Duncan's film story was based on an apocryphal legend going back at least to the Middle Ages – that of a faithful dog wrongly accused of killing a child. The father comes home to find blood on the child's bed, stabs the dog to death, then finds that the blood belonged to an attacker (another animal, often a snake) that the dog has killed to save the child. James English, in his Rin-Tin-Tin biography, said that Duncan heard the story in France, where it was a children's story "among the peasant folk," but that seems unlikely, since Duncan's main characters were a man named Llewellyn and his dog Gelert, both of which are Welsh names. And in France, the wronged dog was often St. Guinefort, the Holy Greyhound, the central figure of a medieval cult in which sickly children were left in the evening near a spring dedicated to the saint; if in the morning a live child was at the spring, it would mean that the child left there the night before had been a changeling and somehow the true and healthy child had been exchanged for it during the night. Duncan eventually changed the story's setting to the American frontier, turned the nobleman into a trapper, and kept the dog alive: Rin-Tin-Tin would not die, but would merely be whipped by his main human character. He called the story "Where the North Begins" and was well along in writing it when he received the letter from Jones.

Duncan may well have read the Llewellyn and Gelert story in a book, *A Present to Youths and Young Men*, written in 1891 by "a gentleman [Edward Shorthouse] interested in Working Men's Clubs – Youths' Institutes, – Sunday-schools & etc." William Robert Spencer's poem, "Beth Gelert, or, 'The Grave of the Greyhound,'" was widely reprinted – for instance, in J. Earl Clauson's *The Dog's Book of Verse* (1916), which was dedicated to an Airedale, one of Duncan's favorite breeds. Rex Beach wrote a story very similar to Duncan's in "The Trapper and His Dog" (*Reader's Digest*, July 1942), which, according to folklorist Ernest Braughman, seems to have been based on an old legend. Perhaps Duncan had read or heard that old legend, too.

All that aside, the story resonates with Duncan's life. Unlike Duncan's, the father cared deeply for his child (even killed for him). Yet he killed the dog the child loved, as Duncan's grandfather killed his pet lamb. It was a terrible mistake, a mistake of revenge for the wrong reasons, and the dog's sense of betrayal, as imagined by Duncan, must have been very like the betrayal he felt as a child from both his mother and father. The child and the dog have a very close relationship, as Duncan did with all his dogs, particularly Rin-Tin-Tin. It is the center of the story, the only relationship that is not flawed.

Duncan said he told his mother and Marjorie he was thinking about giving up "gun work" in order to get Rin-Tin-Tin in the movies. With $100 put aside to live on, he went to Dyas and asked for three months off to develop his idea. Dyas agreed but asked if Duncan had ever been to the studios. Duncan replied that he had not but was confident that he "could make good with Rin-Tin-Tin. You see, I had the Novagraph check in mind and had made it in a few minutes of play for Rin-Tin-Tin and myself, never dreaming I was to be paid for it."

In his *Notes*, Duncan stated that his mother and sister tried to discourage him from pursuing a movie career for Rin-Tin-Tin. He remembered: "To top it all off, after supper Mother and Marjorie had a big cry and told me how that afternoon one of the neighbors had said, 'Why, the idea of him trying to make a living off of his dog!'" Marjorie was afraid that it would "cast a reflection on her school of music" and that he would in the end be only a dog trainer.

Duncan stuck to his guns – the metaphorical ones, not the ones at Dyas. He started working in an "old sweatshirt and overall" with his dogs. In his *Notes*, he said that with his Novagraph money he bought a white enamel stove and new furniture for his mother. "There was a lot of happiness in our little home as a result of this good fortune," he wrote. Where was Sampson, his mother's husband? Where was Charlotte, his wife?

He made another short film with Jones and Rin-Tin-Tin who was supposedly, after several short films and two movies, getting used to the camera. At Pauline Frederick's house at 503 Sunset Boulevard, Jones filmed Rin-Tin-Tin riding on the backs of her jumping horses. Duncan and Fredericks may have met at the Robertson-Cole studios, where she made several forgettable pictures and Rin-Tin-Tin made *My Dad*. Or they may have met through Eugene Pallette, who worked with her in several movies, including *Two Kinds of Women*, in which Rin-Tin-Tin may have had a bit part, if indeed that is the film the *Los Angeles Times* meant when it listed him as featured in *The Flash of Blue Lake Ranch*. (*Two Kinds of Women* was based on a novel, *Judith of Blue Lake Ranch*.) A stage as well as screen actress who had moved in sophisticated circles in her native Boston, Frederick came to California and underwent a metamorphosis. According to her biographer, David Robinson, she fell in love with the West and its people with their "honesty" and "simple natures." She became a horsewoman, with stables of riding horses. Allen Boone, who knew Strongheart, Rin-Tin-Tin's German shepherd rival, and wrote a book dedicated to him, introduced her to the rodeo circuit. She bought herself a cowboy outfit and began to attend rodeos. One of her best friends was Prairie Annie, a tough cowgirl. "[T]ime and again she [Fredericks] turned down a fashionable party because she knew that there was some fun going on in a home where a Winchester rifle stood in the corner," as Robinson put it. It is understandable that she liked Rin-Tin-Tin and Duncan, who presented himself as the epitome of the Western Man.

In another short film, Duncan himself punched a bag with Leach Cross and made $250 doing it. Leach Cross (born Louis Wallach) was a lightweight boxer called the "fighting dentist." In 1918 Cross built a house in Hollywood and started a private gym that was frequented by movie stars and businessmen, which may have been where Duncan met him. In April 1921, Cross came out of retirement from boxing and left Los Angeles until late January 1922. The film with Duncan must have been made either in early 1921 or sometime in 1922 when Leach was in Los Angeles.

Jones also featured Rin-Tin-Tin in a picture in which Rose Heather, "a pretty girl from Hawaii," drove a speedboat pulling him on an aquaplane. I can find no record of this, nor can I find out anything about Rose Heather.

Meanwhile, Duncan rehearsed Rin-Tin-Tin in the part he had written about the wrongly accused dog. Rin-Tin-Tin did it perfectly, "and I think my happiness reflected on him as he went through his part," said Duncan in his *Notes*. The next morning he went to Hollywood with an unnamed friend who took him to United Studios, where he and Rin-Tin-Tin met with indifference. Though he kept making the rounds of the studios while living on "Poverty Row," he had no luck. "To them I was just another dog trainer with his dog. . . . I went on home a little disappointed but not discouraged by any means."

Then came the big break at Warner, a ramshackle studio run on a shoestring on Sunset Boulevard, where Duncan was lucky enough to meet Harry, the sober and conservative brother of the four Warners. Leo Rosten described Harry as a moralist who seldom smiled, a "folksy, homey guy. . . . devoted family man – you never heard about him going to a night club, being mixed up in a scandal." Harry wanted to create (and did create) movies that "promoted old-fashioned virtues" – not that he was averse to making money. Duncan, who called himself a Boy Scout and who led a quiet life, must have appealed to him. Had Duncan first met the cocky, libertine Jack Warner, the story might have been different. (Charles Higham, in *Warner Brothers*, says that it was Jack he met, as does Jeanine Basinger. According to Basinger, Jack is supposed to have said, when Duncan described his dog's abilities, "This I gotta see! A dog that can act!")

At the interview, Duncan showed off Rin-Tin-Tin's quick response to commands and his many tricks. Harry, according to Duncan, liked Rin-Tin-Tin. He probably was also aware of the popularity of dog movies – the German shepherd Strongheart had just made a movie, *Silent Call* (1921), that had received glowing reviews and, though it cost only $100,000 to produce, had made a lot of money. Pictures starring dogs were excellent vehicles for featuring wholesome values like loyalty and courage. James English described this meeting a little differently than Duncan did in his *Notes*. According to him, Duncan and Rin-Tin-Tin found the movie-makers trying to film a scene with a wolf from the zoo. They had spent two days trying to complete it, but the wolf wouldn't cooperate. Duncan dirtied Rin-Tin-Tin's coat to make him look like a wolf, found Harry Warner, who was directing the movie, and told him he could do the part in twenty minutes. He was successful, and Warner was then interested in listening to what he had to say.

In any case, Rin-Rin-Tin was on his way. Warner asked Duncan to give the company thirty days to work something out. During that time, actor William Desmond hired Rin-Tin-Tin at $25 a day for ten days to make a movie on the Feather River and decided to keep him on up until four days of his appointment with Warner. This movie, *Shadows of the North*, produced by Universal, was adapted from Edison Marshall's 1922 novel, *The Skyline of Spruce*, about prospectors in northern Canada.

Two contradictory stories of Rin-Tin-Tin's early movie career thus exist.
One story is Duncan's: He, a poor and unknown dog trainer, enters his German shepherd in a jumping contest; the dog's winning jump is filmed by a Hollywood cameraman in December 1922; with the money from the film, the

trainer quits his job and for three months does more short movies with the dog, writes a screenplay, and finally gets his big break with Warner.

The other story is mine, based on sources from the time: the dog acts in at least three movies from 1921 to 1922, none of them produced by Warner, and is already being touted as a "dog star" when Warner signs him. Duncan is hardly an unknown: he knows movie stars and wealthy (and famous) German shepherd buffs; he marries a socialite horsewoman.

Duncan's story doesn't fit the chronology of events. It took Warner a month to make up their minds to give Rin-Tin-Tin a contract. The first movie he made with Warner, *Where the North Begins* (1923), was a relatively long time in the making – three months on location and "several weeks" after that to completion. It was released in July 1923, so the deal Duncan struck with the company has to have occurred at the earliest by February 1923. The dog show was in December 1922. It is impossible that Duncan compressed the making of several short features, his writing of the story for *Where the North Begins*, three months on leave from Dyas, and weeks of approaching studios in one or two short months. Possibly he and, consequently, English were confused about which dog show Charlie Jones attended – it could have been the one in Pasadena in February or March 1922 rather than the Ambassador dog show in December 1922. If true, that would allow for the sequence of events Duncan said took place – but even so, he left out the movies Rin-Tin-Tin made before *Where the North Begins*.

Whatever story is actually true (and of course I think mine is), it was a go with Warner, though at first Duncan was in limbo about the financial arrangements. Warner, always working on that shoestring then, was, said Duncan, nonetheless fair: they offered to pay him from the profits of the picture six months after it was released, but when he said he didn't know if he could wait that long, he was given a $150 a week draw. As he said, $600 a month was about what he ordinarily made in a year.

Rin-Tin-Tin was on the verge of a spectacular career in the movies. The nobody who knew everybody had brought him there.

3
The Right Dog at the Right Time

"More pleasure he found in a bone than some of his contemporaries in custom-built automobiles, steam yachts and gold-plated baths. His name in electric lights never caused him to swagger, and he was impervious to fan mail. . . . Reno never knew him nor did Gretna Green. His home life was his own business and not a source of income for press agents," said the *Charleston Gazette* in Rin-Tin-Tin's obituary. It went on to add that though he was a phenomenal success, he was "his own romping rough-and-tumble self." Rin-Tin-Tin, a dog, became a Hollywood star, the "Fairbanks of dogdom." Though he was the most popular and successful dog star of his time, he was not the only one. The decade of the 1920s was the era of dog movies, when a dog's name could go up in lights bigger and brighter than his human co-star's name on the marquee for a feature film.

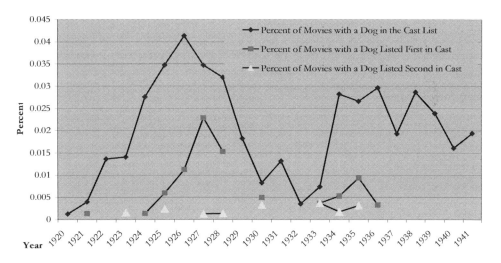

Dogs in U.S. Movies as a Percent of Total, 1920-1941

Until the 1920s, no dog had a starring role in a feature-length movie. Before that, dogs did have bit parts in movies, usually as sidekicks or comic relief, and some did star, but in shorts. There were Jean, a collie trained by Lawrence Trimble; Old Bill, star of Syd (brother of Charlie) Chaplin's *A Dog's Life* (1918) ; Pal, who sported two gold crowns on his teeth and acted in *Who Will Marry Mary?* (1913). Then, in 1921, Strongheart, a German shepherd, was billed as the lead in the feature *The Silent Call*. From then on up until 1930, fourteen dogs, all males, played leading roles in features with top billing above human actors, many of them in more than one film. During this time, forty-two dogs were listed as members of the cast, though not necessarily with top billing, in at least one movie. The overwhelming majority were males.

After Strongheart's first success, three years went by before another movie starred a dog. In 1924, Strongheart had top billing in *The Love Master*. In 1925, Wolfheart was the main lead in *Wolfheart's Revenge*. Rin-Tin-Tin, meanwhile, was billed second in *Where the North Begins* (1923), *Find Your Man* (1924), and *The Lighthouse by the Sea* (1924), though, in advertisements and publicity generated after the release of the movies, he was often billed first. In succeeding years, with only a few exceptions, he was the star of his movies.

By 1923, the year Rin-Tin-Tin became famous for *Where the North Begins*, dogs were big business in Hollywood. The *Los Angeles Times* claimed that the cost of animals to the motion picture industry was $10,000,000. The canine actor Cameo, a bulldog-Boston terrier mix, had raked in enough money to build a mansion for his owner. Buck, the St. Bernard that Hal Roach bought at the dog pound for $5, played the role of his namesake in *Call of the Wild* and became so valuable that Roach "wouldn't take $10,000 for him." In 1925, Catherine Brody wrote an article for the *The Saturday Evening Post* in which she described the ranch a producer kept just for raising animal stars: "He has specially constructed sets with bungalows, street cars, a hotel, a schoolhouse, all fully furnished and cut down to quarter size."

The era of the dog star would not have come about had there not been changes in movie making itself. By the early 1920s, the movies had come of age – in film length, popularity, and technical sophistication – just enough to allow a dog to shine as a hero. In 1910, American movie-makers released over 1500 short films and only forty full-length features. In 1913, the number of American shorts released climbed to a peak of more than five thousand but fell precipitously thereafter, while features began a slow and steady climb. Melodramas and Westerns, which emphasized action, dominated the silent screen. Movie attendance rose very fast. In 1920, 50 million people a week, half the nation's population, went to see a movie; attendance had jumped to 110 million people a week by 1929.

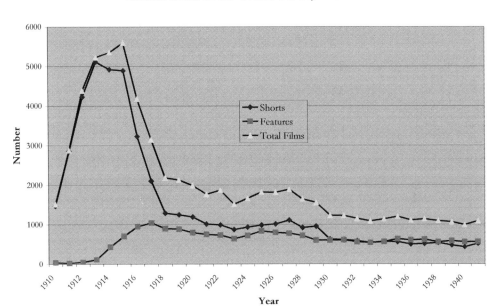

Movies Made in the United States, 1910-1941

Before 1910, movie actors (as opposed to stage actors) were considered to be disreputable folk, but, as the middle class began to attend movies in greater numbers, actors became celebrities. The first cinema star was Florence Lawrence, the Biograph Girl, whose 1910 faked death in a streetcar accident and miraculous reappearance, with attendant media coverage orchestrated by star-system creator Carl Laemmle, made her a celebrity. Within two months after her reappearance, *Moving Picture World*'s "Man About Town" noted the "interest the public has taken in the personality of many of the picture players." Movie-makers were inundated by requests for actors' autographed pictures. The actress Florence Turner said she had three thousand marriage offers in three months. In the 1910s, a roster of movie stars achieved fame, among them Pearl White, Clara Bow, Norma Talmadge, and Mary Pickford, who allegedly made the enormous (for then – and now) salary of $10,000 a week.

Hollywood, the new movie capital, became a place of glamor and scandal. Gloria Swanson supposedly bathed in a gold bathtub. The glitterati gathered at Pickfair, the 22-room lodge of Mary Pickford and Douglas Fairbanks, who after divorcing their respective spouses, had married each other in 1920. In 1921, Roscoe "Fatty" Arbuckle was put on trial for the rape and murder of actress Virginia Rappe, which supposedly happened at a wild San Francisco party celebrating his signing of a million-dollar contract. (He was never found guilty.) In 1922, someone shot director William Desmond Taylor dead; the crime was never solved.

Middle America was titillated and shocked by the stars' shenanigans. In response to criticism, movie-makers created the Motion Picture Producers and Distributors of America (later the Motion Picture Association of America), but disapproval of Hollywood's morality remained rampant.

The aftermath of World War I also affected movies. In the early 1920s, according to Leslie Midkiff deBauche, in *Reel Patriotism: The Movies and World War I*, "War and peace remained in the headlines, on the bookshelves, and in the minds of the American public." Hollywood movie-makers and, to some extent, the rest of the nation were ambivalent about the war. Countering glorification of the war hero were works by writers who decried the war's brutality and seeming senselessness. Hollywood, knowing it was dealing with a mass audience that tended toward conservatism, and afraid, as a fragile new medium, to probe the depths of the war hangover, tended, with a few exceptions, to produce movies that kept it simple. War movies, and there weren't that many of them, usually profiled courageous and sacrificial acts of individual soldiers. A noble German shepherd, who was not really German, saving the wounded from death exemplified this to perfection.

Given this movie climate, what better stars than dogs? Dogs, as guardians of the weak, played in roles that broke no moral rules. They did not frequent opium dens or look lasciviously at women. Their home lives (at least as they were publicized) were a rebuke to Jazz Age sinners, in Hollywood and elsewhere. Moreover, as actors they seemed more natural than humans, who expressed themselves through speech. Dogs' athleticism fitted the demands of silent pictures for action – the daring hero, who solved problems with tooth and claw rather than clever repartee. In short, in an America with an underlying conservative bent, dogs – loved for their innocence, loyalty, lack of pretension, and morality – were a perfect choice as hero. This was especially true of movies for children.

Children's matinees, which began in 1920 as municipal enterprises and were promoted nationally by the Motion Picture Producers and Distributors of America from 1925 on, had something to do with the success of Rin Tin Tin, Strongheart, and other animal actors. Even before the matinee, children were an important part of the movie audience, and a contested one. Richard Koszarski, in *An Evening's Entertainment: The Age of the Silent Feature Picture: 1915-1928*, notes that most children attended movies at least once a week, and the trend was upward. Early on, reformers viewed movies as dangerous to children. In 1919, the Rev. J.J. Phelan, in an admittedly biased study (*Motion Pictures As a Phase of Commercialized Amusement in Toledo, Ohio. Social Survey Series III*), found that movies were detrimental to children in "weakening of morals and development of false ideals in life" as well as "[u]nwholesome curiosity and craving for excitement."

The movies children saw were vetted. Phelan documented active censorship boards not only in Ohio but elsewhere. The National Board of Review of Censorship included a lack of "respect for law," "the social evil," and "picturing of opium-joints" among its prohibitions. There was a National Commission for Better Films for Young People. In Portland, Oregon, a program to censor movies for young people was in operation from 1911. One of its proscriptions was against cruelty to animals, and another was against "[g]irls putting their hands in men's trousers pockets." (Part of the latter concern had to do with the darkness of the movie houses, which could lead towards hanky-panky.)

The content of some movies was considered detrimental, and the studios at first refused to do anything about it. However, they eventually had something of a change of heart. In spring of 1925, Saturday Morning Movies, endorsed by Will Hays, president of Motion Picture Producers and Distributors of America, included fifty-two programs especially made for children. Each began with a one-reel scenic, followed by a feature and a two-reel comedy. According to Kenneth W. Payne, in a 1925 article in *McClure's*, the Hays office took "[o]riginal negatives of many of the best films produced in America. . . . cut, re-titled, and examined and cut [them] again, and finally put [them] together into standard programs of identical length and quality." Standardization included the price of admission – ten cents everywhere – and the length of the program – one and one-half hours. The Hays office chose animal pictures, as well as Westerns and adventure films, all of which are strong on action. Making movies for children freed movie producers. If children had their own movies, said Payne, the movie industry could develop "a truly adult screen art" rather than, like "Coney Island and the comic strip," feel the necessity to "appeal to all ages alike." Payne quoted Charles Morrison, manager of the Palace Theater in Jacksonville, where a similar ten-cent program had been started, as saying, "'We found out that they [children] preferred pictures like *Black Beauty* and *Pollyanna*, and those with dogs such as Rin-Tin-Tin, or with horses as stars." It was not the first attempt to provide programs especially for children. In Albany, New York, the Strand Theater started showing ten-cent Junior movies in 1920. Other cities with children's programs included Washington D.C., Los Angeles, San Francisco, Pittsburgh, Atlanta, and Asheville, South Carolina.

By the 1920s, Westerns were being filmed for the children's matinee audience. Koszarski states, "The change in public taste was predictable, because Westerns had moved from the serious plateau of the early DeMille pictures to a genre clearly intended for children." Young audiences (high school) preferred Westerns above all other genres, according to a 1923 poll. Rin-Tin-Tin's early movies were almost all Westerns, far more suitable for a dog star than sophisticated comedies. So the genre suited both him and his audience. However, adults also attended Rin-Tin-Tin's movies, which played in theaters at night as well as in the daytime – often to capacity crowds.

The lack of sound in silent movies, which removed the language barrier, added to dogs' appeal to foreign audiences. Said the *Bedford Gazette* of Rin-Tin-Tin in 1930:

> Rinty's language is universal and his appeal knows no boundaries. No American star is more popular in Germany than Rinty where his pictures are given gala premieres and run for weeks and sometimes months in important theatres. . . . Man's love for dogs is so general the world over that Rin-Tin-Tin's name and fame have reached corners of the globe where other stars have never yet been heard of.

Dogs had been actors before – on stage, in vaudeville, and in the movies – but not like this. If Rin-Tin-Tin followed a tradition of dogs in entertainment, he and his cohorts also broke through it. In his feature films, he was the hero of a story. He moved the plot forward and was the story's center (though that center was slightly off). Vaudeville and stage animal actors of the past usually were bit actors in a play with human stars, something like Nana (actually often played by a human) in *Peter Pan*, or just did tricks, especially tricks that aped humans. According to Jack London, in his novel *Michael, Brother of Jerry*, the stunts that stage dogs did included back and forward flips, barrel-jumping, waltzing, spinning plates on their noses, hurdle-jumping, walking on front legs, pony-riding, and diving in a tank of water. On film, in a sharp break from traditional canine acting, Rin-Tin-Tin's and other dog stars' physical actions consisted mostly of maneuvers, done on command, that dogs would naturally do in nature (e.g., jumping, running), with the possible exceptions of sitting up on their hind-quarters, untying knots, and opening locks. When Rin-Tin-Tin and Duncan traveled the vaudeville circuit or performed on stage in theaters where his movies were playing, the acts consisted mostly of Rin-Tin-Tin's following commands to do some of the same stunts (e.g., "scratch your left ear") that he did in his movies.

Cinema did not replace vaudeville but coexisted with it. In the beginning of the silent movie era, the Keith vaudeville theaters incorporated silent short films into their shows, and vaudeville performers, including animals, were subjects of shorts filmed in studios. The Library of Congress has preserved some of these on the site American Memory. (They are available through a search of "dog" and "vaudeville" at http://memory.loc.gov/.) The "bag-punching dog," created in 1901 by Thomas Edison, Inc., featured a boxer, Mannie, trained by a Miss Laura Comstock, a vaudeville star. In the film Mannie leaps athletically to swing a punching bag with his body. Another filmed vaudeville animal act includes a baboon playing the violin and a dog jumping rope. The "Dog Factory" (1904) is based on an elaborate joke in which dogs of various breeds are being made into sausages – and back into dogs. A similar film of a vaudeville act features two dogs on their hind legs – one in an apron serving dinner and another in a police officer's uniform – with a third in begging position; these dogs do tricks within a story framework (American Mutoscope & Biograph Co., June 13,

1903). The dogs pretend to be humans by standing on their hind legs and wearing clothes; they are not "stars," and plots are rudimentary. Rin-Tin-Tin does not stand on his hind legs to ape being a human, nor does he wear clothes (except for his Red Cross vest and the boots he wears in *Clash of the Wolves*). He plays a dog, perhaps one with superlative canine senses, but a dog nonetheless, a dog who competes with humans in his perceptions, emotional capacity, and heroism.

Perhaps, too, a dog could become a movie star because American domestic dog culture, so tied to human culture, had changed significantly by the 1920s. According to the 1920 Federal Census, for the first time more than half of Americans lived in urban areas. In the 19th century, the city dog, in addition to sometimes being a pet, was a transporter of goods or pursued other occupations. By the 20th century, the city dog had become mainly a pet, different from the rural dog, who was, and had been, mostly a worker. Mark Derr, in *A Dog's History of America: How Our Best Friend Explored, Conquered, and Settled a Continent*, encapsulates the change: "Dogs and cats were increasingly the primary connection to the animal world for a growing number of urban Americans, and their stature increased accordingly, as did the pressure placed upon them to conform to human desires." In a world going urban, people saw pets as like themselves, part of the family – and therefore expected to act more "human."

Even in the 1920s, people were aware of the similarity between pet dogs and human children. In 1925, a *New York Times* story focused on Central Park, "Care of Children and Dogs Chief Topic of Park Talk," commented on how "keeping a dog in New York is like raising a baby, or worse." According to the writer, "Listening without looking one can hardly tell which is a mother and which is the owner of a dog." The owners talked of food and weight, problems of finding a pet sitter, asking janitors to walk dogs. One park denizen was "considering getting up a playground association for the benefit of dogs." A canine beauty shop (actually grooming parlor) had recently opened on Fifth Avenue.

To some extent, as with children, when the perception of dogs' economic value as workers waned, their emotional value increased. Viviana A. Zelizer's argument in *Pricing the Priceless Child: The Changing Social Value of Children* – that children's leaving the work force "was also part of a cultural process of 'sacrilization' of children's lives" – applies to dogs as well. Zelizer points out that some child labor was acceptable: child actors were "paid to represent the new, sentimentalized view of children." Perhaps something similar, but not exactly the same, was happening to dogs. Though Rin-Tin-Tin and his cohorts were dogs *working* as actors, they represented the new concept of canines valued for more than their labor; therefore it was possible to elevate a dog, as actor, to star status on a par with humans. However, as stars, dog actors were representing not just a new idealized canine but also an *adult human* masculine ideal in a post-war climate where the idea of what a *man* should be had come under question. (See "Overcoming the Limitations of a Dog Star.")

What dogs represented in the 1920s can also be seen as being in a *process* of change. The ways Rin-Tin-Tin was viewed legally in Duncan's divorce from Charlotte Anderson Duncan illustrate the ambiguity of his position as a canine in the human world. According to the *Los Angeles Times*, in a March 1925 article, "Evidently Rin Tin Tin's company was so much pleasure to Duncan that he considered Mrs. Duncan's presence rather secondary." In this instance, Rin-Tin-Tin was seen as a rival for Duncan's affections. The same article reported that a judge gave Charlotte a restraining order so that Duncan could not collect royalties from Rin-Tin-Tin's movies, change his movie contracts, or dispose of community property. She asked for $1000 a month alimony, based on the income of $2000 a month that Duncan derived from Rin-Tin-Tin's acting. Yet the article's headline was: "Dog Film Star May Be Orphan." Orphan? He was the bread winner, source of contested income, and furthermore, he was not the Duncans' child, but an adult dog.

By March of 1926, according to the *Salt Lake Tribune*, Rin-Tin-Tin had become "part of the community property to be adjudicated" in the Duncan divorce suit. At the same time a *Los Angeles Times* article, which was headlined "Rin-Tin-Tin Named in Suit," opened with the following sentence: "Rin-Tin-Tin, dog hero of a score of motion pictures, is the latest film player to be named in a divorce suit." It went on to say that he was named "in a manner that casts not the slightest reflection upon [his] repute. . ." Yet legally the dog actor, so often referred to as "almost human" in his acting, was not a correspondent in the case as some newspaper headlines stated, but an "asset" (property) of

Duncan's. Eventually, Charlotte granted Rin-Tin-Tin to Duncan as his separate *property* so the money he made as part of the dog-human partnership became his.

The interlocutory decree for the divorce was granted on June 1, 1927, the final judgment of divorce on June 4, 1928. The Associated Press story about the interlocutory decree was variously headlined by newspapers, mostly on May 26 or 27: "Rin-Tin-Tin, Dog, Actor, Cause of Owner's Divorce," "Rin-Tin-Tin's Mistress Is Granted Divorce," "Rin-Tin-Tin is Cited as Corespondent [sic]," "Loves Dog Better Than Wife," and "Says Rin-Tin-Tin Is Love Pirate." In an article titled "The Nobleman Revenged," The *Oakland Tribune* featured two photographs: one of Mrs. Duncan sitting on her horse Nobleman, with Rinette, Rin-Tin-Tin's daughter, by their side; the other of Duncan with Rin Tin Tin. It seems that, in the popular imagination, if not legally, Rin-Tin-Tin really was a correspondent in the divorce case.

Rin-Tin-Tin's position as Duncan's dog – and a famous, income-producing one – ranged wide: child-orphan, wife's love rival, community property, asset. This echoes the ambiguity in his success as a movie star, where in his roles he was pet, hero, fighter, and lover, but also in the service of human beings and their desires.

Rin-Tin-Tin was one of many German shepherd stars. Of the fourteen dogs that had leading roles in movies in the 1920s, twelve were German shepherds. In addition to Strongheart and Rin-Tin-Tin, the other German shepherds were Peter the Great, Thunder, Lightning, Wolfheart, Ranger, Fang, Dynamite, Klondike, Champion, and Braveheart. (The two other dog stars were Bullet, a pit-bull or pit-bull mix, and Rex, a collie.) Of the forty-two dogs whose names appeared on cast lists in the 1920s, at least twenty-six (more than sixty per cent if the total) were German shepherds. With the exception of Teddy and Duke, both Great Danes, the other dogs on cast lists tended to be small terriers or mongrels.

The popularity of German shepherds as movie stars cannot be laid entirely at Rin-Tin-Tin's paws or at the paws of his nemesis, Strongheart. It could be just as true to say that the German shepherd's general rise in popularity gave Rin-Tin-Tin and other German shepherds their chance in the movies. Because of the German shepherd's abilities and previous training, it, of all the dog breeds, provided the best fit for the kind of movies that were popular in the 1920s.

On the other hand, one might make the argument that even though the German shepherd was popular and trained in ways that made it a natural for movie acting, another breed of dog, trained in other skills, could also have been successful in movies – a hunting dog, say, who knew how to trail and apprise its owner of game, or perhaps a herding dog, like Lassie, who knew how to alert her people to danger. However, for several reasons, I doubt it.

It is no accident that German shepherds in movie roles gained such general popularity when they did. Turn-of-the-century fear of disorder placed the breed in the spotlight as police and guard dogs, who also showed off their skills in trials at dog shows. After World War I, German shepherds' rise in popularity was attributed to their role as war dogs, savers of lives and guardians of the just, and certainly that did come into play, too.

German shepherds' popularity in the United States follows a curve with a sharp rise from 1910 to 1926 and a slow drop thereafter. *The New York Times*, in its coverage of the Westminster dog shows, chronicled it: In 1910, seven German shepherds were shown at Westminster, but by 1914, there were seventy-two, ninth in number of dogs entered. Commentators noted that it was considered an "innovation breed" at the show and "well known at present in America," especially as a bodyguard for high society. In 1919, again, more than 70 shepherds were entered in the Westminster dog show, and "the competition of the early classes attracted a large gathering around the ring. . . .The breed has come into such sudden favor that many fanciers have spent much time about the benches, which is taken as an indication that in another season this breed will be one of the most popular in the show." By 1922, again at Westminster, the German shepherd led the number of entries (178) followed by 145 Boston terriers. In 1926, the peak year for the decade, of 59,500 dogs registered in the American Kennel Club Stud Book, 21,500 were German shepherds, while Boston terriers counted for 10,700. *Breeds of Dogs* (United States Department of Agriculture, 1927) stated that the German shepherd, after being practically unknown in the United States, had become a "ranking dog breed." By 1931, the breed had dropped to fourth on the American Kennel Club's list of popular dogs with 2,460 shepherds registered out of a total of 46,800.

Ordinary people may have admired German shepherds, but the chances are that they were not buying them, or other pedigreed dogs, in great numbers. Writing about the early years of the 20th century, Mark Derr points out that only about two percent of American dogs were pure-breeds and that only about five percent of Americans could afford the more expensive of them. Pedigreed dogs were a sign of wealth; dog shows were events for high society. Arthur F. Jones, writing in *The New York Times* in 1934, noted that popularity, according to registrations with the American Kennel Club, did not reflect ownership among the "wider public." Steelworkers in 1919 were making forty-two cents an hour, working twelve and fourteen hours a day, which would amount to a salary of around $25 to $30 a week. It would have cost almost two weeks' salary for a steelworker to buy a German shepherd puppy – in the March 1918 issue of *Forest and Stream*, German shepherd puppies were offered for sale in ads at $50 and up. And those were "ordinary" German shepherds. According to a June 1914 article in *The New York Times,* the famous Apollo von Hunenstein was sold by his German owner to Americans for $1,624; his eventual cost was $2,500 when transportation and tariff were added.

As noted by Malcolm B. Willis in *The German Shepherd Dog: Its History, Development and Genetics*, one problem with assessing the popularity of the German shepherd lies in its names, which have included German Shepherd Dog, German Sheepdog, Alsatian Shepherd, Alsatian Wolfdog, Shepherd Dog, and Police Dog. In Britain and France, the German shepherd's name changed to Alsatian when authorities, wrestling with anti-German bias during World War I, found enough evidence to identify the dog with Alsace.

In America, the breed association and the American Kennel Club were at odds over the name of the dog for more than a decade. The term "German Sheep Dog" was used by the American Kennel Club until around 1914, when the animal was rechristened "German Shepherd Dog." "German" was part of its name at the Westminster Dog Shows throughout World War I, but bowing to post-war American hostility towards anything German, the A.K.C. changed the name to Sheepdog in 1919. Further, though the "shepherd" category in dog shows was obviously for German shepherds, there were complaints that it was too general and led some people to confuse the dog with other shepherds, like the black-and-white farm dog (probably a border collie). Also German shepherds were sometimes lumped in with Doberman pinschers and dachshunds, which, to add to the name mess, were rechristened Badger Dogs for the same reason sauerkraut was renamed "liberty cabbage." And to add even more to the confusion, W. Horace Hoskins, Dean of the Veterinary College of New York University, said in 1921: "In Germany they [German shepherds] were also known as the Doberman pincer [sic]."

The breed association, originally the German Shepherd Dog Club of America, changed its name to Shepherd Dog Club right before the end of World War I, in late October 1918. It was not until 1930 that the Club changed the name back to German Shepherd Dog Club and asked the American Kennel Club to follow suit with the breed name.

The name "police dog" also confuses matters. Not all dogs who worked for the police were German shepherds, and not all German shepherds worked for the police. Airedales, fox terriers, and other breeds worked for the police, especially overseas – and people of the time were aware of that. The German shepherd also was called a "Belgian police dog." And this: "Our Common Dogs," a March 1919 article in *The National Geographic Magazine,* by Louis Agassiz Fuertes and Ernest Harold Baynes, pictures the German shepherd in a Red Cross vest with a caption calling it a police dog, while next to it a Belgian Shepherd, also in a Red Cross vest, is named as a Belgian Shepherd. Earlier in the article, though, there are two other descriptions, one of the "German Shepherd, Or Police Dog," and the other of "The Belgian Shepherd Dog."

In the United States, German shepherds were often favored for police work. As *Breeds of Dogs* (United States Department of Agriculture, 1927), said, "[S]pecial training has converted numbers of them [German shepherds] into high-class police dogs, for which work they are admirably adapted, because of a splendid conformation and natural inclination for trailing."

In Europe, dogs of many breeds worked for the police. In 1907, an article in *The New York Times* lauded the work of sixty dogs assisting the police in the city of Ghent, Belgium, a program that began in 1899, mentioning that the most useful breeds for the work were "the big Belgian or French shepherd dog, the powerful and sagacious Briards and Groenendaels." Other breeds used as police dogs were Airedales, Doberman pinschers, Rottweilers, and bloodhounds.

American police actively publicized the work of police dogs. As reported in *Outlook* (1915), the New York police held an outdoor carnival, attended by about thirty-five thousand spectators, at which "highly trained police dogs" showed how they could stop a burglar. Two years later, they gave a show at Carnegie Hall. The audience was "especially responsive to the work of the police dogs, who were shown [in moving pictures] capturing sneak thieves."

Rin-Tin-Tin was also billed as a war dog. Duncan was trading in on an association of German shepherds with war dogs that began quite early in the United States. For example, in November 1919, the sole judge at the open air specialty show of the Shepherd Dog Club of America at Mineola Fair Grounds was Anne Tracy, who, during the war, had been overseas with the Red Cross, where, she said, she had seen German shepherds doing brave deeds. According to *The New York Times*, she came dressed in a "semi-military sport suit." By the 1930s, in the popular press, a German shepherd was the poster war dog. Typical was the statement by Vinton B. Breese in *Country Life and the Sportsman* (1938), "the German Shepherd, more than any other breed, was utilized [as a war dog]. . . .The truly wonderful work of the breed in that connection was doubtless the impulse needed to bring it to more widespread attention."

In reality, many other dog breeds had served the military in World War I. The German shepherd was only one of them – perhaps not the most important one. A 1914 article in the *Los Angeles Times* said that the French used "rustic shepherds" from the Beauce and Pyrenees mountain dogs as war dogs. Walter Mason, in *Dogs of All Nations* (1915), mentioned the German shepherd only when discussing ambulance dogs. "The Dog's Manifold Duties at the Battle Front," an article in *The National Geographic Magazine* (March 1919), made it clear that many breeds of dog served in the war, ranging "from Alaskan malamute to St. Bernard and from Scotch collie to fox terrier." The dogs singled out as heroes included a fox terrier, a setter, a sheep dog "somewhat too coarse for show purposes," two St. Bernards, and an Airedale.

War dogs were popularly portrayed as Red Cross dogs, but in actuality they served in many other functions: No Man's Land patrol dog, watch dog, pack dog, messenger, and ration carrier. Dogs used for hauling machine guns were far less costly – in initial price and upkeep – than horses who performed the same service. In 1914, dogs were trained to signal the coming of suffocating gas by growling signals into a telephone and ringing bells. One English war dog, Jack of Putney, probably a rat terrier, allegedly killed more than a thousand rats in the trenches before he was sickened by poison gas and sent home; he died at age twenty-two. A French army dog supposedly captured enemy dogs by grabbing their ears and marching them along. Yet to the popular press the war dogs of note were the Red Cross dogs, saviors of the wounded. They were portrayed as angels of mercy, who, as the *Los Angeles Times* put it in 1916, "sometimes acquit themselves more nobly than we who insist that they have no souls."

The estimates for the number of World War I European army dogs range from six thousand to ten thousand. In a February 1918 magazine article, "The Dogs of War," Lewis Edwin Theiss bemoaned the fact that, unlike the Germans, British, and French, the United States was laggard in training war dogs. Shortly after the declaration of war, Senator James Brady of Idaho had introduced a Senate bill through which a thousand dogs would be trained for service overseas. Though shepherd dogs, collies, and large Airedales were preferred, Theiss said, dog trainers believed that any good-sized, intelligent dog would be fine. The bill did not pass. American civilians were willing to contribute dogs to the government, but the training of men superseded the training of dogs and the program seems to have been abandoned. In the end, in the United States, only the Red Cross was active in training dogs. Theiss concluded: "so Uncle Sam is preparing to send his soldiers dogless into battle, to let his wounded die undiscovered and unsuccored."

Beyond their reputation as police and war dogs, German shepherds bridged the gap between working country dog and leisured city dog in that they worked in both places, and not just as police dogs. They often served individuals as guard dogs. If society then seemed too free and loose and things were moving too fast, a German shepherd represented law and order and stability. Palisade

Kennels of East Killingly, Connecticut, advertising German shepherds as "police dogs" in 1917 and 1918, called the breed the "dog of the hour – the superdog, the product of Efficiency. A chum, a protector for master, mistress, and children." A 1913 story in *The New York Times*, "Police Dogs for Society," told of how the Getney Farm Kennels were training German shepherds as bodyguards for society folk, such as Mrs. William K. Vanderbilt. Henry L. Baer, their trainer, said Mrs. Vanderbilt's dog would be ready by spring to sit beside her in her auto and go with her on walks around the park and her Newport estate as a protector.

For all these reasons, the German shepherd was a "fashionable" dog from the end of the war all through the 1920s. A 1925 article in *House and Garden* that recommended breeds for "the large estate" noted that besides the fact that a large dog needed space, he looked good there, where he was in "proper scale with his environment." This article – which concentrated on the giant breeds: St. Bernard, Irish wolfhound, Newfoundland, and Great Dane – said of the German shepherd:

> Compared with such mighty fellows the German Shepherd or Police Dog seems almost dwarfed, yet he too is a fitting breed for the large estate. There is something upstanding and capable about the appearance of a good Shepherd which renders him superbly distinctive. He is hardy, active and in every way well fitted to the conditions which spacious country places impose.

The German shepherd was a working dog loved by rich people and elevated to high status partly because of its association with them. Geraldine Rockefeller Dodge bred white German shepherds. Leo F. Wanner and his wife, who owned Lewanno Kennels on Long Island and befriended Duncan and Rin-Tin-Tin when they arrived in the United States after the war, also popularized German shepherds, as did Anne Tracy, who was J. Pierpont Morgan's niece.

Police and war dog training fitted dogs well for playing roles as movie hero: attacking, jumping, running, and other feats of derring-do that were not copies of human behavior but natural to dogs. Also it was not difficult to tailor movie scripts to accommodate the accomplishments of police-trained dogs, who, according to Catherine Brody in her 1925 *Saturday Evening Post* article, came "to the studios with their tricks already learned."

Clearly society was ready for a German shepherd star by the time Rin-Tin-Tin made his first hit movie, *Where the North Begins* (1923), but before him and after him, there were other German shepherd stars. Why was Rin Tin Tin able to eclipse them?

When Oliver Reginald Taviner interviewed Strongheart, the German shepherd movie star, for the *Los Angeles Times*, in October 1923, the dog supposedly replied: "No more 'Where the North Begins' stuff for me: my producer has concluded that the snows most decidedly are of yesteryear . . . and that sheiks are the vogue just now. So my next epic is to be called 'the Love Master' – which is at least intriguing, don't you think?" Leaving the snowy fields of cinematic contention, in which Rin-Tin-Tin had so recently scored a triumph with *Where the North Begins*, Strongheart was moving south to play Valentino. Perhaps he shouldn't have been so ready to cede the field to Rin-Tin-Tin.

Both dogs starred in similar pictures – melodramas set in the frozen north and filmed on location. Both played similar characters – dog heroes, who saved the day, sometimes after making a decision between their wild and human companions. Both received rave reviews for their acting and athleticism. But Strongheart achieved fame and favor first. When Strongheart's hit movie, *The Silent Call*, which reportedly grossed $1,000,000, was released in November 1921, Rin-Tin-Tin was probably being filmed as a bit player in *The Man from Hell's River*, his first movie. When *The Man from Hell's River* was released in May 1922, *The Silent Call* was closing its record-breaking thirteen-week run at Los Angeles' Miller's Theater after 792 performances, playing eight times a day, to a total audience of about 250,000 people. While crowds mobbed Strongheart at stops on a triumphal train tour after *Silent Call*, Rin-Tin-Tin was up in northern California filming *Shadows of the North* and *Where the North Begins*. In July 1922, when Rin-Tin-Tin was relatively (but certainly not entirely) unknown, Strongheart was the "Wonder Dog." in reviews and advertisements. (A year later copycat ads for Rin Tin billed *him* as the "Wonder Dog.") During the next three years both dogs became movie icons. According to an August 1925 *Los Angeles*

Times article that featured a picture of Strongheart "driving" a Hupmobile, he had supposedly already made $2,500,000, a considerable amount of money.

By the middle of the decade, Rin-Tin-Tin had eclipsed Strongheart in popularity, in spite of his rival's early fame and fortune. Jeanine Basinger, who did a study of his reviews in fan magazines in *Silent Stars*, sees Rin-Tin-Tin moving into first place by March 1924.

For the graph below, "Comparison of Popularity of Rin-Tin-Tin and Strongheart," I counted the number of hits for each dog's name in newspapers included in NewspaperArchive.com. At the time I did the count, the number of newspapers included in the archive for years 1918-1936 ranged from 170 to 210. Counting hits for Strongheart as opposed to Rin-Tin-Tin presented problems because Strongheart is a more common name than Rin-Tin-Tin, because a human Chief Strongheart was popular, and because Strongheart dog food was touted in ads. However, I was able to narrow results with the search word "dog."

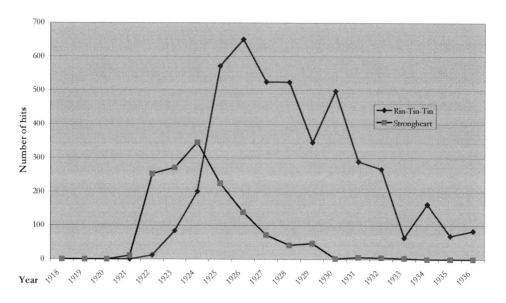

Like Rin-Tin-Tin, Strongheart was a German shepherd with acting ability and with an appealing story of Red Cross service in World War I, but a philistine might say he was even more handsome and had a more solid pedigree. His real name was Etzel von Oeringen, and he was born in Germany, in 1916, 1917, or 1918, depending on the source. The Fort Wayne (Indiana) *News-Sentinel*, probably quoting a press release from Strongheart's movie studio, proclaimed him "champion of the battlefields [who had] won scores of prizes at dog shows on the European continent, and was awarded several medals for his valiant deeds as a Red Cross dog during the great war." He was not the only dog actor touted as a war dog in publicity: Thunder, who acted in six movies from 1924 to 1927, had also been imported from Germany; he wore a military medal on his collar. And while he was not billed as a war dog, Peter the Great had supposedly been educated at the Berlin Police Academy; a rising star in the early 1920s, he had roles in six movies, three with top billing.

Rin-Tin-Tin's early ascendancy shows in ads for other dogs' movies. For instance, an ad in the Zanesville (Ohio) *Times-Recorder* for Peter the Great's *Silent Accuser* (1924) pointed to the fact Rin-Tin-Tin was surpassing him in popularity: "If you have liked the dog pictures with Rin-Tin-Tin we have been showing this season, we know you will be more than pleased with this picture." The Huntingdon (Pennsylvania) *Daily News* even made a mistake and advertised Rin-Tin-Tin himself as the star of *Silent Accuser*. Thunder, too, was often compared to Rin-Tin-Tin in ads for his movies: he was, for instance, "the only dog rival of the famous Rin-Tin-Tin" in an ad for *Phantom of the Forest* (1926). In an ad for *The Lure of the Wild* (1925), Lightning, who doubled for Rin-Tin-Tin in *Rinty of the Desert*, was also billed as "the only rival of the famous Rin-Tin-Tin."

Why did Rin-Tin-Tin become so much more popular than Strongheart and all the other German shepherd stars? Immediately obvious are trivial reasons: the euphony and peculiarity of Rin-Tin-Tin's name as well as his back story – his discovery, found as an abandoned puppy by an American service man, is emotionally appealing. But other reasons are more important.

Rin-Tin-Tin profited by circumstance. Strongheart, Peter the Great, and Lightning died prematurely. Strongheart died in late June 1929, reportedly after developing a tumor as a result of being burned by a studio light. In 1926, Peter the Great was shot by a possibly drunken rival dog fancier who was fighting with Peter's owner, Edward Faust. He died in a Los Angeles dog hospital. Faust sued and, in 1927, was awarded $125,000, more than had ever been awarded before for the death of a dog. Four years later, another jury declared the award excessive because dogs, it said, were not in the same category as human beings. Lightning, who had a short movie career (1925-1927), died in 1929. On the other hand, Rin-Tin-Tin died in August 1932, at the good age of thirteen.

To my mind, the best answer to why Rin-Tin-Tin became top dog lies in an examination of the priorities of the humans who controlled the dogs' careers and the subtle differences in how the dogs were portrayed. Strongheart's human managers were less committed to him than Rin-Tin-Tin's managers were. In publicity, Rin-Tin-Tin came across as a kind and loving father with a middle-class mentality, while Strongheart was pictured as an aristocrat.

Some sources say the director and animal trainer Laurence Trimble and his wife, writer Jane Murfin, discovered Strongheart in Germany; others insist that he was imported into the United States by Bruno Hoffman, an American breeder of German shepherds. A few tell the story that he was given to Murfin before she teamed up with Trimble; however, since she married Trimble in 1915, before Strongheart was born, that cannot be.

Trimble's own story of the finding of Strongheart seems the most likely one to be true, I think. According to him, after a three-year search for the perfect canine actor, he and Murfin discovered Strongheart at Hoffman's kennels, near White Plains, New York, the day after the dog arrived from Germany in 1920. In both 1924 and 1929, he told essentially the same story of their first meeting at Hoffman's place, though in his 1929 version Murfin, no longer his wife, is a "friend" and Strongheart is more frightening. The story according to Trimble: he and Murfin entered a gate to the grounds and were walking towards the house when from a window came "a savage roar; a vibrant barytone it was, expressing such authority that my friend and I came to an abrupt halt." (In 1924, it was just a growl.) The dog came through the window at them. Murfin fled. In looking back at the moment in 1929, Trimble remembered that although he felt fear he was excited because he knew he "was seeing the dog I'd been searching for. I knew him before his forefeet struck the ground." He then cried either "Halt!" (1924) or "Stop!" (1929). And the dog, the future Strongheart, stopped. All remained where they were until a man came from the kennels, shouting. Says Trimble, "The dog rumbled and bristled. My friend began to tread water." The man ordered Trimble and Murfin to stand still, whereupon Trimble, the hero of his own story, told the man *himself* to stand still. After a short time that seemed long, the dog looked from one person to the other, then "calmly walked in front of me [Trimble], circled around me and came to attention at my right hand. Having taken the position he had been trained to take beside the officer in command, he calmly awaited orders." Trimble started to walk away and told the dog to come. Strongheart obeyed – "He came, marching like the perfectly trained soldier he was."

Telling the story in 1924, Trimble said he decided Strongheart was perfect for pictures because of this incident – it showed he could reason. The dog had not been "placed on guard," but had in his mind a line on the ground that only those allowed by Hoffman could cross, and he knew that "his duty was to keep anything inside the deadline from being disturbed."

When Trimble first met Strongheart, the dog had already been trained as a show dog and a war dog, whereas Rin-Tin-Tin was trained, albeit with some of the same methods, by Duncan himself, from puppyhood, to be a performer, at first in dog shows, then in the movies. Trimble admitted that Strongheart's training presented difficulties: "He never made a natural movement. At the sound of my approach he would come to attention and remain that way until I gave him another command."

Therefore, it would seem reasonable to say that one of the reasons for Rin-Tin-Tin's ascendancy over Strongheart, if either Trimble or Duncan can be believed, is that Rin-Tin-Tin was raised more naturally for his profession. Trimble had to convert the "fighting machine" that was Strongheart into an actor, but even so something of the original "soldier" remained. However, it seems that Trimble was able to eradicate Strongheart's early training. Reviewers' extravagant praise of the naturalness and versatility of Strongheart's acting, his lack of ego, and his "humanness" is so identical to the praise Rin-Tin-Tin received during his lifetime that one could consider the two dogs almost interchangeable.

In reviewing *The Silent Call,* a critic for *The New York Times* praised Strongheart as "a magnificent creature, an excellent photographic subject and an interesting performer." A *Los Angeles Times* article was even more extravagant and detailed, praising his intelligence and ability to register emotion "from extreme joy to extreme sorrow . . . naturally and realistically. He protects those he loves with a fidelity that wins the sympathy of all and he fights his enemies both human and animal with a fierceness that brings applause from every beholder." A reviewer for the Fort Wayne *News-Sentinel* commented that Strongheart's "yawning jaws and wicked looking teeth would make any villain run," but was swift to comment on how sweet he is in the scene where, accused of cattle killing, he lays his head on his accusers' shoulders for mercy. According to one against-the-grain reviewer (most praised *Where the North Begins* as a movie and Rin-Tin-Tin's acting in it), *Silent Call* was superior to *Where the North Begins*: ". . . those who directed this picture and looked after Rin-Tin-Tin did not possess the necessary knowledge for real dog actors like the owner of Strongheart." Of a scene in *White Fang* (1925), one critic said:: "Strongheart . . . is the personification of helplessness, the essence of tragedy. And, beneath it all, there is a touch of the quizzical. For Strongheart is the fortunate owner of the most expressive eyebrows, above those brooding, deep-set eyes." And a reviewer for *Variety* praised Strongheart's "splendid" acting in *North Star* (1925), both in attacking the villain, in "comedy by-play" and in escaping, in a "corking scene," from the "tonneau" of an auto rolling down an embankment into a river.

The trainers of both dogs made a point of their special relationship with their canine stars. In their puppyhood, Duncan worked with Rin-Tin-Tin and Nanette; after Nanette's death, Rin-Tin-Tin was his main concern, though he spent time with his other dogs. Trimble worked with many dogs. For example, to make *White Fang* (1925) and *Phantom Pack* (which never was released), Trimble loaded up a train car of canines – wolves (maybe), malamutes (maybe), huskies, and German shepherds, including Strongheart and Lady Jule (Strongheart's "wife"), and took them for four months to the wilds of the Canadian Rockies. Yet in spite of that, he found time to turn Strongheart into a great actor.

Trimble and Murfin had stellar credentials, but those credentials meant little when the breakup of their partnership and marriage badly affected Strongheart's career. The two at first had the advantage of their firm foothold in the movie business, certainly superior to Duncan's more tangential contacts with movie people. Before he and Murfin acquired Strongheart, Trimble had had several years of experience in training movie dogs. For instance, in the 1910s, for Vitagraph, he made several shorts with a collie named Jean (who died in 1916).

In 1910 alone, he starred her in "Jean and the Calico Doll," "Jean the Matchmaker," "Jean Goes Foraging," "Jean Goes Fishing," and "Jean and the Waif." Jane Murfin began her career by writing stage plays, including *Lilac Time* (with Jane Cowl). She had written six screenplays or scenarios by the time *Silent Call* catapulted Strongheart into fame. In her lifetime, she wrote sixty-six of them; her most famous perhaps was *The Women* (1939).

The Silent Call was produced by H.O. Davis, but Strongheart's next two movies – (*Brawn of the North* (1922) and *The Love Master* (1924) – were produced by Trimble-Murfin, a partnership between his husband-and-wife owner and trainer. Robertson-Cole Pictures Corporation produced *White Fang* while the Trimble-Murfin partnership was still active. In early December 1924, with *White Fang* in the can, Murfin and Trimble dissolved their producing partnership. They divorced later, in 1926, and Trimble gave up directing dogs in movies to devote himself exclusively to dog training. Strongheart's pictures were thereafter under the control of Murfin, his legal owner. Lady Jule, Strongheart's mate, went with Trimble, so Strongheart lost both his trainer and his "wife." From then on he lived with Murfin "in a cozy cottage clinging to a Hollywood hillside," where, according to *Los Angeles Times* writer Grace Kingsley, he was "working out each day in the hills and being kept in prime condition for his next picture. . . [which would] give the dog the greatest acting part he has ever had." In spite of the hype, for Strongheart's career, it was a change for the worse.

By July of 1925, Murfin had made a deal with Howard Estabrook, an established screen writer turned neophyte producer, who gave Murfin contracts for a series of major productions starring Strongheart. Murfin, who had once sworn that she would allow Strongheart to make only one picture a year, signed the contracts through which he would make three, all to be distributed through Associated Exhibitors. The first movie on the agenda was *North Star*, based on a novel by Estabrook, with a script by Rufus King. With Strongheart in the starring role, the human co-stars were Virginia Lee Corbin and Stuart Holmes. Clark Gable played Archie West, a secondary character, and Gary Cooper had an uncredited bit part. The movie was filmed on location at Lake Arrowhead in only two months. In early winter, 1925, *North Star* was delivered to New York. It did fairly well, but Estabrook did not make another movie with Strongheart. In fact, *North Star* was one of only two movies Estabrook produced – the other was *The Price of a Party* (1924). He went back to writing, though there seems to be a hiatus in his career from 1925 to 1928.

Strongheart made one more film after *North Star* – *The Return of Boston Blackie* (1927), produced by Chadwick Pictures. In the American Film Institute online catalog, Strongheart's name is last on the cast list. Ironically, the movie is the only one of Strongheart's that survives.

It is clear what happened: Strongheart lost his trainer and director, and his owner gave up control of his destiny. Bounced from studio to studio, he lacked studio continuity and strong consistent promotion.

Meanwhile, Duncan worked hard day to day during the filming of Rin-Tin-Tin's pictures and promoted him fiercely. Rin-Tin-Tin was his main focus. He did not allow his marriage to Anderson, nor his divorce from her, to distract him from the dog's career (and his own), perhaps overworking them both. Rin-Tin-Tin was in four movies between Strongheart's *White Fang* and *North Star*, and in five more movies between Strongheart's *North Star* and *The Return of Boston Blackie*. Overall, Rin-Tin-Tin acted in twent-eight feature-length movies to Strongheart's five, and more, by far, than any other dog star.

Moreover, from 1923 to 1929, Warner was the only studio Rin-Tin-Tin worked for, and it was solidly behind him. The studio gave Rin-Tin-Tin good writers (like Darryl F. Zanuck) and an excellent publicity agent (Hal Wallis); it paid for the tours Duncan and Rin-Tin-Tin took to promote Rin-Tin-Tin's movies. Warner was, according to all accounts, a struggling company when Rin-Tin-Tin came along. Jack Warner's nickname for Rin-Tin-Tin – "the mortgage-lifter" – is mentioned in source after source, though it is questionable whether this is true. In any case, they valued their furry actor.

Like Rin-Tin-Tin, Strongheart made personal appearances and went on tour. The difference between the two dogs' tours lies in the contrast between Duncan's enthusiasm for such promotion and Strongheart's handlers' lackadaisical, even condescending, attitude toward it. Strongheart himself put it best in a *Los Angeles Times* (February 1924) interview with Helen Klumph: "[Strongheart] explained to me that these publicity stunts bored him mightily but that he felt it his duty to his public to put in his appearance when they had gone to so much trouble to do him honor." According to an August 1925 article in the *Los Angeles Times*, Strongheart did very little "Hippodroming," just appearances "conducted in a dignified manner befitting the foremost dog in Dogdom" – probably to his detriment.

The attitudes of Strongheart's handlers towards personal-appearance tours become clear in a lawsuit: In November 1924, J. E. Burch filed a claim with the State Department of Labor against Murfin for unpaid wages of $1557.60, which he said she owed him for taking Strongheart on a three-month exhibition tour in First National theaters throughout the country. Murfin claimed she got no money for showing Strongheart so didn't need to pay; it was the producer who arranged for the tour who should be sued. She also said that the tour was not a success financially and there was no money available to meet the claim.

Like Rin-Tin-Tin and Nanette, Strongheart and his mate, Lady Jule, had an active family life as revealed in the press. Portrayed as pseudo-humans, they sat down at dinner with people. But unlike Rin-Tin-Tin and Nanette, Strongheart and Lady Jule were Hollywood aristocrats, au courant with the latest trends. Lady Jule was an expensive dog, her price of about $800 touted in publicity releases; while the Nanette who replaced the original female puppy was a pedigreed dog from the Wanner stable, Duncan and Warner did not brag about that. In a February 1924 interview in *The New York Times* hinting at child marriage and spousal abuse, Strongheart said:

> I am six years old, which is equivalent to about 42 in a man. My wife, lady Jule, is 2, about 14. Quite a child, what? She's a little petulant, wants all the meat and none of the biscuits, but . . . she's not a bad sort. She's smaller than I am, but I have never put a tooth to her yet.

Jane Murfin, in a June 1923 story in *The New York Times*, stated that Lady Jule acted like a flapper. Flappers were popular figures among the unconventional. They were giddy. They wore shocking clothes and did shocking things. But not all Americans thought well of them. Nanette was never portrayed as a child or a flapper, but as a wholesome wife and mother, a darling of the middle class.

The major papers gave extensive coverage to a visit Strongheart and Lady Jule made in New York to promote their movie *The Love Master* and to attend the Dog Show in February 1924. Though they were officially entered at the show, according to *The New York Times*, they did not participate except to sit "majestically" in "aloof grandeur" on a platform looking down on the other dogs, "quite like stars who have just been crowned king and queen of a movie ball." They were "a law unto themselves and a special attraction."

Hardly a year into his "marriage," Strongheart had a litter of ten puppies by Lady Linda von Lux, owned by a Mrs. Richard Dohring. Meanwhile, at least according to the press, Rin-Tin-Tin remained faithful to Nanette.

Taken overall, Rin-Tin-Tin was a bi-species dog-human, devoted to family, with middle-class values and upper-class income. In print and in his movies, he was portrayed as a kind and loving father to human children as well as to his own, of which he had very many, and a faithful husband to his "wife," Nanette. (The real life Rin-Tin-Tin was another animal.)

Nanette and puppies with the proud father, Rin-Tin-Tin (Courtesy Rin-Tin-Tin Collection, Riverside, California).

Rin-Tin-Tin's puppies played a part in more than one of his movies. In the last scene of *Where the North Begins* (1923), Gabrielle and Felice, the human couple, look into their cabin's fire and wonder what has become of the dog who saved Gabrielle's life. Then Rin-Tin-Tin comes through the door and, tail wagging, runs to them and licks their faces. He sits and barks to bring one adorable puppy after another trotting through the door as he, the proud and happy father, looks on. He barks a final time, and Nanette appears. It is a powerful scene, and critics were aware of it.

Publicity for *Tracked in the Snow Country* (1925) made mention of Rin-Tin-Tin's recent litter of seven puppies. In the movie's happy ending, the human leads marry and have twins, and Rin-Tin-Tin, who is responsible for their bliss,

The Rin-Tin-Tin family advertising Ken-L Ration (Courtesy Rin-Tin-Tin Collection, Riverside, California).

is living with them and "nine cunning little members of his family." (I am not sure where the two other puppies came from.)

Though Nanette combined motherhood with career and appeared in several Rin-Tin-Tin movies, she played second fiddle in the movies and spent a good deal of time at home having puppies and acting as their primary caretaker. When Rin-Tin-Tin went on tour in March 1926, to promote *The Night Cry*, Nanette ("Mrs. Rin-Tin-Tin") and their puppies were unhappy about his impending absence. According to the *Los Angeles Times*, "At the station she [Nanette] emitted a single yelp of sorrow and went about the procedure of herding her offspring back to the portable kennels." A year later, after a personal-appearance tour, Rin-Tin-Tin and Duncan returned home to Los

Angeles just in time for Rin-Tin-Tin's birthday party at the Warner studio. The menu contained raw steak, pork chops, and ham knuckles, along with a birthday cake with candles. Nanette and puppies were there to congratulate the celebrity. Their birthday parties, if they had any, did not make the news.

Perhaps the classic example of Rin-Tin-Tin's public persona as a family man (though a fanciful and impossible dog-human one) exists in a small book, *Little Folks' Story of Rin-Tin-Tin* (1927). It opens with this sentence: "Rin-Tin-Tin, the Marvelous Dog of the Movies, is also Rin-Tin-Tin the Beloved. For he loves children, and he is loved by them." It goes on to say he was the recent father of two puppies and that he was so concerned with their care that he almost gave up his career: "So now you know him as Father Rin-Rin-Tin." His master and mistress entrust him for the day with the care of the human family – two girls (Grace and Alice), a boy (Dick), and a baby (Carol). He is to watch over them and see that they are fed and take their naps. But he does more. He plays hide-and-seek, brings the baby a stick, and delights the children by pretending to be a stuffed animal, a clown, and a monkey in a red turban. He brings the baby the bottle of milk Nurse has prepared for her and feeds his own puppy, holding a bottle of milk in his jaws. He checks over the lunch Cook has made and sits with the children at table, napkin around his neck (not good form except for dogs). He naps with the children. He brings them balloons.

In short, Strongheart represented dissolute nobility and Hollywood loose living, and Rin-Tin-Tin, in spite of the luxury in which he lived, represented a respectable and loving family man. He played that part in movies, in his private life, in his personal-appearance tours, and in literature written about him. Duncan and Warner worked together to publicize him that way. Given the audience for dog pictures, Rin-Tin-Tin had the far better persona.

What tipped the balance between Rin-Tin-Tin and other canine movie stars of his time was his management – its consistency and intensity – by Duncan and Warner. Rin-Tin-Tin made more movies than any of them by far, and those movies were better promoted. As portrayed in publicity, Rin-Tin-Tin was a model family man. Looking at it from the dogs' points of view, though, who fared better? Rin-Tin-Tin, who worked so hard in a profession he could not really have understood, or Strongheart, who spent so many leisurely days in Murfin's cottage in the Hollywood Hills?

4
The Dog of War, The Dog of the West

The prologue for *Where the North Begins* (1923), Rin-Tin-Tin's breakthrough Western, begins with the intertitle, "During the late war, in a dugout near the Hindenburg Line, two police dog puppies were born," and goes on to tell how Duncan, an "observer with the 135th Aero Squadron . . . captured them from their dead German master." Following on the next intertitle, "Rin-Tin-Tin, the famous police dog hero," Rin-Tin-Tin plays himself panting in his Red Cross vest.

After the prologue, we move to a western forest. Dramatic clouds ride above a sunset or sunrise, and wolves roam in the distance as the camera creates a poem to the wilderness. The intertitle: "North of 51 is a land of endless snow and whispering pines, of trackless wastes and brooding silence."

A dogsled carrying a puppy in a crate ("the Cariboo Limited") appears and the intertitle informs us that it is on its way to a trading post. However the crate falls off, unbeknownst to the sled driver, and the puppy is "taken prisoner by the ravagers of the trail." Dog sled gone, the crate sits on a ridge, and along come the wolves, the "ravagers" (a word which not so coincidentally is close to a rhyme with "savages"), three of whom circle the crate. It is easy to find symbolism here: the puppy caught in the cage, a symbol of civilization in all its constraints and safety, threatened, in the middle of the forest, by the timber wolves, symbols of wildness in all its freedom and danger. And yet the idea that the ravaging wolves "take him prisoner" speaks of the ambivalent nature of the movie-maker and the times.

We don't see what happens next to the nervous puppy. An intertitle sums up the next year in twenty words: "A year passes and like a foundling reared by strange hands the puppy grows to maturity among the savage pack." Framed by a snow-covered mountain, the Dog (Rin-Tin-Tin), once the puppy, stands wagging his tail and licking his chops while the wolves eat something. Intertitle: "Though he develops the hunting and fierceness of a wolf, his dog instinct keeps him aloof from his wolf brethern [sic]."

Next, at the trading post run by an evil factor (agent), we meet the human hero, Gabrielle (he has a female name, for some reason), and the object of his affections, Felice. We learn that Gabrielle has agreed to take a load of furs over the dangerous Cariboo pass because the factor has promised him a large sum of money for doing it, enough money to enable him to marry Felice. Gabrielle doesn't know that the factor, who has eyes for Felice, has set him up for ambush at the pass by the factor's henchman, The Fox.

Then we are back in the snow country. A pine branch frames the scene: a dog sled, piloted by Gabrielle, comes along the brow of the hill. The Fox, covered with fur, sits in a tree – all the viewers can see are his eyes. The "wolves," many of which look like huskies or German shepherds, run in the snow. Gabrielle whips his dogs to hurry. The Fox shoots Gabrielle from the tree, then from the ground, and Gabrielle's dogs run off with the sled, leaving the wounded Gabrielle behind. The snow turns into a blizzard, and Gabrielle lies unconscious with snow half over his face.

Along comes Rin-Tin-Tin. Dog meets man. "To this dog raised by wolves, man is a kind of prey he has never seen before." Wolves circle as Gabrielle tries to crawl to shelter, and Rin-Tin-Tin fights them off. After holding off the wolves, Rin-Tin-Tin, with his ears back, approaches Gabrielle, a step at a time, in stalking mode. Gabrielle creeps away, but Rin-Tin-Tin grabs his leg and shakes it. He barks (silently, of course). Gabrielle passes out. The intertitle: "Something within him, heritage of dog ancestors, said NO. MAN was not his enemy, but his MASTER and FRIEND." Rin-Tin-Tin's eyes squint against the glare of the snow, and he seems to be half-smiling. He licks Gabrielle. The wolves are back and Rin-Tin-Tin lies on top of the man – to protect him. The wolves gather around, ready to fight. As they approach, he gets up and stalks them, nose in the snow. Vanquished, they leave. Rin-Tin-Tin goes back to Gabrielle, puts his front feet on the man's prone body, and howls.

It is a great victory: one dog, raised feral but turned miraculously tame, fights off a whole pack of "savage" wolves. He has never been wholly part of their pack, but is a maverick, both in the human world and the wilderness. And at the end of the scene, he stands victorious on top of the human he has saved.

When The Fox, gun in hand, returns to finish off Gabrielle, Rin-Tin-Tin attacks him from a rise. In a long scene, The Fox keeps trying to get at his knife, kicking at Rin-Tin-Tin, while Rin-Tin-Tin, clearly besting the man, clamps his teeth on his throat. The Fox departs, leaving a piece of his pants, crucial evidence, in Rin-Tin-Tin's mouth.

An intertitle signals a change of scene: a cabin, outpost of human civilization, where a fire burns in the fireplace. Sitting in a chair, Gabrielle holds out his arms as Rin-Tin-Tin looks anxiously at him, then Rin-Tin-Tin comes over, jumps up, and puts his paw on Gabrielle's leg. Gabrielle holds him. "Man's companionship, nothing he has ever known.".

That night Rin-Tin-Tin hears the howl of his wolf mate, played by Nanette, and he feels himself "torn between two loves – love of master and love of mate . . . like calling to like." Romance with his wild mate trumps the allure of human companionship. He finds his way out of the cabin, where Gabrielle remains asleep, and joins the wolves. The hill, at dawn, with pines and clouds, is beautiful. Yet Rin-Tin-Tin returns to join Gabrielle, and the story continues. Back at the trading post, Rin-Tin-Tin is falsely accused of murdering a baby, and Gabrielle whips him for it. (We don't see the whip touch his body.) Rin-Tin-Tin crawls out the door – "[h]eaded for the wilderness, his great warm heart broken by the one creature he'd learned most to love." However, he doesn't actually leave the trading post for the wilderness until he jumps on the villain's horse to save Felice from abduction and later forces the villain off a cliff. In the touching last scene, after a long absence, the Dog comes back to the post and lures his eight puppies and his mate into the cabin. Duncan describes the closing scene: "every wrong had been righted and all had been forgiven." The dog, who lives in two worlds, not only saves the day but represents the noblest of the noble (to humans, anyway): the freedom of the wild, the loyalty of the tame. He has brought a wild animal, a female wolf (albeit *played* by a dog), into human habitation, reconciling savage sex and domesticity, and all is well.

Where the North Begins has two inter-related themes found in many other Rin-Tin-Tin movies. One, played out on the frontier, is the struggle between wilderness and civilization. The other is ambivalence about World War I, in the background but nonetheless there. The 1920s Western embodied contrary attitudes about the American West – awe at its untouched beauty and fear of its dangerous wildness where the untamed lurked; the impulse to preserve it and the hunger to tame and exploit it. Yet, in the Western, civilization always triumphs over wilderness, even though the wilderness is loved (not only by the cameraman), and the good-guy civilizers always defeat the bad-guy outlaws. In the end, law and order reign and there is nothing ambiguous about it. Many Americans in the 1920s wrestled with the same polarities when contemplating the Great War: the blurring of lines between human civilization and human savagery, even the overturning of ideas about those polarities. The war to save civilization almost destroyed it and left doubt in people's minds that civilization, in the first place, was civilized and that, in the second place, it would always win over what its adherents identified as savagery (usually on the opposite side).

While I certainly don't mean to imply that the film makers were consciously obsessed with the war and decided to deal with it obliquely in Westerns, Rin-Tin-Tin's Westerns themselves do suggest a link, however subconscious. Moreover promotion from Warner, as well as independent reviews, juxtapose Rin-Tin-Tin's so-called experiences in the war and his roles in his movies in ways that seem intentional. In both Rin-Tin-Tin's usual movie role in the Western and in his supposed role in the war, as a dog – a *beast* and a beast without a political affiliation – he saves the day and fights for civilization with no other motives but the heroism and sacrifice so often attributed to dogs by humans. To complicate matters, as a tamed wolf or wolf-dog, which he plays in several of his movies, he represents domesticated wildness, and as such a canine character, he reverses some ingrained attitudes toward wildness.

Where the North Begins is not about World War I, yet it opens with reminders of the star's alleged real-life part in that war as mascot and Red Cross dog and of the defeat of the Germans, as symbolized by "his dead German master." (The Dog, the part he plays, does not, of course, have any war experience.)

Promotion for the movie, much of which originated at Warner, played up Rin-Tin-Tin's supposed war record and tied it, though obliquely, to the theme of civilization/savagery that the war, the frontier, and the wolf-dog represented. For instance, a story in the September 1923, *Modesto Evening News* (California), "Rin-Tin-Tin Rescued from Throes of War," claimed that Rin-Tin-Tin "served under fire"; in the same issue was an ad for *Where the North Begins* that described the film as "[a] story of backbone and brawn where a dog's instincts are pitted against the cunning of a man who is more brute than man."

Rin-Tin-Tin made only one war picture, *A Dog of the Regiment*. In it, he, a German dog, rescues an American pilot, whom he knew before the war. A *Chicago Tribune* review had him saving the pilot "from the whole German army" and pointed out that Rin-Tin-Tin held no brief with nationality: "Once a pal, always a pal is his dog logic, and Rinty lives up to it despite the fact that had he been a human he would have been called upon to pay the supreme penalty of treason under arms." The film, which aired about the same time as *Wings*, uses Rin-Tin-Tin, the supranational dog, whose loyalty is to those he loves, not a nation, to foster a sentimental notion of international reconciliation, a bringing together of the "savage" enemy and "our" civilized side. Promotion for the movie inevitably refers to Rin-Tin-Tin's supposed past, mentioning that he "actually saw the battlefields of France," that he is (in the movie) a "dog of war" and that the movie "portrays the actual events of his own early life."

In other movies, especially the Westerns, the character Rin-Tin-Tin plays has a past in which he was a war dog, often made explicit in the prologues, and the promotion hammers away at his romanticized past as a war puppy. It was not uncommon for 1920s movies to have such reminders of war in subplots, flashbacks, and bits of dialogue, even though far fewer films dedicated to war themes were made in the early part of the decade than later. (The second half of the 1920s saw the war films the decade is known for: *Big Parade*, *What Price Glory?*, and *Wings*.) The pattern in several of Rin-Tin-Tin's movies is the same: references to the war are peripheral and not important to the plot, except that the relationship between man and dog has usually been cemented by their wartime experiences together. For instance, in *Find Your Man* (1924), Rin-Tin-Tin plays Buddy, a dog found during the war by a soldier and brought back to the United States. Promotion, ads, and reviews for the movie tied his fictional war service to his supposed actual war service. In a review, Grace Kingsley of the *Los Angeles Times* said that "somebody conceived the bright idea of letting this police dog do his war stuff – something that hasn't apparently been thought of before. . . . There was an additional tang to the tale of this dog when you saw him actually working in No Man's Land, just as he did overseas with his master, Lee Duncan, who was a soldier." The story went on to say that Duncan and Rin-Tin-Tin ("in flesh-and-fleas") had appeared in person on Theater Row and that Duncan gave "a most spirited little story of their experiences overseas."

Another example is *Tracked by the Police*. The movie is about the saving of a dam, but, like *Find Your Man*, it begins by flashing back to World War I and the dog character's part in it. The camera focuses on Rin-Tin-Tin (Rinty) standing on a rock. After the list of credits, the intertitle reads: "It is known that brotherly love born under the stress of battle and bloodshed never dies – that wartime comrades and front-line friendship carry on forever." Intertitles let the viewer know that Rinty had saved his wartime buddy and present-day master, Dan Owen ("late of the A.E.F."), in the war. Through a flashback, we see hazy smoke eddies and flashing shells going off, as Rinty, again in his Red Cross vest, on his belly in the mud, crawls to a wounded man (Owens) and puts his paw on the man's chest. Back at the dam, Owens says, "I've never forgotten, old pal. And I never will." Later, we see a picture of the dam: "The dam was one of a series built to stem vicious floodwaters and divert them into useful irrigation channels." In those first scenes, *Tracked by the Police* sets up a correspondence between the dog's war experience as savior of man and his duty to preserve the dam, which channels "vicious floodwaters" into "useful irrigation channels." The adjectives tell the tale. The movie links the bravery of the dog in the war (on the "civilized" side) to the taming of raw "vicious" nature in the West into usefulness (by the "good guys").

If as an actor Rin-Tin-Tin does not play war roles in most of his movies, the fiction of his role as a war dog comes up repeatedly in promotion for at least eighteen of them. In 1919, at the dog show in Los Angeles, before Rin-Rin-Tin ever saw the eye of a movie camera, Duncan presented him as a military dog, "trained in war and police work." It glamorized the dog to think of him as a shivering puppy terrified of "screaming shells" then, as he grows up, learning bravely to ignore them, flying in planes doing reconnaissance, saving lives on the ground. Duncan elaborated on his original story in 1925, stating that Rin-Tin-Tin was trained for Red Cross service and did "sentry, dispatch and guard duty." For Armistice Day in that year, the *Los Angeles Times* ran a picture of Rin-Tin-Tin in Red Cross vest "saluting" an American flag. And, in a 1926 story, "He [Duncan] made a graceful, modest, confident little speech, telling how, while serving as an aviator in the World War, he had come upon the mother of Rinty in the battle area, and how Rin-Tin-Tin had been born in the trenches and taught to be a soldier – a good and faithful soldier." As late as

1930, a newspaper article (about Rin-Tin-Tin's first and next-to-last serial, *Lone Defender*) tells the story of Duncan finding Rin-Tin-Tin and Nanette on the battlefield and rearing "them through the vicissitudes of the war."

The roles Rin-Tin-Tin played in Westerns as hero are similar to his supposed roles in the war in that he is a savior on the side of civilization, but they are more remarkable because as a dog on the frontier he is more easily able than a human to cross from his domesticated life into wild nature and live within it. In *Where the North Begins*, he is a wolf-dog, raised in the wilderness by wild animals, and, like Tarzan of the apes, he holds deep within himself his genetic domestic nature. (In early twentieth century fiction, "blood" never forgets.) Despite stories like *Tarzan* (and the legend of Romulus and Remus), a human baby would not be likely to survive in the wilderness. At least in our imagination, a puppy, even though born in the human world, might be greeted as a fellow creature by his cousins, the wolves, unaware of his domestic heritage. Of course, it is difficult to find true stories of puppies raised by wolves in the wild. And, given the importance of puppy/cub development to the adult behavior of a canine, it may not be factually true that those puppies raised by wolves would so easily embrace humanity. Yet, if a human goes alone into the wilderness, Tarzan aside, he usually does not find a group of primates to befriend him, while a dog can find a whole pack of wild creatures closely related to him. In fiction a dog who associates with wolves always knows somehow that he is a dog. He is the best of the tame, the best of the wild.

Little is made in this kind of fiction of the idea that the dog, in the end, betrays those wild creatures who took him in and cared for him, and Rin-Tin-Tin's movies are no exception. Grown up, without any human nurture, when it comes to the choice between killing the downed hero, Gabrielle, as wolves would supposedly do, and saving him, as dogs would supposedly do, he protects the human and turns on his wild saviors to keep them from harming the man. He has changed sides, in one short moment rejecting those who have nurtured him from puppyhood in order to save the life of a member of another species. Though he is a betrayer, the movie doesn't question his about-face.

Rin-Tin-Tin's wolf-dogs seem able to switch from feral to tame as needed. In *Tracked in the Snow Country*, Rin-Tin-Tin is half-wolf, and his "wolf blood" comes to the fore when he has to fight for his life after being falsely accused of murder, but vindicated, "he once again becomes a gentleman pup, bidding adieu to his wolf instincts forever" (*Variety*). In the domestic world that he has so quickly embraced, the wolf blood is useful in a fight but a liability otherwise.

To some extent Hollywood was aware of the messages implicit in *Where the North Begins* represented by the wolf-dog who can bridge the gap between the "civilized" human world and the wilderness, and his superiority over humans turned more bestial than the "beast" he is. In the promotion for the movie, Rin-Tin-Tin is billed as a Wolf Dog. An ad in the *La Crosse Tribune and Leader Press* (Wisconsin) talks of how "rugged brute men" behaving "outside the pale of law and order" are thwarted by "a dog's true instinct." The Liberty Theater in Cumberland paid for a one-page ad that described in purple prose the "surge of primitive impulses beating against the restraints of civilization. Real men and real women battling for dear life in the wild, forbidding wastes of the north, where man and beast obey their instincts." And a wolf-dog "resolves the plot by taking sides."

Rin-Tin-Tin was a wolf-dog, or a dog gone feral, in four of his other films: *Hills of Kentucky* and *Jaws of Steel* (1927), *Rinty of the Desert* (1928), and *Frozen River* (1929). In all four, as in *Where the North Begins*, he is lost as a puppy and grows up into a feral dog, but in a departure from *Where the North Begins*, where his domestic instinct takes over instantly, it takes human kindness to entice him into tameness.

In *Hills of Kentucky*, the "primitive" ignorance of the hill folk pitted against the educated school teacher mirrors the savagery of wild dogs opposed to the reformed and domesticated Grey Ghost (Rin-Tin-Tin). According to publicity, the movie shows "the primitive passions of primitive people . . . the hill folk as they really are with their corn pones, sowbelly, beans, moonshine liquor, home-cured tobacco and ever-present rifle." (It is true that every male in the movie, even the "good" one, carries a long, phallic gun.) The teacher's crippled little brother, Davey, unafraid, brings Grey Ghost water, and as the intertitle says, "With the first touch of kindness from human hands – hatred and fear departed from a bewildered dog." In that instant of transformation, the grateful Grey Ghost "shakes," barks, lays his head on Davey's leg, and licks his hand. As the boy's love changes the dog from wild to tame, so, the movie promises, learning will change the "hill folk" from savage and ignorant to civilized. In *Frozen River*, as in *Where the North Begins*, Tin-Tin-Tin leaves his wolf pack, but in this movie he actually searches for human beings. The first humans he comes across are cruel to him and so he turns into a killer until he meets a little boy, who tames him instantly.

In *Clash of the Wolves* (1925), Rin-Tin-Tin is Lobo, a wolf-dog who leads the wolves in his pack down from the mountains into ranch territory when a forest fire threatens them. He impales his paw on a cactus thorn, and, in a take on "Androcles and the Lion," the hero, Dave Weston, removes it (against Lobo's wishes). Lobo, finally recognizing the human's kindness, becomes devoted to him. The intertitle says: "To young Weston's friends, Lobo is the personification of affection and gentleness, to his enemies, a fiend of retribution and revenge."

Rin-Tin-Tin was not alone in playing wolfish characters. *The Silent Flyer*, a 1926 serial starring Silver Streak, another German shepherd, steals the plot of *Clash of the Wolves*: a half-dog-half-wolf, his paw healed by a man after it is caught in a trap, fights spies with his master. Strongheart, too, took on one such role – as Flash, the wolf-dog – in his first movie, *The Silent Call*. Flash is torn between loyalty to his pack and his human "girl." An ad described the movie as: "The wonder story of the giant wolf-dog, pulling between the blood-call of the wolf pack and the dog-devotion to the girl." And a review echoes the idea: the movie "centers on a ferocious half-breed wolf-dog and the struggles within himself between the civilized and the primitive instincts." As for Peter the Great, one must assume that he played a wolf at least once – in *Little Red Riding Hood* (1922).

The wolf and wolf-dog as characters in Rin-Tin-Tin's and other movie dogs' Westerns have ambivalence partly because of human attitudes toward wolves, which were not simple then (and still are not). *Clash of the Wolves* has this memorable and sentimental closing title: "Wolf heart or human heart, they are just the same, wherever love sets." Yet as one article about *Clash of the Wolves* pointed out, "On account of wolves and cattle, wolves aren't popular." In 1908, Ernest Thompson-Seton said in *The New York Times* that the wolf was the most intelligent wild animal in North America and the dog the most intelligent of the domestic ones. In a sentence reminiscent of Montaigne's and Rousseau's reverential admiration of the Noble Savage, he added, "But the dog is merely the wolf's brother with a college education. It would be obviously unfair to judge the dog and the wolf by the same standard, for while the dog has gained by his long course of instruction under the tutelage of man, he has suffered woefully in morals." He was relatively alone, however, in holding to this idea. For instance, William T. Hornaday, in a book published in 1904, said, "Of all the wild animals of North America, none are more despicable than wolves. There is no depth of meanness, treachery, or cruelty to which they do not cheerfully descend." Theodore Roosevelt, in 1905, described wolves as vermin, displaying a not uncommon attitude among sportsmen, many of whom, though they loved the wilderness and its animals (especially those they could hunt), thought of wolves as outcasts, both from civilized and natural society, to be hunted down and killed, not for sport, but as in a war against an enemy. By 1931, the federal government could claim that wolves were virtually eliminated from "every national park in the contiguous United States." In "American Attitudes Towards Wolves: A History of Misperception," an 1989 article in *Environmental Review,* Valerie Fogleman identifies two major reasons for antipathy toward wolves: a long history of anti-wolf lore, including their tendency to hunt in packs (the size of which that lore greatly exaggerates), and wolves' predation on livestock.

A purebred wolf has a different cultural meaning than a feral wolf-dog. He has no genetic history as a domesticated dog to fall back on, and he has a bad reputation to overcome, so it was no wonder that Rin-Tin-Tin and his fellow actors so often played wolf-dogs who led packs of supposedly purebred wolves.

As German shepherd dogs, Rin-Tin-Tin, Strongheart, and Peter the Great were naturals to play wolves or wolf-dogs because, with their pricked ears and general conformation, they *looked* like wolves. Moreover, it was generally assumed that they were genetically closer to the wolf than they actually were. In 1913, the *The New York Times* noted: "These dogs look something like a wolf, and come from the antique origin of the wild dog." During the late 1920s and the 1930s, this assumption was questioned. In 1927, when British authorities were contemplating a ban on the breeding of German shepherds for their "alleged lupine taint," Arthur F. Jones Jr. noted that the Germans had traced the ancestry of the dog to the Bronze Age and "[I]n the modern history of the shepherds there is no indication of the wolf . . . The 'Killer' instinct which is so feared in the Alsatian occurs only in exceptional atavistic cases." In a 1929 article for *The New York Times*, Reginald M. Cleveland brought the idea home: "There is no more wolf blood in the breed than in the Boston terrier. The shepherd dog is not 'wild.' He cannot 'go back to the wild,' as the ignorant love to say of him, for he did not come from it. He is just a dog." In a twist noted by *The New York Times* at the death of Rin-Tin-Tin in 1932, the wolf roles Rin-Tin-Tin and Strongheart played affected the reputation of their breed:

> Oddly enough, however, while the performances of the dog heroes got national publicity and, to a degree, stimulated the breeding of better specimens [of German shepherd dogs], it also spread widely the false impression that these dogs have wolf blood. Nearly every scenario made its chief character "half wolf" or "descended from the wild" or "reverting" to a feral state from which he never came.

Actually, according to a recent article in *Science*, the German shepherd is genetically very far away from the Gray Wolf. Breeds closest to the wolf are Arctic, Asian, and African, not European. Interestingly, the German shepherd is closer genetically to mastiffs, bulldogs, and boxers than the herding breeds.

In *Where the North Begins*, the frontier between wild and tame is also exemplified by a human character with an animal name – The Fox (Charles Stevens), a "half-breed Indian." (A parallel exists between the polarity of wild-tame in terms of the Western landscape and the polarity of savage-civilized that exists in the anti-Native American racism of the early part of the 20th century.) The "enemies" in the movie are the factor and The Fox. The factor, a white man, is exploiting the wilderness by dealing in furs; in addition he is clearly a "bad guy," in that he steals (furs) and leers at an innocent and unwilling woman. He sends out his minion, The Fox, a trapper, into the wilderness; he doesn't go himself. The Dog (Rin-Tin-Tin) puts an end to the harassing of innocent women and killing of innocent men (though he kills those who kill), but not the trapping, which delivers death to the wild.

While Rin-Tin-Tin is "The *Dog*," at least by name an animal deserving only of a generic term, he stands higher in the estimation of the movie-maker than The Fox does. He can easily return to the wild but never forgets that he is a dog, "friend to man," fully in the human "civilized" (white man's) world. He stands above The Fox, whom he defeats, on the 20th century Western's Great Chain of Being, as, in Jack London's *Jerry of the Islands* (1915), the pedigreed Irish Terrier Jerry, "no common bush-dog, but a blooded Irish gentleman" stands higher on the status ladder than a human "black."

In *While London Sleeps* (1926), the villain is The Monk (played by George Kotsonaros, the world's light-heavyweight wrestling champion), a "savage ape-man" from the Indian jungle, a slave to his master (a criminal), as was the so-called monster to Frankenstein. (Rin-Tin-Tin almost kills him before the police arrive.) Though played by a white actor, he is supposed to be Indian. To be fair, some white men go by animal names in Rin-Tin-Tin's films, but they are usually villains: "The Wolf" (Wallace Beery) in *The Man from Hell's River* (1922) and "Wolf Man" in *The Lightning Warrior* (1931). While Ben "Wolf" Darby in *Shadows of the North* (1923) is the hero, "Wolf" is just a nickname in the middle of his very human first and last names.

The heroes of most Westerns of the 1920s, including the unwitting Rin-Tin-Tin, were on the side of the West's exploiters – its ranchers, miners, loggers – as at the same time, they, and the cameramen, gloried in wilderness. It is interesting that Rin-Tin-Tin, in *Where the North Begins*, comes out of the forest depths – the domain of wild animals – to save the life of a trapper, who kills wild animals for profit. What Rin-Tin-Tin fights for is law and order – the defeat of the villain, who also seeks profits from fur – not the end of trapping. (This is true also in *Land of the Silver Fox* [1928].) But trapping does not profit Rin-Tin-Tin – he wears no fur that is not his own.

Rin-Tin-Tin also made several films in which mining was featured and approved of – 1923's *Shadows of the North*, 1925's *Tracked in the Snow Country* and *Clash of the Wolves*, 1930's *The Lone Defender*, and 1931's *The Lightning Warrior*. *Find Your Man* (1924) is about lumbering, and the good guys are loggers. In *The Man Hunter* (1930), Rin-Tin-Tin prevents the wrong people from taking ivory, but his "side" is not against killing elephants for it.

Duncan – like the films Rin-Tin-Tin stars in – showed an ambiguity about the wilderness. In his *Notes*, describing the filming of a scene in *Find Your Man* in which the crew blows up logs, the inert remains of the trees he so loved, he said that "[t]his made one of the big thrills of the picture." Later, he described how when still on location for *Find Your Man*, he saw baldheaded eagles, pelicans, and wild ducks and geese, in what was to him "a bird-heaven on earth." He rhapsodized:

> What a picture, a wild duck mother swimming with her new family only a few days old. My work at the store used to give me a chance to be out for a few days at a time but I was always out shooting and killing these beautiful birds that were now giving me so much pleasure in an entirely different way. I was out 'shooting' this time, too, but harmlessly, with a camera.

Yet Duncan also talked of killing two "nice buck" during a later pack trip on his way out of the mountains.

Love of unspoiled wilderness is apparent in the camera work on location. In a way Rin-Tin-Tin's films preserve the West before it became very populated. As Deborah A. Carmichael says in *The Landscape of Hollywood Westerns: Ecocriticism in an American Film Genre*: "In studies of the Western, the importance of the landscape itself . . . often receives supporting-role status." This is certainly true of Rin-Tin-Tin's films. Perhaps without thinking of their significance, his cameramen captured scenes that might never again occur: for example, in *Where the North Begins* (1923), the camera records the movement of a large herd of "cariboo" (probably elk, because caribou did not exist that far south then) seen as prey for the wolves that our hero, Rin-Tin-Tin, was then associating with. *Tiger Rose* (1929) was set in Canada but filmed in Yosemite National Park. Duncan's *Notes* waxed poetic about Yosemite's waterfalls, the mountains, and picnicking under the pines; to him, it was a time that would likely never come again – a summer or fall when people from all over the world mingled freely with deer, elk, and bear that roamed "day and night." The cast and crew stayed at the Ahwahnee Hotel, a magnificent edifice built in 1927 after a remark from Lady Astor that the Park needed a luxury hotel. It is (and was) a mishmash of Art Deco, Arts and Crafts, Native American, and Middle Eastern influences, with a granite facade, log beams, and stone fireplaces. As Duncan put it, from the dining room the cast and crew could see mountains from every window and the grass-covered valley floor "dotted here and there with a mother deer and her family or else a big elk whose call can be heard all over the valley, or a family of tourists feeding the young bear who sit up or stand on their hind legs to receive the food."

As for Rin-Tin-Tin himself, the dog? Duncan remarked in his *Notes*: "These location trips on the rivers and lakes gave us a chance to combine business and pleasure and there never was a happier dog than Rin-tin-tin." It is quite likely that Rin-Tin-Tin was in his element on location more than he was at home in his kennel, exercising on his wheel, on stage, or in front of the camera. During the filming of *Where the North Begins*, Rin-Tin-Tin played in the snow: "It was so clean and he loved to jump and roll in it," said Duncan, who added that Rin-Tin-Tin also chased and somehow captured a silver fox escaped from a fox farm.

Rin-Tin-Tin was at home in that wilderness landscape. Though he is ostensibly acting in the scenes in which he explores the forest with wild joy – licking snow off trees and "fishing" in streams – the cameraman is only recording a dog set free in a place he does not question but recognizes.

Rin-Tin-Tin snowshoeing with Myrna Loy and another friend. (Courtesy Rin-Tin-Tin Collection, Riverside, California).

5
Overcoming the Limitations of a Dog Star

In 1926, Rin-Tin-Tin granted a bizarre interview to the *Los Angeles Times* about his leading ladies and other human females who were attracted to him. He started with: "During my hectic career in motion pictures, many of the screen's most beautiful women have opened their hearts to me." After mentioning several "great girls," he added, "They have all loved me and shown it in their own individual way," but it was different with Alice Calhoun, his co-star in *A Hero of the Big Snows* (1926). She had not paid attention to him off-camera so he decided to pay more attention to *her*, a new role for him. He said that "All the other girls had made love to me" and it had spoiled him, then concluded with, "I wouldn't trade places with any man I know, although lots of them would give a lot to have even part of the attention I get." Taking into account that "making love" meant something less physical then than it does now, and leaving aside the issue of implied bestiality, this revealing interview does more than delight us with the imaginative genius of a publicity agent. It hints at the essential problems of putting a dog in a role ordinarily played by men: what to do with the issue of romance between a dog hero and a human heroine? Shouldn't the male who saves the girl at least get to hug and kiss her? It was a worse problem than Rin-Tin-Tin's inability, as a Western hero, to carry a gun.

As "The Right Dog at the Right Time" argues, Rin-Tin-Tin's stardom was not an anomaly. For roughly ten years, several other dogs – big male dogs – were also movie stars playing lead roles. Yet no matter how big or how male or how talented, a star of the Rin-Tin-Tin kind (a dog in a largely human role) was still a dog. No matter how "riproaring" the Rin-Tin-Tin film stories were or how clever his scriptwriters and directors, the scope of his movies was circumscribed by his necessarily limited ability as a canine actor. Perhaps a *Variety* reviewer described the dilemma best in a 1928 review of *A Race for Life* when he said that the movie could be "recommended for the very apparent skill it demonstrates in the art of constructing a theatrical scaffolding around a quadruped leading man."

Of course, there was one obvious reason it was possible to star dogs in 1920s movies: while the technology of silent movies – the hocus-pocus of the camera and the sleight-of-hand of editing – had advanced to the point it could partially compensate for some of dogs' limitations as actors, humans' natural abilities were cramped because the technology had not gone far enough. Silent movies, empty of language except through printed intertitles, which interrupted the story and were often stilted, were a natural for animal actors, who did not have to forego a major means of communication as human actors did. Human actors compensated for lack of sound by using exaggerated body motions and facial expressions and by talking without being heard by the audience. It was unnatural, and it made animal actors' "acting" seem even more authentic. Miming as humans did was not in a dog's ken. If a dog barked during the filming of a scene, he did not know that the sound would not register on the screen. He did not even know there would be a screen. Consequently he was unselfconscious about what he did.

However, the success of dog stars did not come about entirely because of the lack of sound. One popular theory goes that when talkies came along, it meant the end of the dog star. In actuality, as I will argue later in this chapter, that was not exactly true. Rin-Tin-Tin's popularity started to wane a bit *before* talkies came along, and talkies even gave his popularity a brief boost because audiences wanted to hear him bark. Also, the 1930s saw another peak, though a much smaller one, in movies – talkies – starring dogs. (See "Rin-Tin-Tin's Last Years and the Career of His Son.")

To some extent, the melodramatic plot suited dog heroes so well that their limitations were not so apparent to audiences. The plot pattern of Rin-Tin-Tin's movies was set in his first major film, *Where the North Begins* (1923). He is the undisputed star. Compared to the human hero, even though he is called just "The Dog," he is a god: without using language, he rescues the heroine from abduction, he saves the day by exposing the villain's perfidy and sending him to his death, he remains loyal to his inherent values (according to a human values system), and with his puppies he even out-reproduces the hero – eight to zero – in the process solving the bestiality problem in that his sexual interest is another canine. The male human lead, Gabrielle du Pré, is a poor example of a leading man. He sets off on a dangerous dogsled trip in order to earn the $500 that will enable him to marry the heroine, who is also being courted by the villain, the manager of the trading post, but fails to complete the trip successfully. French-Canadian, Gabrielle "speaks" in fractured English; he is low on the scale of class as measured by 1920s Hollywood. Moreover, his character is very flawed. He is so involved in hanky-panky with his girlfriend that he forgets the canine friend who has saved his life when he leaves The Dog outside the door waiting to get in. He is far too quick to judge The Dog as a killer when he finds bloody baby clothes. It's the evil factor, Galloway, the man in jodhpurs (a Hollywood trademark), who has the power – until Rin-Tin-Tin comes along. And Rin-Tin-Tin defeats him, too.

Melodramatic plots suited a dog star because they emphasized athleticism and action. Rin-Tin-Tin, the "Fairbanks of dogdom," could perform some athletic feats better than Douglas Fairbanks himself – and certainly was furrier. (Strangely, in his movies he makes little use of his superior canine senses of hearing and smelling.). In fact, it was his athleticism that got him into movies. The first trick Rin-Tin-Tin became famous for was the leap he performed at the March 4, 1922 dog show sponsored by the Shepherd Dog Club of the West; the *Mansfield News* (Ohio) said it was responsible for his being chosen for *The Man from Hell's River* (1922), which "called for a dog that could make a long leap over one man and strike the throat of the second, fighting with him." That crucial scene is the final one, where Rin-Tin-Tin goes to the aid of his friend, Pierre de Barre (Irving Cummings), takes over the fight with the villain, Gaspard the Wolf (Wallace Beery), and with "jaws of steel traps and eyes ablaze with fire," leaps at Gaspard's throat and ends up shoving him off the cliff to his death. Newspaper reviews applauded this scene at the expense of others.

Rin-Tin-Tin was an action hero, more popular with children (and many adults) than any other type of star. As a "man" of action, he needed no words to make an impact. George N. Fenin and William K. Everson, in *The Western: From Silents to the Seventies*, outline the series, in early Westerns, of complex predicaments from which a cowboy hero almost wordlessly extricated himself with ingenious escapes based on his athleticism and stunt work, assisted by a little trick photography. Rin-Tin-Tin's movies were similar in structure.

Athletic ability and great acting talent (if indeed Rin-Tin-Tin possessed it) could not compensate for the sticky problems presented by a dog playing opposite a human leading lady playing opposite a dog. For one thing, it placed the human below the canine in importance, because male lead trumped female lead, whose role was on the whole limited to looking pretty and being threatened by vague rape. For another, physically romancing the female lead was left to the male actor billed below both Rin-Tin-Tin and her.

Rin-Tin-Tin bringing a valentine to one of his co-stars (Courtesty Rin-Tin-Tin Collection, Riverside, California).

June Marlowe, "the girl with the soulful eyes," was Rin-Tin-Tin's main female co-star. Under contract to Warner, she starred with him in five films from 1925 to early 1926 (*Find Your Man, Tracked in the Snow Country, Below the Line, Clash of the Wolves,* and *The Night Cry*). After a four-year hiatus, during which she went to work for other studios, mainly Universal, Marlowe came back to star with Rin-Tin-Tin in *The Lone Defender* (1930). In that same year, she was chosen to play Miss Crabtree in the *Our Gang* comedies. Rin-Tin-Tin had top billing in reviews and ads of movies he made with Marlowe. For instance, a *Los*

Overcoming the Limitations of a Dog Star

Angeles Times review of *Tracked in the Snow Country* was mostly about Rin-Tin-Tin. June Marlowe, it said, had her usual "quaint wistful charm," but of course, "The heroine of a dog picture . . . seldom has any great dramatic moments to attract the attention of the audience."

The task of male human leads in Rin-Tin-Tin's movies was to play gracious second fiddle to Rin-Tin-Tin. Why did actors agree to do this? Sometimes they were relative unknowns at the time they made the movies (Eric St. Clair, Walter Merrill, Charles Farrell), or they were not the type to play leading roles (William Collier, Tom Gallery), or they were under contract with Warner and therefore couldn't choose their own roles (John Harron, Don Alvarado, Jason Robards). For instance, Eric St. Clair, the little brother of the much more prolific and famous writer, actor, and director Mal St. Clair, was at the beginning of his career when he played the male human lead in *Find Your Man* (1924). According to Grace Kingsley, writing in the *Los Angeles Times*, he was an "engaging juvenile, who is sure to grow in power as he goes along with his film work." (However, *Find Your Man*, his third movie, was also his last. He changed his career to writer, creating the story for "Flies Ain't Human," a Popeye short, in 1941.) If the leading man moved outside his role of romancer into action hero, he could end up looking ridiculous. In *The Lighthouse by the Sea* (1924), the ectomorphic William Collier, playing Albert Dorn, tussles with muscular Matthew Betz, playing bad guy Joe Dagget; this mirrors a fight between Rin-Tin-Tin and the Yukon Killer, a bulldog who could whip "its weight in alligators," according to one of the movie's villain rum runners. As Fred, of *Variety*, said, "The scenes with young Collier besting the heavy are almost funny as it is dead open and shut little Collier could never have handled Betz any day."

At least one actor, Jason Robards (father of the Jason Robards of *All the President's Men*), chafed publicly against being put in the shade by a canine hero. He voiced his objections in a *Los Angeles Times* interview, which though tongue-in-cheek, had a subtext of real anger. He had broken his contract by mutual agreement with Warner because he was "weary of leading 'a dog's life'" after acting in three Rin-Tin-Tin movies: *Hills of Kentucky*, *Tracked by the Police*, and *Jaws of Steel* (all released in 1927). Noting that not all his movies were dog pictures, he spoke of going to Warner to complain:

"I said, "Is that nice? What have I done that I should deserve such treatment? Rinty is as nice a dog as ever barked up a tree; Rinty is a man's pal; Rinty is a great deal more than that.

"But, gentlemen, enough is enough. I have a wife and kiddies to support. I want their faces to light up when I come home o' nights, and when they say to me, 'Daddy, what are you doing these livelong days,' I want to be able to answer, 'I am not, praise be, acting with Rin-Tin-Tin.'"

Some critics of dog pictures didn't like the supplanting of male heroes with dog heroes either. As early as 1925, a *Los Angeles Times* reporter was particularly brutal (as well as skeptical), panning not only Rin-Tin-Tin movies but dog pictures in general for the way they displaced human actors from stardom and drove screenwriters to devise ridiculous turns of plot: "Personally, I'm devoted to animals, but when I see actresses like Louise Fazenda and juvenile sheiks of high voltage like Buster Collier, not to mention sweet old troupers like Charles Hill Malles, and vivid character actors like Matthew Betz, put to support a canine matinee idol, I'm just plain mad."

To critics, though seemingly not to the public, the logical problem of a dog hero in a leading role was apparent early on. In 1922, in a review of Strongheart's *Brawn of the North*, the *Los Angeles Times* writer noted the strangeness of a dog being portrayed as more sensible than a human, without "faults and follies . . . noble, pure, and true." Though in the movie Brawn went "almost as far as the humans" in his lovemaking with his mate, he was more devoted to his humans – and he had to be because the humans were "muddle-headed." Brawn defeated the villain because the hero couldn't. The hero and heroine "even left their baby about carelessly, so that wolves were after it, and Brawn had to play nursemaid and rescue the infant." The audience ridiculed the human actors by laughing at dramatic moments meant to be serious, "[b]ut Brawn got a hand every time he dashed in and straightened out the hero's and heroine's affairs."

Rin-Tin-Tin's *Find Your Man* (1924) attracted similar criticism: the reviewer for *Variety* also noted that a dog star could be a constraint: "the story necessarily curtailed by the limitations of its star." And did it work to write a part in which a dog was so smart? *Variety*, in a review of *Tracked by the Police* (1927), doubted it: "Titles get weak at times, explainable in the fact that it's hard to tell just why a dog is gifted with human intelligence." While it seemed unbelievable that a mere animal could best human beings, it was also unbelievable that the human beings could be so dumb. The implication was that they had to be dumb to compensate for the fact a dog really wasn't as smart as a human. After all, why didn't villains drown or poison the dog but instead "tie[d] him up or put him in a net, and he eats up the rope and gets away in time to kill the villains, whole nests of them, and save the hero," asked the *Los Angeles Times*.

By 1928, the fact that Rin-Tin-Tin had "been a star and a moneymaker for a longer time than any other woof-woof hero" made it "not surprising that there [was] a certain factory-like efficiency in the turning out of these pictures," said *Variety* about *A Race for Life*. And the plot of *Rough Waters* (1930) was, also according to *Variety*, "just a group of situations hooked together to show how far Rinty can leap and how well he can swim."

Given these limitations, why did Warner set Rin-Tin-Tin up to compete with Douglas Fairbanks, Rudolph Valentino, and John Barrymore? Perhaps it was because he kept those human leading men in their place. It was a reminder they could be supplanted – by a dog. Also, in a context bigger than Hollywood, a dog represented values that male humans had violated by fighting a bloody war where they fearfully huddled in trenches, by drinking illicit booze, by committing adultery, by not keeping women in their place.

In *Manhood in America: A Cultural History* (1991), Michael Kimmel, discussing the effects of World War I on the masculine ideal, points out that "military glory had proven elusive to the typical G.I. Joe [sic]" many of whom instead suffered the shell shock that came with the helplessness and horror of trench warfare. He also points out that, while in the 1920s middle-class men worked at uninspiring jobs, "the traditional image of the heroic toiler had become tainted by associations with bolshevism" and that the machine (metaphoric and otherwise) had turned men powerless to the point that even those who did not work with machines felt like cogs in the engine of corporate culture. He adds that women were seeming to feminize the public world. In summary, he says: "American men tried to come home, both literally and symbolically. And yet try as they might, they couldn't seem to ground their manhood on a firm footing."

Rin-Tin-Tin appeared to transcend the emasculating changes of the 1920s. He didn't put on a suit, run a machine, buckle under to the Company or to a woman. He couldn't. His onscreen world was almost always outdoors, where, with only his wits and his body, he overcame villains and righted wrong. The irony is that without the movie technology of the 1920s, Rin-Tin-Tin would not have existed except as a vaudeville star, someone's pet, or a guard dog. So in the end, he, too, was the slave of the machine.

If this reason for movie-makers' elevation of the male dog star is true, and I think it is, it also explains why no female dog starred in movies in the 1920s and 1930s. It took another mindset, a decade later, to produce a Lassie, who was, nevertheless, played by a male.

In any case, Rin-Tin-Tin was important enough to Warner that the studio went to great lengths to ensure his continued popularity by adding at least one new situation or stunt to each Rin-Tin-Tin movie, by increasing his dramatic range, by setting his films in different locales, and by changing genres. But there were just so many stunts, and an older dog could not do all of them (thought a double could); besides, a dog's part was limited by some settings (the big city, for instance) and certainly by some genres (like romantic comedy). Yet only a few times during the heyday of his career did the studio demote Rin-Tin-Tin to second or third place in the cast line-up. It didn't work with audiences, who loved him in spite of his limitations.

The plots of Rin-Tin-Tin's movies capitalized on his athletic ability and kept it interesting by changing context. Rin-Tin-Tin leaps into second-story windows and over chasms and out of deep wells. In *Tracked by the* Police (1927), he climbs up (and down) a ladder, a very difficult and dangerous feat for a dog. More than once, he climbs a tree. In *Below the Line* (1925), the tree is "bent and old," probably making it easier for him to scale than one with a straight trunk, and as usual he fails the first time but finally succeeds, adding to the suspense. He does the same thing in *Clash of the Wolves* (1925). (If you go to YouTube, you will find many videos of contemporary tree-climbing dogs. Max von Stephanitz's book *The German Shepherd Dog in Word and Picture* [1925; in German,

1905] includes material on how to train a dog to climb trees.) And Rin-Tin-Tin jumps, high and long: *The Reel Journal* has a photo of a scene from *Below the Line* – Rin-Tin-Tin leaping, back legs high in the air, over several men below him.

The new stunt Warner added to each movie often did not demand athletic prowess, but still Rin-Tin-Tin chews through ropes and unties knots. He escapes through chimneys and through a hole in the wall in the back of a grandfather clock. He turns a wheel to work the locks of a dam. He hides in hollow logs and spies on the villain.

Perhaps it is in *A Dog of the Regiment* (1927) that the balance shifts from Rin-Tin-Tin's athletic feats to pure acting. The publicity for the picture emphasizes his heroic acts in all the elements – earth, water, and air – particularly the fact that he "flies," taking to it "like a duck to water" (a strange simile given the context), and as easily as Lindy. (Here the movie capitalized on the enormous fame of "Lucky Lindy," Charles Lindberg, who had flown the Atlantic Ocean from New York to Paris, nonstop and alone, on May 21-22, 1927.) But flying as a passenger in a plane demanded no special athletic ability from the dog. Besides, by this time, Warner had run through its bag of tricks. Though promotion for *Rinty of the Desert* (1928) promised "new tricks," nothing was really new, though contexts were different. *Variety* was impressed by his leap into a pit, but he had done that before – in *Tracked by the Police* (1927), for instance, he jumped into a deep mine shaft.

In his movies, even though he is a dog, Rin-Tin-Tin always bests the villain, finding him out and causing his death, often by urging him over the edge of a cliff or into water (*Tracked in the Snow Country* [1925] and *Hills of Kentucky* [1927]), but his victories are almost always somewhat different from the ones in previous movies. The only thing he doesn't do that a human actor might is kill the villain with a gun. The gun was an integral part of the Hollywood Western, but in his movies Rin-Tin-Tin doesn't wear a gun belt or shoot a gun. He doesn't need to. Human weapons (knives and guns) are no match for him. Rin-Tin-Tin always "gets his man" (or survives) with teeth, claws, body blocks, speed, or ingenuity, and, in some cases, through eliciting the sympathy of the one holding the gun. In *The Western*, David Lusted talks about the power of weapons in the Western movie to represent human skill and romantic masculinity. None of that symbolism applies in the case of Rin-Tin-Tin.

Rin-Tin-Tin rescues the heroine from the villain by feats of derring-do, but never exactly in the same way. For instance, he saves a heroine from drowning in rapids in *Find Your Man* (1924), but in *Hills of Kentucky* (1927), he goes to further lengths to do the same thing: in a turbulent river, he swims not only to recover the little crippled boy's crutch but to drown the villain and save the catatonic heroine, who, Ophelia-like, is being borne swiftly on a raft down the rapids toward a waterfall.

While it is true that there were just so many plot situations in which a dog could replace a human lead, Warner found ways to make them seem different. For instance, Rin-Tin-Tin is often falsely accused, but not always for the same crime. In *Where the North Begins* (1923), he is accused of killing a baby, in other movies for killing sheep and/or people. Of course, he is always innocent and is always vindicated.

Rin-Tin-Tin also played different roles, often within the same movie: In *Find Your Man* (1924), recalling the polarities of World War I, he is hero, friend, and enemy. In other movies, he is a loving father to puppies and human babies though he also heroically trounces the villain. Comedy was popular with audiences, so Warner introduced it into Rin-Tin-Tin's movies, but with limited success. Rin-Tin-Tin didn't seem to understand or enjoy being funny – at least in a non-canine way. In *Clash of the Wolves* (1925), Warner used Heine Conklin, a rubber-faced slapstick comedian, as comic relief. Conklin puts a disguise – a fake beard – on Rin-Tin-Tin. The beard is meant to make Rin-Tin-Tin look foolish – and funny. Boots are put on the dog's feet, ostensibly to protect them after he has had a thorn removed; in reality the boots turn him into a clown. Rin-Tin-Tin, being a serious German shepherd dog, is obviously embarrassed at having things attached to his body. And it embarrasses audiences (at least it does me) to watch him try to climb a ramp as the boots on his feet cause him to slide down at every attempt. However, according to reviewers, he could be funny in a dog fashion, as when, in *Land of the Silver Fox* (1928), he clowns around, distracting a crying baby with antics in the snow.

Warner also tried giving Rin-Tin-Tin a change of genre later in his career. Of Rin-Tin-Tin's twenty-eight full-length films, half are Westerns (or Northwesterns); the others are dramas of various sorts, at least five of them crime dramas. The ratio of Western to drama changed over time. The first half of Rin-Tin-Tin's full-length movies (1922 through 1926) were mostly Westerns (ten of twelve), while the second half (1927-1931) tended to be more varied (only eight of fifteen were Westerns). It was part of a general trend. In *Filming of the West* (1978), Jon Tuska points out that by 1929-1930 "the silent Western was finished and the sound Western reputedly impossible. Only Rin-Tin-Tin was working at Warner Brothers." *Rinty of the Desert* (1928) broke away from the traditional Western by combining that genre with underworld melodrama. Also it was not a "snow picture," as so many of Rin-Tin-Tin's movies were – theaters were now air-conditioned, which to some extent undercut the appeal of cold climate settings in the summer.

Though most of Rin-Tin-Tin's movies were set in the West (the Frozen North; the California wilderness, shore, desert, or ranch country) and filmed on location, several were set in far-away places (the eastern United States, London, and Africa, for instance) but were probably made in California. An example is *Below the Line* (1925), which according to several reviews, was set in a "sleepy southern village" below the Mason-Dixon Line with "simple people" and "pastoral scenic beauty" – as well as "alligator-infested [sic] swamps" – "the background for as much excitement as any small town has witnessed since the evolution trial at Dayton, Tenn."

The studio's attempts to star Rin-Tin-Tin in city dramas did not do so well – the dog needed a landscape in which to run. The critics gleefully panned the crime drama *While London Sleeps* (1926), a movie Duncan wisely never mentions in his *Notes*. The reviewer for *Reel Journal* said of it that "very slight demands are made on the uncanny cleverness, the almost human (if one is not too cynical) intelligence which the dog has displayed in the past. He is called on to do merely the conventional and does that naturally well." The shtick of the cop movie *The Million Dollar Collar* (1929) – that secrets were hidden in Rin-Tin-Tin's collar – shows how much Warner was reaching for new ideas for Rin-Tin-Tin's pictures. *Variety*'s reviewer "Waly" noted that the movie gave Rin-Tin-Tin something different to do besides "dashing over the plains," while it "automatically forces a story which . . . provides another stellar vehicle for Rin-Tin-Tin." He went on to say, somewhat irreverently, "Love interest of lad who books crook's clothes and noble sister of twisted brother have the gyrations without the heat. . . . Dog is improving."

Occasionally, Warner tried to solve the monotony problem by giving a human actor top billing over Rin-Tin-Tin, thus allowing more scope in plotting, situations, and genre. It didn't work, because audiences wanted Rin-Tin-Tin to be the star. In 1924, after being listed second in the cast list for *Find Your Man*, Rin-Tin-Tin was relegated to the end of the cast list in his next picture, *The Lighthouse by the Sea*. He was supplanted by William Collier Jr. and Louise Fazenda, though Fazenda got most of the publicity. Known as a comedienne second only to Mabel Normand, Fazenda later married producer Hal Wallis, who according to lore, was called "The Prisoner of Fazenda," a pun relating to the title of late 19th century novel *The Prisoner of Zenda*. (Coincidentally, Wallis was Rin-Tin-Tin's publicity agent on his way up the Warner ladder – how many lives Rin-Tin-Tin touched!) Fazenda made almost three hundred movies between 1918 and 1939, and this was the only one with Rin-Tin-Tin. Some reviews that showed up in the newspapers (most likely from Warner's press releases) touted her and Rin-Tin-Tin as "the pivot around which the exacting photoplay revolves." Behind the attempt to give her coequal stardom may have been studio rivalries as well as a desire to lift Rin-Tin-Tin's movies out of the category of "dog picture." As early as this, his seventh picture, only a couple of years into his career, anxiety about his ability to carry a picture by himself was manifest in a 1926 review: "It is unlike many of his previous pictures, in that there is an interesting story, and the dog isn't everything."

However, the studio's plan to elevate their female star did not work. At first Fazenda was given top billing, as in a December, 1924 notice in the *Billings Gazette* "The famous comedy queen, Louise Fazenda, will have the starring female role in 'Lighthouse by the Sea' . . . while the famous dog star of the movie, Rin-Tin-Tin, will play opposite her in this photoplay." Even then, the ad accompanying the article on the same page clearly featured Rin-Tin-Tin above her, both in the type size for his name and the tag line: "Thrilling adventures woven around the Wonder Dog and the raging sea. With Louise Fazenda and William (Buster) Collier, Jr." In some publicity, Fazenda was billed as a supporting actor, but Rin-Tin-Tin often received sole mention.

At least in the beginning, publicity for *Jaws of Steel* (1927), Rin-Tin-Tin's fifteenth movie, also made an attempt to dethrone Rin-Tin-Tin from his position as main and only star by mentioning the "unusually strong human cast to support him" – Jason Robards, Helen Ferguson, and the child actress Mary Louise Miller. The *Los Angeles Times* contained two lengthy articles about Ferguson, once a WAMPUS baby star and sometime stage actress, claiming that her acting in *Jaws of Steel* had achieved new heights after months of stage work. However, the writer made it clear that the story was Rin-Tin-Tin's and that Ferguson was "assuming the featured feminine role for Warner." A second article, ten days later, went into more detail about the six months Ferguson had spent on stage as ingenue in a play, locally successful, which had brought offers from stage producers in the east. The prospect of making the movie with Rin-Tin-Tin was, supposedly, what convinced her to go back to the screen, where her work proved that "[t]he much mooted question of whether or not players should confine their work to either stage or screen has been definitely answered to [her] satisfaction." Yet in spite of the attention paid to Ferguson, when the movie played in Los Angeles at the Broadway Palace for a week, Rin-Tin-Tin was billed first, with mention of a "good [unnamed] cast seen in support." And a later article noted that: "The cast [named] in support of Rinty is one of the best that has ever appeared with him in pictures."

In *Frozen River* (1929), Warner once again tried to give another star equal billing with Rin-Tin-Tin. Not surprisingly, the other star was a human child, four-year-old Davey Lee. Like a dog, a child could play a part that a human adult could not. Both dogs and children were revered for their innocence and goodness, while at the same time, they were ostensibly under the firm control of human adults. In a boy-and-his-dog movie, Rin-Tin-Tin did not have to act as melodramatic hero. He could play a dog, without any questions about his ability to romance his co-star. This was Rin-Tin-Tin's first real boy-and-his-dog movie, though *Below the Line* (1925) has a boy-dog theme, as does *A Race for Life* (1928). Davey Lee had made his mark in *The Singing Fool* (1928) with Al Jolson and in *Sonny Boy* (1929). The epitome of sweet innocence and naturalness, he was a beautiful child with "fine seal-brown hair, perfect teeth, blue eyes shaded by long brown lashes." A reviewer for the *Gleaner* (Kingston, Jamaica) waxed lyrical about the little boy, comparing his laugh to a line in a poem by Swinburne: "All the bells of heaven may ring." Theater patrons loved his baby talk. He was "'cute' without being altogether intolerable." In the beginning, Warner elevated him to co-stardom with Rin-Tin-Tin, but the attempt to unseat the dog star failed. By summer of 1929, in ads, Rin-Tin-Tin was again the main star of *Frozen River*, and Davey Lee had been demoted to supporting cast.

In spite of the nay-sayers, Rin-Tin-Tin survived the perceived waning of the dog movies' popularity and the switch to talkies. While it seemed natural that when human actors talked on screen, animal movies would be immediately less appealing, evidence says otherwise. Talkies did not end Rin-Tin-Tin's career. Perhaps in the long run, they would have done his career in, but talkies were slow in coming of age, and his own run was short (he died in 1932).

Warner was the pioneer of talking pictures, the first to include speech and synchronisation with Vitagraph (Vitaphone) sound-on-disc. When Al Jolson said, "Wait a minute. Wait a minute. You ain't heard nothin' yet," in the masterpiece *The Jazz Singer* (October 1927), he ushered in the talking-picture era. This is the crucial moment in the coming of talkies, even though the movie was silent with only some sound, as were most talkies in the last years of the 1920s, and even though *The Jazz Singer* was not the first full-length movie to use the new Vitagraph technology. (*Don Juan*, which premiered on August 6, 1926, had a soundtrack with a musical score and sound effects, but no dialogue.) In 1928, the year Warner premiered *Lights of New York*, the first all-talking feature, *Motion Picture Times* credited Warner Brothers with being the leader. By early 1929, all the major Hollywood studios were including sound in their pictures, but they continued to make movies that were partly silent, and as late at 1930, they were making movies in two versions – silent and talking. (By 1930, dog actors were speaking English in comedies through special effects, but Rin-Tin-Tin never did.)

The New York Times blamed the waning of dog pictures on talkies, warning in early 1930 that Rin-Tin-Tin had been "a great dog in his day," but "[n]ow that the talkies have come, unemployment in the best animal circles in Hollywood is simply appalling." According to the reporter, the problem came from lack of control over the noises animal actors might make, like barking at the studio cat. This notion persisted: In 1963, more than thirty years after Rin-Tin-Tin's death, Fred Childress, writer of the "At the Theatres" column in the Youngstown *Vindicator* (Ohio), claimed that "Rin Tin Tin was the mainstay of the company [in 1924]. Within a few years, of course, Rinty was replaced by sound."

Certainly Warner executive P.A. Chase thought Rin-Tin-Tin's days were over when, on December 6, 1929, he wrote a letter to Ralph E. Lewis, of the Los Angeles law firm Freston and Files, about cancelling Rin-Tin-Tin's contract, saying that after completing the movie the studio was about to start, Warner Bros. did not intend to make any more pictures with Rin-Tin-Tin. His reason:

> . . . since the talking pictures have come into their own, particularly with this organization . . . the making of any animal pictures . . . is not in keeping with the policy that has been adopted by us for talking pictures, very obviously, of course, because dogs don't talk.

In 1930, Warner released Rin-Tin-Tin's last three Warner movies – *On the Border* (March 15), *The Man Hunter* (May 3), and *Rough Waters* (June 7).

I think Chase was wrong. So does Jon Tuska, who says in *Filming of the West*, "Competition hurt Rinty, but not the coming of sound." In 1929, before Chase wrote his letter, Rin-Tin-Tin had already barked in five talking pictures – *Land of the Silver Fox* (1928) and *Frozen River*, *The Million Dollar Collar*, *Tiger Rose*, and *The Show of Shows* (all 1929) – and quite successfully. A laudatory article in the *Los Angeles Times* (1929), titled "The Dog Star," noted that Rin-Tin-Tin's "voice registers superbly" and suggested that he "do all the talkies," remarking that he worked cheap and was always willing to act for hamburger. "We are in favor of bigger and better talkies – for Rin-tin-tin. We are talking about the dog star. So this is supposed to be Sirius."

Of course, the new technology presented obvious problems for dog actors, who were used to voice cues. Trainers had to switch to gestures, but this meant that the dog would look at them rather than at the camera to see what they were supposed to do, which could create a problem in itself. Directing a dog required great subtlety and timing – the director had to signal the dog *before* he started acting, and the signal often had to trigger a very complex action. According to James English in *The Rin-Tin-Tin Story*, Duncan originally used voice signals to train Rin-Tin-Tin. When, in 1926, Quin Martin reported on Duncan's stage act with Rin-Tin-Tin, he said, "Lieutenant Duncan spoke in a soft, high voice, without a trace of threat in it, but rather only a tone of mild entreaty. He used his hands not at all." However, for the talkies, Duncan taught Rin-Tin-Tin to respond to hand signals. In 1935, Duncan explained how he accomplished the transition — by first giving simultaneous voice and hand signals, then dropping the voice signals. To tell a dog to run, he dropped his hand, but raised it when it was time to stop; he spread out his fingers as a cue to snarl. Often he used actors' scripted words as a signal for a certain action from the dog — e.g., "Get him, Rinty" as a cue to attack.

The 1932 Fox Movietone News film about Rin-Tin-Tin's death includes a scene of Duncan and Rin-Tin-Tin entertaining a group of children at the German-Catholic Orphan Asylum in Buffalo, New York. In it, you can see Duncan using hand signals. For instance, Rin-Tin-Tin rolls over, cued by Duncan rolling his hand, and leaps into Duncan's arms, cued by Duncan holding his arms wide open.

Talkies also demanded training for dogs's voices. According to a story in a June 1930 issue of *Lima News* (Ohio), by the time of *The Man Hunter* (1930), Duncan had succeeded in softening Rin-Tin-Tin's sharp bark and had taught him to "speak" with his throat. Also Rin-Tin-Tin varied his bark according to mood and learned a range of sounds "from caressing noises to awe-inspiring growls."

The first picture in which Rin-Tin-Tin spoke and was heard by audiences was *Land of the Silver Fox* (1928), set in the snowy Canadian wilderness. Though the movie had "speaking sequences," with a "thunderous" synchronized score, it was silent except for several scenes for which the voices of the main actors and Rin-Tin-Tin were recorded. The *Ogden Standard-Examiner* (Utah) found that Rin-Tin-Tin had "a somewhat heavy voice in the speaking sequences although his enunciation is very good." And what did he say? "Woof! Woof! — He's in the Talkies Now!" (In Oakland, California, the movie was accompanied by other Vitaphone acts — a playlet, a tenor, an orchestra, and news, including a League of Nations session and President Calvin Coolidge "doing a little ox-cart hunting in the old south.")

Frozen River (1929) was also partly silent and partly talking. There was little dialogue. The child star Davey Lee did not speak at all, nor did he sing; his dialogue was corny — for example, he was reputed in an intertitle to say, "I faw down." *Variety* panned the movie's sound, saying that Rin-Tin-Tin's barking was not well synchronized and only slowed the story down, therefore the movie, billed as a talkie, was overpriced. However, *The Sheboygan Press* did not agree with

Variety: "Rin-Tin-Tin is another screen star whose popularity will not wane because of the talking pictures. He has an excellent bark for recording purposes as was proved last night at the Majestic theatre."

The Million Dollar Collar (1929), in which Rin-Tin-Tin barks, yelps, and growls, made him "the first dog star of the talkies!" – at least according to the *Daily News* of Huntingdon, Pennsylvania.

In *The Show of Shows* (1929), a spectacular talkie partly in Technicolor, with seventy-seven luminaries (including John Barrymore, Ben Turpin, Beatrice Lillie), Rin-Tin-Tin had a small part introducing Myrna Loy and Nick Lucas in "Chinese Fantasy." You can see this on YouTube: He trots onto the red-curtained stage, sits, barks twice, then walks to a screen and yanks a cord with his teeth to reveal another screen saying that he is proud to introduce the act.

On the Border (1930) was Rin-Tin-Tins's first *all*-talking picture. *Variety* gave it a lukewarm review ("weak entertainment") but awarded a thumbs-up to Rin-Tin-Tin: He was "[b]ack again with new thrills as you hear him growl and snarl in desperate battle." Mordaunt Hall of *The New York Times* commented, "He barks his way through danger and love."

Audiences were not as bored with dog movies as some critics assumed they were. Even in 1930, publicity releases bragged about how Rin-Tin-Tin's fan mail – several thousand letters a month, "one of the heaviest fan mails in the motion picture industry" – had "steadily increased since his entry into talkies." He was receiving mash notes "sent by feminine chows, police woman dogs and owners of hot dog stands."

True, Rin-Tin-Tin was not *always* the star of his movies, but it was not because talkies came along. What happened to him in *Tiger Rose* (1929) seems to presage the end of his career, but it was just a glitch. Except for listing Rin-Tin-Tin as part of the cast (in last place), the review of the movie by *The New York Times* did not mention him once, which may have been a good thing, because the reviewer didn't think much of the picture – it was so corn-ball it was unintentionally humorous. *Variety* mentioned Rin-Tin-Tin only in the third paragraph of its review, saying he was:

> a much less prominent doggie than in the days when mutts were glorified by Hollywood. . . . . Rinty (as his fans used to call him when

art was art) has been scissored almost out of the picture. He now merely peeps through his paws and gets petted a couple of times. No more saving the express train or racing miles for the United States Marines.

Warner placed Rin-Tin-Tin at the top in the cast list in his last three movies for them, all released in the first half of 1930 (*On the Border, The Man Hunter,* and *Rough Waters*), and he was the star in his two serials for Mascot Pictures – *The Lone Defender* (1930) and *The Lightning Warrior* (1931).

An obituary that ran in several newspapers in 1932 gave the lie to the coming of talkies as reason for Rin-Tin-Tin's supposed loss of popularity:

> This remarkable dog even survived the talkies, and brought to the sound screen a loud and euphonious sort of woof-woof-woofing that was several degrees superior, as the standards of voice culture go, to the adenoidal artistry of half the movies' human stars. If Rin Tin Tin's bark was worse than his bite, it was still infinitely better than much that passed as elocution, and one could always be certain, whatever else this canine thespian might do, that he would never lisp or croon or chew his lines.

In 1928, thirteen of Rin-Tin-Tin's films were playing at various times across the country. By 1929, there were only eight. But he was popular to the end of his life, weathering the advent of talkies and child stars, the prematurely announced death of Westerns, the end of dog pictures, the canceling of his contract by Warner. He was an actor who could always astonish audiences, no matter what motivated him.

6
Rin-Tin-Tin, the Magic Actor

In *The Night Cry* (1926), Rin-Tin-Tin, falsely accused of being a sheep killer (though he does not know that), limps home after a fall from a cliff, opens the door of his family's cabin by releasing the latch with his teeth, slinks in, and shuts the door after himself. The family – father, mother, and baby girl (all humans) – are seated at the dinner table. Expecting the usual love and recognition, Rin-Tin-Tin goes first to the husband (John Harron), who ignores him. He rears up and puts his paws on Harron's body in supplication, but it is as if he – Rin-Tin-Tin – doesn't exist. The wife (June Marlowe), seemingly more conflicted but resolute, also refuses to recognize his presence. With his chin and paws on the table (something like a pathetic Kilroy), Rin-Tin-Tin looks piteously from under his eyebrows to the man and then the woman for acknowledgment, but again he receives no response. The baby (Mary Louise Miller) alone seems to know he is there. She pats his head, giving him some relief from his anxiety. It is heart-wrenching.

Critics have noted the power of this scene. Nearly forty years after the scene was filmed, George N. Fenin and William K. Everson wrote in *The Western: from silents to cinerama*: "All of the later Rin-Tin-Tin films had at least one situation in which he had to *emote*, to rely *entirely* on facial expressions. In *The Night Cry* in a single take, [he] expresses hope, grief, tolerance, and finally joy, when at least one friend is found in the person of the couple's baby."

Watching the same scene, a number of my fellow academic friends and I expressed similar reactions, as we let loose with a spontaneous empathetic "Oohhh" at Rin-Tin-Tin's bewilderment and sorrow. However, at a later screening, Jt Clough, a dog trainer, pointed out to me that a plate of food out of camera range could well have elicited the same look of anguish and puzzled sadness from Rin-Tin-Tin. This is, of course, conjecture, but any dog owner will instantly recognize its possibility, once reminded. The eyes of a dog begging at the table look yearningly intelligent and deep. That look of supplication can crack the most resolute of us, if we are not on our guard.

While watching the scene again, alone, in a more analytical mood, I noticed for the first time that Rin-Tin-Tin licks his lips at least twice, which would indicate that a plate of food indeed might have been present. Also he looks toward the camera for direction before appealing to the child, then drops to the floor – it is clear he has heard a command. (Fenin and Everson note, correctly, that in his later films, he did not to seem to be obviously reacting to commands.) Moreover, the only expressions I saw on Rin-Tin-Tin's face in that scene were supplication, hope and joy, not the grief and tolerance Fenin and Everson did.

For further verification of the plate-of-food theory, try setting up a plate-of-food scene with your own dog. – if she begs at the table, that is. Is there not a hard-to-resist appeal from her as you ignore her supplications, and is there not joy on her face when you do give in?

Obviously, film made it possible to put dogs in sustained starring roles because of the short takes and off-camera commands and inducements (like that plate of food) that had little to do with the supposed onscreen emotions of the actors. When we watch a movie, we tend to forget what happens out of range of the camera and how the movie is put together from separately filmed scenes. As Richard Koszarski says in *An Evening's Entertainment: The Age of the Silent Feature Picture, 1915-1928*:

> Soviet Director Lev Kuleshov had demonstrated that traditional acting was irrelevant in silent pictures because the editing process imposed its own structure regardless of the intentions of the original performer. This idea would not have surprised the producers of OUR GANG comedies or the many animal films starring Rin-Tin-Tin.

So the plate of steak can be placed out of camera range, the scene filmed, the steak eaten, and all the audience sees is a soulful Rin-Tin-Tin in apparent despair. Similarly, as a January 1925 *Los Angeles Times* article claimed, when Rin-Tin-Tin snarled and leapt to the attack on screen, the off-camera stimulus might have been something other than a villain: "those marvelously intelligent expressions that the dear old ladies love to remark on the face of Rin-Tin-Tin are brought forth by the sight of – a stuffed cat? Some time the dog is going to find out that the cat is dead and then he will probably stop acting."

The camera also made other magic possible – editing to cause athletic feats to seem more dangerous than they actually were, using stuffed animals to replace the dog or the dog's animal "enemies," and compressing many dogs into one by the use of doubles.

In *Clash of the* Wolves (1925), Rin-Tin-Tin (Lobo), pursued by a posse, leaps across a seemingly bottomless chasm about eight feet wide. An eight-foot broad jump is a not impossible feat for most trained German shepherds. (My German shepherd, Louis, could do a six-foot broad jump when we were taking agility classes and could have been taught to do more.) But a misstep was certainly possible. Did the director really put this valuable dog at risk of falling that far down, or use an understudy, or fake it somehow? After many replays, I decided that, while Rin-Tin-Tin did make the leap, the chasm itself was edited to look far deeper than it was. Other Rin-Tin-Tin movies contain similar scenes.

Stuffed dogs are stand-ins for Rin-Tin-Tin in more than one movie. It's a stuffed dog that jumps on the back of a galloping horse in *Where the North Begins* (1923), that falls spiraling to the ground in a death grip with a condor in *The Night Cry* (1926), and that leaps through the air into a moving ore car that is hundreds of feet above the ground in *The Lightning* Warrior (1931). Duncan himself admitted using a stuffed dog to represent Rin-Tin-Tin in dangerous situations. The stiff, stuffed puppies Rin-Tin-Tin carries to safety in *Clash of the Wolves* are unintentionally funny.

Rin-Tin-Tin also fought against stuffed animals in more than one movie. "Fred," reviewing for *Variety*, was aware of that. In his column on *Below the Line* (1925), he noted that "stuffed animals used in certain shots were all too noticeable." He later commented that in *Hills of Kentucky* (1927) "the 'fake' dog stuff, when the Grey Ghost [Rin-Tin-Tin], perched on a ledge, fights off the pack" would not be noticed by "the majority of the audiences. . . as it is done so well." Indeed the "dogs" fighting Rin-Tin-Tin in that scene do look suspiciously artificial, with their large puppet heads lunging from out-of-camera-range bodies.

While Duncan denied that Rin-Tin-Tin had doubles, several sources (and evidence from his movies) say that he did. Jack Warner, in *My First Hundred Years in Hollywood* (1965), serialized in the *Los Angeles Herald-Examiner* in that same year, said:

> It had occurred to us, when we realized Rinty's earning capacity, that our investment would be lost if anything happened to him. Therefore, with Duncan's consent, we agreed to breed and train a kennel full of doubles who could be used if our hero were ill or injured or even killed in some of the dangerous stunts that we had planned.

He added that the studio ended up with eighteen Rin-Tin-Tins that had various specialties – like attacking, jumping, acting as "a gentle house dog,"

In his serials for Mascot, made starting in 1930, Rin-Tin-Tin clearly had doubles. In at least some of the action scenes, we can see that the dogs who run are not Rin-Tin-Tin, not just because Rin-Tin-Tin was by then an old dog and not that agile, but because some of the running dogs are lighter in color with different markings. In *The Filming of the West,* Jon Tuska mentions Rin-Tin-Tin's doubles casually twice: "Rinty's major double struck Yak [stunt man Yakima Cannutt] as a better action player" and "The animal – that is, the real Rin-Tin-Tin and not his many doubles." However, Rin-Tin-Tin Jr., when questioned in a newspaper interview on August 13, 1932, three days after Rin-Tin-Tin's death, said that the notion that his father depended on doubles was a "ridiculous rumor," a Hollywood story like those "they circulate about Garbo. My father never used a double in his life, even for the most dangerous scenes. He leaped from the top of fast-moving trains and rushed into burning buildings."

Possible tricks of the camera and director aside, Rin-Tin-Tin gave the impression that he was acting from the bottom of his heart. Tuska says:

> Rin-Tin-Tin . . . [was] able to depict by physical posture and facial expressions very subtle feelings and sudden shifts in mood. And then there were his eyes, deeply sensitive, variously bright, fierce, sad, a mirror to moods seemingly beyond the ken of his comprehension. . . .his success stemmed most precisely from the touching, tragic, and tender moments he portrayed on the screen.

In another of his books, *The Vanishing Legion: A History of Mascot Pictures*, Tuska discusses the reactions of two of the people who worked with Rin-Tin-

Rin-Tin-Tin, the Magic Actor

Tin – Darryl F. Zanuck, script writer for Rin-Tin-Tin, and Ross Lederman, who directed five of Rin-Tin-Tin's movies. According to Zanuck, "Rin Tin Tin could do anything." And Lederman said that Rin-Tin-Tin seemed to act on his own without cues from Duncan except for physical movement:

> That dog knew just what was expected of him . . . He couldn't tell time. But as for emoting, or playing a scene right, he didn't need any coaching. That's the unusual thing about that dog. He actually seemed to understand the story line well enough to bring off his role better than most of the other actors in the picture.

And Tuska himself says that after Rin-Tin-Tin starred in *Where the North Begins* (1923), he outshone Strongheart, Peter the Great, and other dog actors "because while they might all have an interesting bag of tricks, none could breathe human meaning into his performances for the screen as could Rin Tin Tin."

Lederman wasn't the only person who found Rin-Tin-Tin magically aware of human stories and emotions. Columnist Harry Carr, in a September 1924 *Los Angeles Times* article on a D.W. Griffith interview about acting, said that Rin-Tin-Tin could "register eagerness or fear or anger as no actor, living or dead, has ever been able to." He attributed this to the fact that Rin-Tin-Tin was "completely without self-consciousness and . . . his imagination [was] a natural and perfect quality of his mind and soul." He could "forget himself," which human actors could not completely do.

Others also saw Rin-Tin-Tin's acting as a mystery that made him "more than human" in his uncanny intelligence, sagacity, and unselfconsciousness, as well as his ability to portray a wide range of emotions: fear, sadness, joy, puzzlement, anger. After seeing *Clash of the Wolves* (1925), a *Photoplay* reviewer wrote, "This dog is the most sympathetic and human creature on the screen today. There are times when we think the dog actually shed tears."

Is all this really true, or did Zanuck, Lederman, and studio publicists romanticize canine sensibility? How could a dog follow a story line? The camera, a machine that Rin-Tin-Tin probably understood about as well as my dog understands a vacuum cleaner, was the "eye" to which he played a scene, but he couldn't have understood what it was doing. After all, he was a subject of a different species, who, though he made more money and achieved more fame than almost all Americans of his time, had no sense of the meaning of a dollar or a good review – or a movie. He could sit in a dark theater and look at a screen on which one of his movies was playing and perhaps see nothing but odd flickering on a flat space.

According to some modern experts, dogs cannot recognize themselves, especially when shown on a movie or television screen But maybe not. James English, in *The Rin Tin Story*, based on Duncan's *Notes*, says that when Rin-Tin-Tin attended the showing of *Where the North Begins* (1923) in Glendale, he was bored until "about midway, when he suddenly recognized himself on the screen" and started barking. "From then on Rin Tin Tin was his most ardent fan, getting an immense delight out of seeing his own movies." The September 18, 1929 issue of *The New York Times* contained an article that would indicate that other dogs could respond to images on the screen: the proprietor of the Marble Arch Pavilion Cinema in London arranged a special performance for dogs, who, it turned out, weren't interested in a reel showing dogs doing tricks, but barked "with approval" at a film with Charlie Chaplin and Rin-Tin-Tin. (I cannot find such a film listed in any Rin-Tin-Tin source). The last reel showed a stag pursued by hounds (silent film) and in the theater "three big deerhounds tore their leashes from their mistresses' hands, jumped to the stage and began clawing and biting at the canvas behind which they thought the quarry was concealed, to a chorus of approving barks by their friends in the audience."

Could Rin-Tin-Tin really act? At first, pondering this question made me wonder about what all acting – whether human or canine – really is. Was Rin-Tin-Tin a canine Method actor who manifested emotions believable to the audience by plumbing some deep reservoir of past emotions in his heart, or did he become so immersed in the scene, not knowing it was simulated, that he was not even acting but reacting to something that seemed like real life to him? Maybe he responded to, or mirrored, fellow actors' emotions (even though feigned), as almost all dogs respond to humans who approach them with love, anxiety, fear, or hate. I asked my "dog-people" friends about this, and their answers made me realize that all dogs "act" – it's natural to them to pretend.

Canine play, in which puppies engage a good part of their waking life, involves acting. Dogs understand that a game is a game and, like all gamesters, are capable of subterfuge. The dog who tussles with a toy, growling and gnawing and tossing it about, knows the toy is not animate. (Duncan used Rin-Tin-Tin's squeaky toy as a motivator.) Begging at the table is a game. Like most people writing about dogs, I find myself going to personal experience: Hugo, a Hovawart, who brings wrestles mightily with visitors for possession of a tug toy; Sprocket, a long-legged collie mix, who pretends to be unable to rise smartly from his haunches until he sees a cat; Louis, who has no idea what happened to that baguette he stole from the counter and buried in the back yard.

Dog training – for acting in movies or other purposes – usually involves taking advantage of dogs' natural proclivities. The police dog who attacks on command is playing a game prompted by his handler. He feigns his ferocity and after a word from the handler, returns to his normal calm self. The Chesapeake Bay Retriever is following a natural inclination to bring back that dead duck when he plays fetch with an inanimate ball. (Louis, a German shepherd, will pick up a ball only when it is bobbing in the surf, looking alive.) Even when they may not want to, trained dogs will, on command, sit, lie down, and roll over, and so on, but those actions are natural to them. Most of Rin-Tin-Tin's stunts were based on such movements, but he performed them better – he could jump higher, run faster, attack seemingly more ferociously, and respond quicker than the vast majority of dogs.

Through Rin-Tin-Tin's life, Duncan trained him intensely – over and above the usual – unlike those of us who become lax and then, seeing our dogs are failing to obey as we want, go back to giving them lessons. Rin-Tin-Tin's training was as thorough and unrelenting as that the talented child professional undergoes, and it produced the same spectacular results it sometimes can with them. There was little magic in Rin-Tin-Tin's versatility except in the extraordinary capacity of the dog to learn and in the tenacity of his trainer.

No matter what the method (for hunting dogs, police dogs, war dogs, or family dogs), training in the 1920s involved establishing an intimate bond with dogs, in which they learned to mirror their trainers; it involved teaching a series of commands by modeling, voice, and gesture, to which the dog responded with appropriate actions. It all fitted beautifully into movie making.

Rin-Tin-Tin: The Movie Star

Certainly Duncan used police and war training methods with Rin-Tin-Tin, as made manifest in his performances, beginning as early as October 1919, at German shepherd shows, which are based on those methods. Tangible evidence also exists that he did so: In Box 2 of the Rin Tin Tin Collection of Lee Duncan's personal papers in Riverside, California, is a small book called *Training the Sanitary Service Dog*. It has a very plain inside cover except for the title; the name of the German publisher (Deutsche Verein fur Sanitats Hunde, a German association for the training of Red Cross dogs in World War I) and city of publication, Oldenberg; a wax seal reading "Ville de Paris B.H. Dyas"; and the name of the translator, Anne B. Tracy. No copyright date exists either on the cover or within the book, but I judge that it was published in the late teens and that Duncan came to own it after early 1919, when Dyas bought the Ville de Paris building, and sometime before Duncan quit working at Dyas. During that time, Anne Tracy was a breeder of German shepherds and active in the Shepherd Dog Club of America. Well aware of police and war dog training, she had served during World War I with the Red Cross for two years and often judged German shepherd trials.

Outer cover (Courtesy Rin-Tin-Tin Collection, Riverside, California).

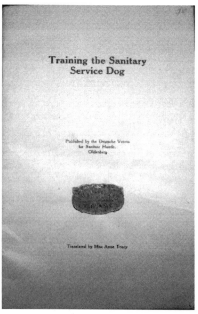

Inside cover (Courtesy Rin-Tin-Tin Collection, Riverside, California).

"Sanitary service dog" is a literal translation of "sanitats hunde." The more accurate translation would be just "service dog." The book may well be a translation of all or part of *Der Deutsche Schäferhund Als Diensthund (The German Shepherd as Service Dog)*, published in 1910 in Germany by Max von Stephanitz, the grand old man of German shepherd dog breeding and training, though that book is much more extensive.

By the tattered state of the outside cover, it seems someone used the book, and it is most likely that that someone was Duncan. I find its presence in the Rin Tin Tin Collection significant because it is the only *material* evidence of how Duncan trained Rin-Tin-Tin for movies. (Of course, we also have contradictory evidence in his own testimony, publicity, movie people's comments, and the viewer's interpretations of Rin-Tin-Tin in his movies that are still available.)

Because Duncan was an active member of the Shepherd Dog Club in Los Angeles, I would guess that he once owned a copy of Tracy's other translation, *Schooling and Training the German Shepherd Dog: After Von Stephanitz Book Der Deutsche Schäferhund in Wort Und Bild* (1917), which was taken from Chapter VI of von Stephanitz's mammoth tome on the German shepherd (translation: *The German Shepherd Dog in Word and Picture*). Published in German in 1905, von Stephanitz's book is still available in a 1994 English reprint. Chapter VI was considered the gold standard for training German shepherds and appeared in English in other places.

Information about German dog training methods was also readily available outside of books. Max von Stephanitz said that before the Great War officials came to Germany from within Europe and from overseas for information on training German shepherds, often going home with "fully trained dogs" and German instructors.

Dog trainers in general recommended creating a bond between human and dog, one in which the dog became a reflection of the man, the dog's will subjugated to the human's will. And yet they also promoted mutual cooperation between human and dog, especially in instances where the dog's native talents surpassed those of humans (in scenting, for instance) and therefore the dogs needed a certain independence. Von Stephanitz, who advocated a Germanic soul-to-soul foundation for German shepherd training, said that the trainer should try "as far as possible to enter into the innermost mind of the dog," knowing how to "short-circuit, for the time, all his purely human points of view." Indeed, often he imaginatively took his reader very far into a dog's mind. For instance, he described "water work" from the dog's point of view: "It must be remembered in every exercise in the water, that the dog lying deep in the water, has only a limited circle of vision, that the mirror of the water dazzles, and that there is no such thing as scent." For him, even beyond getting into the dog's mind, *"dog and man must form one indivisible whole."* And yet this sentiment seems to war with another statement von Stephanitz made: "The aim of training and schooling is to subordinate the dog to our will, and to make of him a helper in accordance with our wishes" with his obedience "to *appear* [italics mine] as voluntary service." Many other dog experts said that in the end no matter how much attention was paid to the dog's individuality, it mirrored its owner. For instance, Theo F. Jager in *Scout, Red Cross and Army Dogs: A Historical Sketch of Dogs in the Great War and a Training Guide for the Rank and File of the United States Army* (1917) stated: "'A dog that is worth while, a dog that we have fussed over for a long time, becomes in the course of many months a second edition of our very being."

The trainer worked with paradoxes: he needed to maintain the dog's essential nature (rooted in Nature) yet train the dog to mirror him (a creature of another species and culture); he needed to recognize the dog's individuality and at the same time insist on absolute obedience.

According to James English in his book about Rin-Tin-Tin, when Duncan was training the puppies in France, he used "kindergarten" lessons, which were exactly those proposed in manuals for training dogs for any role – war dog, police dog, hunting dog. He would kneel so the puppies weren't intimidated by looking at his feet, then hold out his arms and motion them to come, speaking gently "from the heart." All this was aimed at winning confidence and affection so that the dogs would trust him enough not to question commands. Supposedly from a German sergeant, Duncan learned to anticipate what the dogs would do and give a fitting voice command, "[their] involuntary action fitted to [their] master's order." This resonates with Jager's observation that the dog should "by instinct" [sic] learn and anticipate the wishes of his master." Duncan kept extending the periods in which the puppies were held in a position. Knowing they were eager to please and would not knowingly disobey but were merely misinterpreting, Duncan sometimes even apologized to them. He kept training Rin-Tin-Tin after the war and, "Later he learned how to reason with a dog and in every sense to treat him as a human and an equal."

English comments that the companionship between Duncan and Rin-Tin-Tin led to an "intuitive understanding that far surpassed Duncan's relationship with any of his previous dogs." As a result, he says, Rin-Tin-Tin was "not a trained dog but an enthusiastic one, to whom work was play and companionship with his master and friend was ample reward." Yet Duncan claimed to have learned training methods from a German sergeant, and we can be pretty certain that he learned them from his friends in the Los Angeles Shepherd Dog Club and/or of the several books available on training police and war dogs – certainly his copy of *Training the Sanitary Service Dog*. And both war and police training methods went beyond canine enthusiasm, play, and friendship for the master.

Perhaps also picking up from police dog training according to von Stephanitz, dog trainers readied dogs for movies by modeling the action, that is, demonstrating to their canine actors what they wanted them to do by doing it themselves. For instance, Von Stephanitz had trainers jump over things to demonstrate barrier-jumping to dogs. For a 1933 article in *Popular Science Monthly*, Andrew R. Boone interviewed Rennie Renfro, a trainer of animals for silent pictures. Renfro told Boone he led his charges through "intricate scenes by personally showing them the action, by talking to them constantly, by pointing out the route they were to travel or objects to be moved." He said that training for the camera could take up to a year and should start from infancy; it involved teaching the puppy that he (Renfro) was master, friend, and father, and in the process the puppy would mimic him. As he modeled an action and the puppy followed, Renfro talked to him: for example, he himself would roll over, saying, "Roll over, little fellow," while also rolling his hand. Eventually, he eliminated the modeling and voice signals so that all that was left were hand signals.

Duncan demonstrated Rin-Tin-Tin's ability to perform certain acts and portray certain emotions on command when he took him on personal-appearance tours. In 1926, Quin Martin of the *New York World Digest* gave what is perhaps the best and most detailed (if quaintly written) eyewitness accounts of their act: "'I thought you people who love dogs, as I do, might care to see Rinty as he really is,' the speaker [Duncan] went on. Then as handclapping began he stept to one side, peered into the wings and said: 'Are you there, Rinty? Are you . . .'" At this point, Duncan wordily reminded Rin-Tin-Tin of a scene in *The Night Cry* where he scratched his ear, then asked the dog to duplicate it, which he did, by scratching his right ear. Duncan said that it was his left ear that itched, and Rin-Tin-Rin shifted to his left. Duncan went on to put Rin-Tin-Tin in a down position, ears down, showing fear. He then asked Rin-Tin-Tin to "bark" without noise; to pose for a photograph and hold the pose; to catch a piece of candy placed on his nose. He was to show anger (ears moving, lip curled, teeth showing, looking "every inch the wolf") followed by happiness (eyes opened wide, ears up, mouth open, tongue out, prancing).

In Chicago, in May of 1926, Quin A. Ryan reported on a similar demonstration which Duncan commanded and Rin-Tin-Tin responded: "Rin, go over to the chair and rest your head and left paw on it, and then come and lie quiet under the piano. Scratch hard, now, as we used to do in France." In a demonstration in San Antonio in August 1931, Duncan asked Rin-Tin-Tin to "play dead," whereupon the dog "rolled over on his side, closed his eyes and completely stopped breathing." He knew his directions, according to the reporter, especially when Duncan told him there was something on his right leg – and, to the dog's surprise, there wasn't. Rin-Tin-Tin wasn't the only dog to know right from left: Albert Hochwalt (*The Working Dog and His Education*, 1921) and von Stephanitz both suggested that the trainer build on previously learned lessons in teaching directions – left, right, straight ahead – with arm motions. Knowing directions was a skill important in scouting as well as in movie acting.

Clearly, Duncan's demonstrations would seem to substantiate the theory that, when acting, Rin-Tin-Tin might have been merely responding to commands – that is, he was not really afraid in the down position, and he was not angry when he growled, but he knew how to arrange his face and body in such a way that he portrayed those emotions to someone else.

Perhaps the magic of Rin-Tin-Tin's acting had something to do with the directors. The *Port Arthur News* (Texas) said of *A Hero of the Big* Snows (1926), which was directed by Herman C. Raymaker: "A dumb animal can be turned into an almost human actor if the right director takes it in hand. Rin-Tin-Tin, the wonder dog, apparently found the proper instructor, for the popular canine screen star rises to even greater heights in the 'Hero of the Big Snows.'" By the time *Rough Waters* (1930), which was directed by John Daumery, came along, late in Rin-Tin-Tin's career, the *Variety* reviewer proved the point from the other side: "Directing the dog in the matter-of-fact way that the animal is handled here will injure the appeal."

The story mattered, too. Jane Murfin, in an article about writing scenarios for dogs, suggested that the script be tailored to the dog: that is, that the writer should observe the dog's manner of expression, then write scenes that capitalize on it. This could be true of the scripts for Rin-Tin-Tin's movies as well.

Rin-Tin-Tin captured audiences not just with his emotive ability but also with his quasi-ferocious attacks on villains and his athleticism – his beautiful loping run as he chases down a villain or races to save a heroine; his spectacular leaps across chasms; his effortless scaling of walls. German shepherds excel as athletes, and Rin-Tin-Tin was the gold medal winner of German shepherds. Rin-Tin-Tin's movies, if viewed as a series of acts or tricks, show how much of his training was training for shows and police work: he sinks his teeth into bad guys; he barks to alert the good guys; he jumps barriers, he scales walls and fences, he leaps over rivers.

A 1923 newspaper article about Rin-Tin-Tin described the kind of training he was reputed to have had: to face pistol fire "unflinchingly, leaping savagely to attack," to find hidden objects, bark in announcement, identify and guard criminals, and search through houses and alleys for evildoers. It added, "The well-trained police dog can leap a 7-foot obstacle and can broad jump a small stream of 12 to 15 feet in width." Incidentally, not all trainers of police dogs thought that jumping was necessary. While von Stephanitz did teach jumping, to him it was an unnatural skill because dogs tend to go *around* – not over – artificial obstacles. Evidence of Rin-Tin-Tin's police dog training exists in his movies. For instance, Jt Clough was able to determine that Rin-Tin-Tin was performing as a police dog in *The Night Cry* (1926) when he stood at the base of a giant rock and barked at the threatening condor above. ("Bark and guard," she said.)

Training German shepherds in performing athletic feats, in conjunction with the mock attack and arrest of criminals, took over in the United States when clubs began to engage in training dogs for trials at shows. In 1913, *Forest and Stream* said of German sheep dogs (trained police dogs) imported to the

United States: "Most of them [German police dogs who compete at trials] are able to make a standing high jump of at least eight feet, can trip a man with remarkable ease and once they get a hold cannot be shaken off unless killed or ordered to let go by their masters." The trials usually fell into two phases: in one, the dog showed off his athletic prowess, which was connected to the arrest of criminals; in the other the dog trailed a criminal ("footpad," "vagabond," "miscreant"), took him down, and guarded him.

A leader in the movement was a wealthy Scranton man, Benjamin H. Throop, who owned the Elmview Kennels in Elmhurst, Pennsylvania, and established a place for training police and war (Red Cross) dogs near Hempstead, Long Island, in 1915. His trainer, Rudolph Hauri, who had trained police dogs in Switzerland, claimed that in 1913 he imported the first "genuine" German shepherd, who was expert at tracking criminals. Hauri refused to separate police training from war training but trained dogs "for anything. . . . All that's necessary is to develop their intelligences up to the point of making them understand what you want them to do. Then they'll do it. You can train them to be your personal guardian, to do police work, or to discover wounded bodies in a field." He taught his dogs to jump a seven-foot barrier without touching the boards, and a twelve-foot barrier *with* touching, essential to taking a short cut over a fence or other obstacle. He had them follow trails, guard objects, trip a criminal. His dogs were "one-man dogs, recognizing no one but their owners, to whom they are devoted."

In 1915, in front of a crowd of more than five thousand, field trials sponsored by the German Shepherd Dog Club were held at New York's Van Cortlandt Park "for the purpose of demonstrating to the public the extent to which that particular breed of dogs could be used by the police in running down criminals." Prominent in this were Throop and Hauri, as well as Anne B. Tracy. The exhibit began with obedience and the scaling of fences (up to nine feet). A demonstration of protectiveness followed in which a dog owner was attacked by a "highwayman" armed with a club in padded clothes "that resembled those worn by the people of arctic regions." The dog responded with a counterattack, "sink[ing] its fangs in the padded clothing and roll[ing] the criminal to the ground." Then came another performance in which a supposed criminal "attacked" a policeman with a brick and left him unconscious. After being notified by citizens, a policeman appeared on the scene with a police dog, who trailed the criminal though the crowd and treed him.

In a 1926 article in *Collier's*, John B. Kennedy gave a detailed account of one of Duncan's live movie-theater demonstrations of Rin Tin Tin's talents, which, though somewhat suspect as to its accuracy, is instructive because it shows that much of what Rin-Tin-Tin did that so astounded the author was the result of standard dog training then and now. The article noted that Duncan trained Rin-Tin-Tin on a sheep farm in Beverly Hills, "a modest patch of prairie [sic] boasting forty head." While this would not have been impossible, given the rural nature of the area from 1919 to 1925, one doubts it because Duncan did not buy property there until 1924 and that property consisted of only three lots. The article also claimed that Duncan had "no set plan of training Rin," but we know that he trained the dog with the Shepherd Dog Club. Those caveats aside, it might be true that, as Kennedy suggests, Duncan taught Rin-Tin-Tin using word association, a common technique with dog trainers. "When Rin would bristle at the night wind tapping the ranch door, Duncan would cry, 'Villain.'" And "when Rin was threatening or friendly to approaching strangers Duncan tagged snarling emotion 'bad' and bubbling welcome 'good.'" Kennedy said it took three months to train Rin-Tin-Tin for the camera. In describing the demonstration, Kennedy talked about how Rin-Tin-Tin associated "window" with jumping up on a window sill (something German shepherds do naturally when something interests them) and how he could scratch his left and right ears on command. Here again, police dog training included training in directions. Other "tricks" included playing dead and refraining from eating a bit of food (our "leave it"?). According to Kennedy, Rin-Tin-Tin could do a twenty-two-foot broad jump and could leap a seventeen-foot wall "making second-story rescues without a scaling ladder" – an obvious exaggeration.

Rin-Tin-Tin's athletic accomplishments astounded audiences. Though anything he did was something almost any dog could be trained to do, he did everything better – he jumped higher, leapt across bigger chasms, even seemed to run faster. He was prowess measured in the large. If anyone were to ask if the stunts were all about trick photography, Rin-Tin-Tin's German shepherd dog show wins and stage appearances proved otherwise. On the other hand, the cabin wall he scaled in *Where the North Begins* (1923) was constructed to make the feat easier for him, and it is possible, even probable, that that wall was not the only structure made especially for him.

Of course, Warner churned out press releases that lauded Rin-Tin-Tin's athleticism, and the material found its way into local newspapers. However, on his own, the reviewer for *Variety* found much to admire: "The animal's main forte would seem to be jumping, and a couple he cuts loose are corkers, as is also the leap up a chimney which runs from the ground. . . . Mal St. Clair, director, has balanced nicely, without making the feats of Rin Tin Tin too impossible." Articles about *The Man Hunter* (1930) remarked on "the remarkable agility of this 12-year-old dog" who performed "with all the speed and alertness that he seemingly ever did." He still had the "smooth, low-running stride that distinguishes Rin-Tin-Tin from any other dog that has ever appeared on the screen." (Actually, many German shepherds have such a stride, and it is beautiful to see.)

Rin-Tin-Tin's natural abilities and Duncan's persistent training turned the dog into a superlative performer. There was a price.

7
Rin-Tin-Tin Carries Fire

Rin-Tin-Tin grabs a long piece of burning cloth in his teeth and runs up the lighthouse stairs. Spewing fire and smoke, the cloth trails and twists alongside him. At the top of the stairs, he stands up on his hind legs and drops the flaming cloth into the maw of the tall glass globe. His head leans over the fire as it leaps up. Outside, the light illuminates the sea, foiling the forces of evil (rum runners who have doused the light), and civilization is saved. Rin-Tin-Tin is, according to publicity, "a flashing sword of heroism," the key player in the "cruel struggle between the keepers of right and light, and the illegal and criminal band that trades on prohibition." And the act of carrying the burning cloth "is the most marvelous thing ever done by a dog," said the *Staffordshire Sentinel* (England) in its review of the movie, *The Lighthouse by the Sea* (1924).

Audiences loved the scene. Even on New York's Broadway, they burst into applause.

The difficulty of staging it is apparent. Dogs fear fire, and Rin-Tin-Tin had to be no exception. The forest fire scene in *Clash of the Wolves* (1925) testifies to that: Rin-Tin-Tin stands in the middle of a grove of trees being consumed by flame, and ears back, mouth open and tongue hanging in a grin of terror, he swivels his head from side to side as he seems to recognize the helplessness of his position. When a burning tree crashes behind him, he makes a terrified spontaneous leap out of camera range. In *The Lighthouse by the Sea*, this same dog, so well trained that his impulse to obey overcomes his visceral fear, performs an act – carrying the burning cloth – that must have seemed senseless to him. James English told in *The Rin Tin Tin Story* how the scene was filmed: "after being paced with an unlighted torch through several practice runs, the dog hesitated a second when the torch was lighted, dashing through the part he had rehearsed just as though he had no fear what-so-ever of fire."

This dangerous feat might have been less dangerous for Rin-Tin-Tin had his owner and employer thought ahead more carefully. Warner paid $350 for a specially blown glass globe for the tower light where Rin-Tin-Tin would drop the flaming cloth. They measured Rin-Tin-Tin standing on his hind legs to see how high he could reach and sized the globe accordingly. However they forgot to take into account the fact that the cloth would hang down six inches from Rin-Tin-Tin's jaw so that he had to strain to lift it up high enough to get it over the rim of the globe. Duncan later wrote "those who saw Rinty running up the spiral stairs with the lighted cloth in his mouth will perhaps remember how he had to struggle to get it over the top and light the light, yet not get burned." According to James English's biography, Rin-Tin-Tin *did* get burned in performing the feat – the fire singed some hair off his shoulder and eyebrow on one side of his body, and he lost some whiskers. One reviewer reported that he burned his feet.

According to Duncan himself, Rin-Tin-Tin almost died in another scene in the movie, which was filmed partly in Laguna Beach, an artists' colony about sixty miles south of Los Angeles. As planned, Rin-Tin-Tin pulled up a stake he was tied to in order to run and save an old blind man teetering on the edge of a cliff. Still attached to his collar by a rope, the stake caught in a railing while Rin-Tin-Tin was running, and, propelled by his own acceleration, he flew out over the ocean. Luckily the stake held, and he boomeranged back to safety on land, where he continued the scene. Danger was also present on the set when Rin-Tin-Tin fought the strong-jawed bulldog Yukon Killer and when he fought the villain, both on a slippery boat deck and in the ocean water.

The entire company of *The Lighthouse by the Sea* often gathered at night on the Laguna Beach pavilion, where they partied and watched the lights on the water. "We were all like one big family on locations and it [sic] was seldom . . . any discord," Duncan said in his *Notes*. "In fact, I think it would have been impossible to work Rinty if there had been such a thing as discord." However, this warm, family-like atmosphere failed to draw Rin-Tin-Tin in, at least according to Anthony Cassa, who, writing in *Hollywood Studio Magazine* (June 1981), said that Rin-Tin-Tin attacked and bit the movie's crew members and that "[m]any times they had to be forcibly restrained from killing the nasty pooch."

Why did Rin-Tin-Tin run up those stairs carrying fire? Why did Duncan put him at risk? What motivation made Rin-Tin-Tin fight the bulldog and circle in the water attacking the villain? And if it is true that he attacked members of the crew, why did he do it?

Rin-Tin-Tin Carries Fire

The answers, I think, lie in Duncan's "you-and-me-against-the-world" relationship with Rin-Tin-Tin, the way Duncan trained Rin-Tin-Tin, and the life that Rin-Tin-Tin led on and off the set. That Duncan made Rin-Tin-Tin a one-man dog no one disputes, and as a one-man dog, Rin-Tin-Tin's attitude toward the world was often adversarial, in spite of the coerced, sometimes fake affection he showed actors on screen and ordinary individuals on promotional tours. I would argue, too, that, like almost all dog trainers of his time, it is possible Duncan used mild pain and humiliation to discipline Rin-Tin-Tin into obedience and submission so that the dog's fear of the consequences of disobedience overpowered his fear of fire and other dangers. There is no doubt in my mind that he attacked people and animals from time to time. In acting, Rin-Tin-Tin repeatedly feigned attacks on humans and animals, continuing the attacks for theatrical value long after the trainer would have stopped them in real life, then did it over again, perhaps more than once, for retakes. Even trainers of dogs for the police warned against such excess because it could contribute to ferocity. Maybe other things in Rin-Tin-Tin's life also caused him to be less than friendly. For instance, for insurance reasons, Rin-Tin-Tin could not run free, except sometimes in his own yard, on location, or on vacation trips; instead, for exercise, he was forced to spin himself like a hamster in a wheel-like contraption. He was relegated to living in a kennel, even though his food was served in a silver trough. (The money he made paid for the house he was not allowed to live in.) He was overworked in that he was required to perform long hours, not only on camera but in front of live audiences, sometimes doing his act with Duncan three or four times a day on promotional tours.

Duncan acknowledged that Rin-Tin-Tin was trained as a one-man dog. As a one-man dog, he was taught to treat the world with caution, if not suspicion. I think it contributed to Rin-Tin-Tin's aggressiveness. Duncan didn't let others befriend, pet, or feed his dogs except during filming or when he otherwise allowed it – as, for instance, when on visits to crippled children's homes he told Rin-Tin-Tin to put a paw on a wheelchair-bound child's knee and allow the child to pet him. After all, Duncan said, just as it was difficult to prevent a police dog from responding to the wiles of a food-bearing criminal, it was "difficult to direct a dog to attack a villain who has been feeding him off the set." Long after

Rin-Tin-Tin's death, when Duncan saw that war dog Rin-Tin-Tin III, not trained as a one-man dog, was as teachable and as good an actor as any, he changed his mind.

In researching this book, I consulted eleven contemporary (1907-1930) dog training manuals, all that I could find in libraries. Almost all advocated one-man dog training. Ed. F. Haberlein, in *The Amateur Trainer: Force System without the Whip* (1907) warned against any dog becoming "everybody's dog" during training, and to forestall that, he suggested having someone not well known to the dog step on its forefeet "hard enough to cause a yell and retreat." Max von Stephanitz's *The German Shepherd Dog in Word and Picture* compared some dogs' lamentable lack of standoffishness to "our ignorant 'Masses' who wax eloquent over 'World Brotherhood,' and prefer it to loving their Native Land and their Home." He also suggested that family friends should rebuff a friendly dog and that dogs should be punished for taking food from strangers, as did Fred Kollet (*Training the Shepherd Dog*, 1924) – by whipping – and Albert Hochwalt (*The Working Dog and His Education*, 1921) – by putting peppered meat in the stranger's hand to give to the dog and by muzzle-slapping.

It would be nice to believe Duncan's claims that he treated Rin-Tin-Tin with nothing but kindness, but evidence otherwise exists in first-person accounts by those who knew Duncan and Rin-Tin-Tin, though some of them are overwrought, that Duncan did indeed inflict pain on Rin-Tin-Tin. It also exists in subtle movements of the dog and Nanette, his mate, in his movies.

Certainly, ideas about training animals and children were changing during the period after World War I. Though by the 1930s methods leaned very strongly toward kindness and rewards, this was not always the case during the interim, when they were in transition. Those early twentieth century dog training books that I have been able to find, including those on police and war dog training, sanctioned the deliberate infliction of pain in training dogs once out of puppyhood (and to a lesser degree while they were puppies) in order to achieve faster results and punish willful behavior.

The question – puzzling to us twenty-first century people – arises: How could someone who claimed to love dogs and see into their souls use pain to train them? Perhaps our bafflement has to do with our difficulty in putting ourselves in the past. To 1920s child-raisers as well as dog-raisers, love and physical discipline often were handmaidens, not necessarily antithetical to each other. Yet it was a time of transition: the waning Old Guard vs. the New Morality. The trend in child-raising was away from physical punishment and dominance, and toward nurturing with kindness and understanding. In those years, hundreds of thousands of requests for pamphlets on child care flooded the U.S. Children's Bureau, and *Parents' Magazine* was created. The resulting "new family" featured child-centeredness. Some experts still criticized the move toward democracy in the American family and praised military training for boys and "character training" for all children. Members of the Child Study Association of America debated about which was worse: the indulgent mother or the stern father. Others were appalled at harsh treatment of children. A 1930 Children's Bureau pamphlet, "Are You Training Your Child to Be Happy?," contains this sentence, "A wise mother does not need to spank or slap her child very often," indicating that some physical punishment, as a last-ditch resort, was still considered acceptable at the beginning of the new decade.

An example of the societal tension about corporal punishment of children shows up in a 1924 controversy: the superintendent of schools of Elmsford, New York, defended his schools' use of a rubber hose as a punishment device and said he would quit his job if it were outlawed; thirteen of his twenty-three subordinates agreed with him, but *The New York Times* did not:

> There is something to be said, of course, for corporal punishment of children by both parents and teachers, but members of either class who cannot maintain their authority without it thereby confess to incompetence, at the very least, and cannot claim the respect that goes to those better equipped for their duties. They are survivals from another age – the age when the beating of children for every departure from adult standards of infantile propriety was done as a matter of course, and physical torture was regarded as the best of inspirers for youth.

The transition in dog training was similar. Society's ambivalence about how humans should relate to dogs in general was mirrored, for instance, in attitudes toward war dogs. Theo. F. Jager, in his 1917 book on their training, expressed those conflicting attitudes well: "Dogs should not be used, at least so some claim, as a direct combatant," and "We know how efficacious they would prove [in combat]. As long as we sanction the use of savage and cruel weapons against white men, why should not man's best friend, the dog, be given a chance to aid his master." The reasons, given later in the book, for not using dogs in combat or to go on suicide missions reveal another point of view:

> To train the infantry dog[s] in the last two mentioned requirements (in combat and suicide missions) would, scarce as the dogs will naturally be for some years to come, prove suicidal for the dog's interest. When the time arrives that we have a surplus of dogs and are unable to stand the losses naturally the result of using them in active fighting, we might consider such additional service.

The dog was a fellow soldier – and at the same time, a replaceable commodity. (The same ambivalence existed in discussions about the use of human soldiers as well.)

Trainers of dogs for police duty, as guard dogs, and for hunting were in agreement: in some ways the dog, with his superior abilities, was a valued companion, but in other ways he was an inferior to be disciplined forcefully and to be disposed of if he was not useful. For example, Haberlein said: "A puppy at the age of four to six months . . . who is docile, lethargic . . . and has no ambition than to gorge himself, should be hastened to the dog heaven without delay."

The creature being trained was of less significance than the method. Trainers emphasized that, with both children and dogs, violent methods often did not work. Said Albert Payson Terhune in a 1920 interview:

> If you were trying to teach a three-year-old child to talk or to learn a rime, you would not accompany your teachings by kicking the youngster in the ribs, by banging him over the head, or by swearing and yelling at him when he became tired and

confused. If you did that, you'd soon have an imbecile or hopelessly injured baby on your hands. . . . It is the same with teaching a dog.

In short, inflicting too little or too much physical punishment on any creature was not efficacious, and in the early part of the twentieth century, efficacy was a prevalent underlying principle of most dog training, no matter what kind – as well as of training children. Efficacy appealed to dog trainers as a way of achieving the proper results as fast as possible without ruining the dog, and by "ruining" they meant producing a dog that would not perform well for them because of too much submission or fear. Methods of inflicting punishment were often designed so that the dog would not associate pain with the trainer, and the trainer was cautioned not to lose his temper. In *Training the Dog* (1914), Robert S. Lemmon blamed dogs' owners for permitting "formation of bad habits, and then, when the trouble has gone too far to be easily remedied, either give it up as a bad job or else, considering the dog an utterly unreasonable and unreasoning brute, adopt the unfair method of trying to beat it out of him by main strength." Briton E.H. Richardson, author of *Watch-Dogs: Their Training and Management* (1925), adhered to reward ("cupboard love") and affection training, but nonetheless recommended "a smack" when the dog disobeyed knowingly. Kollet argued that a dog who attacked his owner with growling or attempts to bite should be whipped "until the dog lays down and whines, as it is a case to show who is master."

The principle of efficacy applied to the training of hunting dogs as well as police and war dogs. Duncan does not say how he trained his Airedale and foxhound puppies before World War I. Sending dogs out to an expert to be trained was not uncommon then, so perhaps he relegated the task to the person who owned the turkey ranch. Whoever the trainer was, he probably used the prevailing method: modified force training, common at least from the turn of the 20th century and on into the 1920s, as exemplified in Ed. Haberlein's book, *The Amateur Trainer: Force System without the Whip*. (The title is misleading because Haberlein does recommend hitting the dog on certain occasions.)

According to this method, puppies were to be treated kindly. Any harsh treatment and the trainer risked breaking the puppy's spirit and thus rendering him useless. However, if puppies seemed willful, then physical punishment was called for. Once the puppy was older, real training began. While trainers avoided outright cruelty, they favored the use of pain as a learning device because the dog learned faster. Most claimed that while persuasion training worked, it took longer and was not as reliable. Lemmon recommended force and the infliction of pain so that the dog would know the penalty for "leaving the straight and narrow path of rectitude." Haberlein and Hochwalt both emphasized that the force method gave permanent results – the lessons learned would remain in the dog's mind.

Force training involved the use of various devices that inflicted pain when the dog didn't do what it was supposed to do. The main device was a spiked collar something like the prong collar some trainers use today. It was studded inside with beveled spikes (usually six). The collar was more efficacious than the switch because it inflicted pain when the dog disobeyed and, unlike whipping, was not associated with the trainer.

Force training began with basic commands. The dog was kenneled, attached to a five- or six-foot chain, then left alone except for training sessions and exercise runs. Trainers expected that the dog would yelp and try to escape. If, after a command to lie down, he continued to resist, the advice was to "tap" the dog with a switch, switching harder and faster until he went into his kennel, then order him again to lie down and keep switching the side of the kennel. If the dog jerked against the force collar, the trainer did nothing: the dog, after flailing around, would figure out that the pain stopped when he slackened up.

If Duncan's first experiences were with hunting dogs, which were probably trained with the force method, his adoption of Rin-Tin-Tin and Nanette, a different breed, might have changed his focus somewhat concerning training, but I still think it is possible – indeed, probable – that he used pain as a training device. According to dog trainer Jt Clough, Rin-Tin-Tin's body language in *The Night Cry* (1926) when he shows fear reactions indicates that he was compulsion-trained – that is, trained by using the infliction of pain. That he was sometimes unwilling to do what he was asked to do shows in the fact that his tail was between his legs, a sign of fear – as it was in some of his fights and in the photograph on the cover of this book. This is even clearer with Nanette, who often acted with her tail between her legs.

Training the Sanitary Service Dog, which we know Duncan owned, recommended correction by hitting the dog with a switch and stepping on its toes and if further action was needed for excitable dogs, through the use of a studded or choke collar. If a dog failed to come when called, the book suggested that the trainer should launch ten small grapeshot at it with a slingshot, and when, on being hit, it "yelped with fright," the trainer should call it over affectionately as if he was not responsible at all for the pain the dog suffered.

Max von Stephanitz suggested the use of several tools for training German shepherds: a choke collar, a spiked collar, a "torquatus" (a prong collar), and Hegendorf Training Collar, which included a studded collar with loops to the forelegs so that the dog could not get up. Jager also recommended the spiked collar – "he [the dog] must be taught that any objection to the will of his master, expressed silently through the leash and the spiked gag collar, causes pain." If a dog failed to execute left face properly, Jager's advice was to step on his toes – with "soft-soled shoes or rubbers" – and if he "howl[ed] considerably" it would be only because he was surprised. Yet Jager also states quite firmly that a dog should only be trained by "a natural dog lover."

Most of the books I looked at recommended specific punishments for disobedience. Von Stephanitz's were extraordinarily varied: whipping the dog on the flanks with a light whip; putting cayenne pepper on the dog's mouth; tying the dog up; chaining the dog short and high so he could neither sit or lie ("care must be taken that the criminal does not unexpectedly and unintentionally commit suicide by hanging himself"); stepping on the dog's toes for jumping up; placing food just out of reach; making him crawl; using a slingshot to hit him with grapeshot.

Jon Tuska, in *The Vanishing Legion: A History of Mascot Pictures 1927-1935*, says that "Lee Duncan, according to Yak [Yakima Cannutt, a stunt man], would have to hit his dogs in order to get them to obey; on one occasion he used an iron chain." When I first read this statement, knowing that Cannutt had something of a grudge against Duncan, I doubted that it was true. Yet I changed my mind when I later read von Stephanitz's suggestion that a trainer punish disobedient dogs by throwing a chain at them while being careful not to hit their legs.

Trainers were aware that a "down" position was submissive and dogs didn't like it. Creeping or crawling on the belly, as Rin-Tin-Tin did in several of his movies, was part of training. According to *Training the Sanitary Service Dog*, "Crawling should be used frequently during training and while in service, as there is no better means of making him submissive and obedient." Crawling was also a penitential act (as for the murder of a farm animal) "more efficacious than a whipping," particularly when used to subdue hard-to-manage dogs. Trainers forced dogs to learn crawling by whipping them or by pulling them with a leash passed through a ring, close to the ground, ahead of the dog.

In on-stage appearances, Duncan denied ever being cruel to Rin-Tin-Tin and claimed the accusation arose because Rin-Tin-Tin "has been pictured as groveling in the dust, shrinking away, his tail between his legs, his eyes expressing fear." Then Duncan went on to ask Rin-Tin-Tin to crawl, squeak, roll halfway over, and roll over toward him. His argument seemed to be that if the dog responded to a command by acting in a way that seemed fearful when he was not, then he had never been punished physically. Logically, the fact that Rin-Tin-Tin had been taught to "act" afraid certainly does not mean that he had never performed the "act" while also feeling afraid.

During the filming of *The Lighthouse by the Sea* (1924), ss I noted earlier in the chapter, Rin-Tin-Tin was put in extreme danger at least twice. This was not the only time. In *The Night Cry* (1926), Rin-Tin-Tin fights a condor. One reviewer, puzzled by the fight, said, "A person unacquainted with the methods of film producers can hardly comprehend how this part of the picture could be filmed without fatal results either to dog or bird." Duncan himself reported that Rin-Tin-Tin knew he was in danger and defended himself, especially his eyes, from the bird. While filming *Rinty of the Desert* (1928) in Colorado, Rin-Tin-Tin was supposed to run out over the Laguna Dam's spillway on a catwalk made of metal plates and then chew the gate-lever rope controlling the water flow. On the way, he slipped on some oil that had gotten on the plates, lost his balance, and slid to the edge, falling to his knees. Somehow he was able to pull himself up. If he had not, he would have dropped down into a raging torrent of water.

Why was Rin-Tin-Tin willing to perform these dangerous acts? Probably some of it was because of his desire to please Duncan, but it could also have been fear of punishment if he resisted.

Rin-Tin-Tin Carries Fire

Rin-Tin-Tin with a punching bag (Courtesy Rin-Tin-Tin Collection, Riverside, California).

Duncan's statements in his *Notes* about Rin-Tin-Tin's aggressiveness vary. On the one hand, he portrayed Rin-Tin-Tin as sweet-natured. On the other, he bragged about Rin-Tin-Tin's tendency to fight: "He had three or four fights and was so full of life and vigor it is no wonder when he made his first public appearance, the critics came out with a story in the paper that Rin-Tin-Tin came into the ring with his tail up over his back like a grey squirrel, snapping and barking at the judges, etc. " (A German shepherd's tail is not supposed to curl up over its back, according to the standards for the breed.). In general, according to Duncan, "Rin-Tin-Tin loved a good fight with man or beast," but hurt no one, partly because he and the other animals he fought on screen wore "light muzzles," which statement on the face of it seems false because the muzzles would show up on film.

Duncan also reported that during one of their tours, while talking to a friend on a Boston street, he heard Rin-Tin-Tin growl and turned to see him attack a Mexican hairless dog who was lying in the sleeve of a woman's caracul coat with only its head showing. Rin-Tin-Tin grabbed the dog's ear and ripped it open, then tore a hole in the coat sleeve. The Mexican hairless "looked for all the world like a rat," commented Duncan. "Now Rinty had already grown quite accustomed to finding and killing rats in the alleys behind the theaters." The woman filed a suit, which was settled for $25 – $10 for the veterinary bill and $15 for fixing the coat. This incident made Duncan take out $25,000 more insurance on Rin-Tin-Tin, in addition to the $75,000 he already had. This insurance required that Rin-Tin-Tin be on a leash in a city.

While most of those who interviewed Rin-Tin-Tin found him to be friendly, some said otherwise. In 1926, Quin A. Ryan reported that Rin-Tin-Tin came into an interview muzzled, led on a leash by an attendant, and while "gracious" at meeting people one-on-one, growled when confronted by a crowd.

Rin-Tin-Tin reportedly bit several actors, usually during the filming of a fight scene. (One source says he bit four-year-old actor Davey Lee during the filming of *Frozen River* [1929], but I found no other source that mentions this.) According to a newspaper reviewer, one of Rin-Tin-Tin's favorite tricks was to "pull the seat out of the villain's pants." Did Rin-Tin-Tin think "pulling the seat out of the villain's pants" was just a game, or was he serious about inflicting harm? After all, he seemed serious when he attacked those crew members during the filming of *The Lighthouse by the Sea* (1924). In practically every movie he made, Rin-Tin-Tin attacks a "villain" and he keeps attacking as the "villain" tries to get away, usually using such control that he never actually hurts the actor – most of the time; how serious was he then?

Reports from a variety of sources contradict each other. English says that no one was hurt in Rin-Tin-Tin's movie fights because he responded so quickly to commands. A Rin-Tin-Tin obituary implied that he was always in control of his teeth: "[H]e never bit anyone, his viciousness being entirely assumed as a feature of his technique as an accomplished actor." In an effusive quotation about Rin-Tin-Tin, "the film star that held my heart to the exclusion of all the human ones," the Baroness Ravensdale said, after visiting the set of *While*

London Sleeps (1926): "After some tremendous performance, in a fierce fight, or jumping sixteen feet through a window, or saving a woman bound in chains, he would come round to his master and Mr. Morosco, the director, and to the tune of loud applause wag his tail and make his bow, like Gerald de Maurier or H.B. Warner." Yet in that same movie, Rin-Tin-Tin reportedly went beyond a "game" in a fight scene with George Kotsonaros, the world's light-heavyweight wrestling champion, who weighed 180 pounds to Rin-Tin-Tin's 70. According to *Los Angeles Times* writer Grace Kingsley in a September 1926 article, Rin-Tin-Tin bit Kotsonaros on the head, hand, and shoulder while the cameras were rolling, and the scene, as it was, made it into the movie. The "acting" turned into a real-life attack. Kingsley went on to say: "And the actor still has a scene coming in which the animal is supposed to kill him, but Kotsonaros feels that realism has gone quite far enough and that he has sacrificed himself enough on the altar of art, so he will strive to keep the tragic end of the story from coming true." In the making of *The Lightning Warrior* (1931), Rin-Tin-Tin allegedly bit stunt man Yakima Cannutt, missing entirely the protective pad Yak wore over his arm.

Daphne Hereford, who raises Rin-Tin-Tins, said in a 1992 interview with Katia Hetter for the *Wall Street Journal* that "he bit most of the actors he worked with." Charles Higham, in *Warner Brothers* (1975), attributes reports about Rin-Tin-Tin's supposed docility to studio publicity. On the contrary, Higham says, Rin-Tin-Tin "would attack members of the cast without warning, savage his directors and answer a friendly pat with a menacing growl and perhaps a serious bite" and that "[e]veryone who worked with the celebrated quadruped is agreed that he was a monster: ill-tempered, vicious, dangerous." Higham's assessment of Rin-Tin-Tin's propensity to bite cast and crew members during filming needs to be examined critically. How could the dog who was allegedly so tractable and loving in the 1920s and 1930s become so vicious in retrospect?

More to the point, Higham's blanket statement that "everyone" agreed that Rin-Tin-Tin was a monster is not really true. For instance, the female actors who starred with him did not complain of being bitten; two of them, June Marlowe and Virginia Browne Faire, signed up for more than one movie. Veteran actor Pat Hartigan, who acted as the villain in six movies with him, had no complaints that we know about. If it were no so perplexing, one story might make you believe Hartigan should have been anxious about acting with Rin-Tin-Tin. The story, as told by James English, goes like this: during the filming of *Where the North Begins* (1923), Rin-Tin-Tin grabbed Hartigan's pants in his teeth. Why? Hartigan had sat in aniseed syrup, which dogs love. It's true that dogs like anise, but English does not explain what the aniseed was doing on a chair. In any case, after that, English says, actors playing the villain demanded padded pants and made an effort to befriend the dog before playing scenes with him, something that Duncan discouraged. If Rin-Tin-Tin had been as dangerous as Higham claims, it is doubtful Hartigan would have signed up for more than one movie with him. He was a well-known character actor who didn't have to put his life in danger to make a living. On the other hand, many actors who acted in films with Rin-Tin-Tin had Warner contracts, and, under those contracts, they had little to say about what parts they played.

John B. Kennedy, in his 1926 article in *Collier's*, claimed that Rin-Tin-Tin never hurt anyone but Duncan, "who suffered face and forearm bites in the early days when the dog's primal instincts were unmodified." I don't believe this statement any more than I do Higham's. Most people who have dealt with puppies know how, in puppyish, uncontrolled playing, their sharp teeth can slice into a forearm, but puppies don't tend to attack faces. Moreover, in the same article Kennedy wrote somewhat fancifully that Rin-Tin-Tin's "appreciation of his [own] prowess" was exaggerated because filming was managed so that he always defeated the foe; consequently, he once attacked a Fifth Avenue bus and thought nothing of attacking other movie animals, including a cowardly lion, who "turned tail at the first myopic sight of Rin's dripping fangs and bounded deftly over the horizon."

Rin-Tin-Tin's fight scenes with men on land depended heavily on his police training. He grabs pant legs, "goes" for the throat, rolls around on the ground in a hostile embrace. In press releases, perhaps written by Hal Wallis, audiences were reminded of how his police training taught him to keep people at bay, attacking only when necessary, "that most difficult reversal of thought which demands quiet and inaction up to a certain point, and then ruthless lunging and fighting." But screen acting, unlike police work, demanded that the dog continue the attack for dramatic value and perhaps do the scene more than once, straining his capacity to hold in check any innate ferocity generated by the attack and causing him to forget that this was, after all, maybe just a game. Von Stephanitz, who emphasized training the protection dog or police dog to attack on command and to stop attacking on command, which demands great and sensitive control on the part of the dog, also warned against allowing protection dogs to fight humans too much, or

> the Dr. Jekyll of the service dog gives way to the Edward Hyde of the beast of prey. The notion of 'Man' should convey to his mind something sacred and inviolable. We have already founded the whole of his education . . . on this principle, and he must only make an exception to this in the most unusual circumstances, and then too only on the word of command.

Warner and Duncan had a stake in Rin-Tin-Tin's cinematic fighting. In nearly every movie he vanquishes at least one villain single-footedly or with the help of the human hero. He also engages in fights with animals – wolves (in several movies), bulldogs (in *The Lighthouse by the Sea* [1924] and *Rinty of the Desert* [1928]), a sheep dog and a condor (in *The Night Cry* [1926]). From the beginning of his career (even before he worked for Warner), fights, part of the appeal of his movies, were touted in advertisements and highlighted in press releases. It was not just the defeat of the villain that seemed to thrill audiences but the violence and savagery of the fight itself – ads often show a ferocious Rin-Tin-Tin with his teeth bared. It was part of the dramatic polarization in his roles: loving with his friends, dangerous to his enemies.

According to James English, Rin-Tin-Tin Jr. bit Jackie Cooper the first day of filming *Tough Guy* (1936), leaving a scar: "like his daddy, Junior could be vicious when strangers made a sudden move toward him." Yet a newspaper story in *The Gleaner* (Kingston, Jamaica) said that Rin-Tin-Tin Jr. was "gentle, tractable, and playful, whereas the original was always dangerous to strangers, and to human actors. This, explains Duncan, was because the original dog was trained to fight in earnest and the new dog trained only for pictures, is taught to regard fighting as a game, and does it as play."

Rin-Tin-Tin in his exercise wheel (Courtesy Rin-Tin-Tin Collection, Riverside, California).

Keeping Rin-Tin-Tin in a kennel may also have led to his aggression. Duncan kenneled his dogs so that they would then be rested enough to learn better – a dog on the loose, he said, was like a child who uses up his energy playing. It wasn't unusual then to kennel dogs routinely. Lemmon, whose method originated in training hunting dogs, suggested having dogs live in a kennel because it was supposedly healthier and more natural, but he was not against dogs living indoors. However, von Stephanitz warned against kenneling a dog because "like a beast caged for show," it could become "dull, hysterical, even mad." In spite of his statements about his closeness to Rin-Tin-Tin, Duncan felt that the dog really did belong "in his place" – his kennel outdoors.

According to some sources, Rin-Tin-Tin was, if not vicious, certainly temperamental, perhaps because he was leading an unnatural life. Columnist George H. Beale, in "The Film Shop," (November 1928), wrote that Rin-Tin-Tin was becoming a spoiled dog and hard to work with: "Temperament,

Hollywood's most pernicious ailment, has attacked the most famous member of the screen colony's animal family. Rin-Tin-Tin has reached the state where he works only when his dog emotions feel like it and when his demands are conceded." When the studio decided to substitute an accordion for the portable organ usually brought along for Rin-Tin-Tin's listening pleasure as he worked "on a mountain location," he rejected it and a portable organ was carried in. Also Rin-Tin-Tin refused to work unless his toys were visible – a whistling doll (and the doll had to whistle), toy dog, and tennis ball. Beale added: "Although Rin-Tin-Tin is credited with almost human intelligence and has accumulated a lot of almost human temperament he still enjoys the baser pleasures such as a good roll in the dust or an innocent chase after his own tail."[i]

Uncertainty about Rin-Rin-Tin's temperament and Duncan's treatment of him may have another reason for being: the rise of organizations dedicated to the prevention of cruelty to animals that dovetails with the changes in attitudes toward training that were taking place in the 1920s. In 1915, "Be Kind to Animals Week" became a national holiday. By 1924, twenty-three states made humane education compulsory, and humane education flourished through the 1920s. The concern extended to the treatment of animals in entertainment.

As early as the late teens, stories about animal cruelty in movie-making were in the news. In 1915, in a case brought by the Society for the Prevention of Cruelty to Animals, the William Fox Amusement Company was fined $25 for cruelty to an animal in the making of a movie: it forced a horse to jump forty-five feet into the stream that runs through New York's Ausable Chasm. The horse escaped unhurt but Arthur Jarvis, the actor who rode the horse, broke his leg. A 1919 article in *Life*, noting that the Massachusetts legislature was debating a bill outlawing the use of animals doing tricks for entertainment, said that, because the lawmakers thought the animals learned tricks without cruelty, the populace did not protest the exploitation of animals for the stage. The article concluded differently, and added, "now the 'movies' are guilty." The following year, *Life* ran a satirical story in which a movie "magnate" is kidnapped by four animals, one of them a collie, who says, "Don't be alarmed. It will all be over in a couple of days. We're going to throw you over a precipice, drag you along the ground, trip you up, lasso you, fire off a few bombs in your ears, and, in short, have as much fun with you as you movie people like to have with us." To this the magnate says, "The exploiting of animals for commercial purposes has become one of our great necessities."

Popular protest against cruelty to animals began at least by the early 1920s though it wasn't until the infamous scene in *Jesse James* (1939), in which a horse was sent to its death over a cliff, that the American Humane Association began to fight so strongly against such abuses that movie-makers were forced to face the problem head-on. Maine (in 1921) and a few other states passed laws that protected movie animals, but by and large the protests were sporadic. By the time that Rin-Tin-Tin and Strongheart were starring in pictures, studio publicity actively denied animal abuse.

In June 1924, the Association of Motion Picture Producers refuted animal cruelty charges made by the American Defense League. The movies under attack were *The Ten Commandments* (1923), *Ashes of Vengeance* (1923), *Sundown* (1924), *The King of Wild Horses* (1924), and *The Covered Wagon* (1923). The secretary-treasurer of the Association signed a statement asserting that an investigation "disproved the charges." There was talk of bringing suit. The investigating committee was composed of, among others, Fred W. Beetson, secretary-treasurer of the Association of Motion Picture Producers, and Hugh M. Bole, attorney of the Los Angeles Society for the Prevention of Cruelty to Animals. Hugh J. Baldwin, chief investigator of the State Humane Association of California, found no indications of cruelty to animals. A humorous paragraph in the *Los Angeles Times* two days later said, "It may look cruel to bump a goat on the bean with a baseball bat, but the chances are the club is stuffed with hay and the animal enjoys the exercise. . . . At any rate, a full and complete investigation covering virtually all of the studios would indicate that the only wild animal that got really bumped was Roscoe Arbuckle."

In Germany, in 1926, director Hans Schwarz tried to force two horses to dive off a fifty-foot cliff. When they refused, even after "inhuman" beating, Schwarz built a trap that gave way when the horses stepped on it, and they fell off the cliff. The horses writhed in agony as cameramen filmed them; finally they were shot. Schwarz, fined $40, boasted that he could "afford any number of horses at the same price." People in the court protested. The Society for the Prevention of Cruelty to Animals sought to ban all Schwarz's films everywhere.

Because any hint of cruelty to animals hurt the box office, most 1920s American movie-makers tried to confine themselves to non-abusive methods. If those methods didn't work, it was not unusual for them to resort to harsher ones. Because tame animals were easier to train, wild animals suffered most. According to a 1924 article in *Popular Mechanics Magazine*, "seldom is anything more than the *electric whip* or *tough lash* [italics mine] used to subdue [wild cats]."

The best evidence that animal abuse did indeed exist in the movies in the 1920s comes from the 1930s. In 1933, Andrew R. Boone wrote an article for *Popular Science Monthly* that listed as practices then forbidden by a studio (which implies that they had been used before that): overwork and lack of food and water; wiring (using a wire to cause certain performances); use of drugs, liquid smoke, and electric shocks; trussing, spiking, doping, and setting on fire; use of knotted wire, spiked bits, running wire, trip ropes, and pitfalls. Certainly wires were used to control dogs. According to Catherine Brody, in a 1925 *Saturday Evening Post* article, one technique was to attach one end of a wire to a windlass and the other to the dog's foot. The trainer commanded, say, that the dog run toward the windlass, and immediately thereafter he started cranking the windlass so that if the dog didn't obey, he'd be jerked off his feet. This is reminiscent of training methods for both hunting dogs and police dogs – and certainly for dogs who worked in vaudeville and the circus.

The problem of determining when movie trainers used truly cruel treatment was complicated by the fact that movie-makers, through the use of technology, could film scenes that portrayed cruelty but in actuality did not harm the animal actors. In 1920, *The Literary Digest* ran an article entitled, "Cruelty Charged in Training Trick Animals for Stage and Movies." The author laid out his objection: the portrayal of cruelty to animals, no matter how it was arrived at, including a trick of the camera, was wrong because it could brutalize the viewer, especially a child, by giving him "the right to make any creature in his power a plaything and a puppet." This was not a new idea. The notion that human beings can be brutalized by observing or participating in cruelty to animals goes back to classical Greece, according to historian Keith Thomas (*Man and the Natural World: Changing Attitudes in England, 1500-1800*).

The author of the article in *The Literary Digest* quoted Dr. Francis H. Rowley, president of the Massachusetts Soceity for the Prevention of Cruelty to

Animals, who cast doubt on the claim that apparent cruelty to animals was all in the camera work: "No one familiar with facts will question the skill of the expert moving-picture photographer to make the camera do a lot of things that fool the spectator of the film. But when a man claiming to be a motion-picture director . . . writes that there is no cruelty practiced in the preparation of films, that what seems like cruelty is only an illusion and clever trick of the camera, his statement appears like trifling with the truth in the light of the facts."

Rowley backed up this statement with somewhat questionable evidence, which sounds like yellow journalism (but perhaps isn't): a producer's alleged statement in an advertisement that the "approximate valuation of animals actually slain during the production of the film was $95,000" and his own statement that abuses were legion: a big cat shot to death, a horse run over a cliff, a dog with a board hanging on its tail.

Yet some movie animals were treated well, according to the same article. Curley Stecher employed several trainers to teach dogs to act, adhering to the principle that "If a dog knows what you want him to do, he'll do his best to do it." Stecher, who had two movie-acting huskies, claimed to train dogs through kindness because the animal "who works through fear is a pathetic spectacle and is useless before the camera."

Certainly movie-makers used camera tricks rather than cruelty to show animals being hurt – a tail attached to a tailless dog so that "street arabs" were able to tie a can to it in a painless way, a double exposure to show a dog being knocked out by a chair that broke into pieces on the screen.

While Rin-Tin-Tin's fights were, of course, staged, some critics noted that they might cause controversy. In a *Variety* review of *The Lighthouse by the Sea* (1924), the reviewer commented that the fight between Rin-Tin-Tin and the bulldog was unnecessary to the plot: "It's all right to build up your dumb hero by having him worst the heavies of the cast, but it is bad business to stage a dog fight in any picture and the chances are that in some localities it will mean that the A.S.P.C.A. will get after that sequence. Besides nobody should pit an English bull against a shepherd at any time." (Modern sources say that a German shepherd would beat an English bulldog in any contest.)

The Animal Defense League and other organizations kept an eagle eye on Hollywood for signs of animal abuse. Movie-makers and trainers of movie dogs pushed back, denying that it happened. In June 1924, Jane Murfin, Strongheart's owner, wrote a letter to the *Los Angeles Times* promoting her star's latest picture, *The Love Master* (1924). In it, she praised the Animal Defense League, whose representative watched over the filming, and added, "The motto of the league, 'Trained by Kindness,' applies literally to Strongheart's entire training."

Some journalists and reviewers backed up statements like Murfin's. In 1921, the writer Helen Christine Bennett argued in *Collier's*:

> After six months about the studios in Los Angeles I can testify that, as far as I was able to see, most of the intelligent animals like the work; and I can make a still stronger statement as to abuse . . . The animals are not beaten except in two instances: when they are a menace to a human being, and when their trainer or keeper loses his temper. If the latter happens often, he loses his job.

Humane societies enlisted Rin-Tin-Tin and Duncan for campaigns against cruelty to animals (Courtesy Rin-Tin-Tin Collection, Riverside, California).

Catherine Brody in 1925 commented that dog actors brought in "the golden shekels" and were treated while filming like "well-bred children." She went on to describe the dogs' cushy living conditions on the set and their short working days.

Over time, Warner became aware of the issue of cruelty, too. A press release for *Land of the Silver Fox* (1928) said that Rin-Tin-Tin "pounces [on the villain] with such venomous fury that he is glad to get away with his life. . . .[It looked] more like the real thing than make believe." By the time *The Man Hunter* (1930) came along, Rin-Tin-Tin's acting as a fighter against men needed explanation: "Strangers are sometimes alarmed at Rin-Tin-Tin's realistic savagery in fighting scenes but those who have worked with him in other pictures knows [sic] that he is always conscious that he is only acting."

Aside from physical pain, I think that Rin-Tin-Tin might have suffered psychologically. Yes, he lived in luxury by human standards, but he worked hard. One might argue that he was a working dog and enjoyed what he did, which certainly could be true. However, my observation of my own German shepherd is that entertaining people wears him out quickly, perhaps because that activity goes against his nature, as it might have with Rin-Tin-Tin. During his heyday, Rin-Tin-Tin made as many as four movies a year, and, when he was not making movies, he was often on tour. He and Duncan took their first tour right after *Where the North Begins* aired in Glendale in fall, 1923. With the blessing (and money) of the Warner studio, they traveled the country presenting an on-stage, in-person act to accompany showings of the movie. The program included a jump through a window eight feet above the floor. Often Rin-Tin-Tin performed day after day – for the matinee and for three shows at night.

In 1930, two years before Rin-Tin-Tin's death, Duncan set up a vaudeville tour and arranged with Radio Keith Orpheum Company for a five-week trial to open January 25, 1930 A story found its way into the newspapers that after the tour Duncan and Rin-Tin-Tin were going to Europe, then would retire.

Critics were aware of Rin-Tin-Tin's age – one pointed out that the "canine marvel must be as old as Norma Talmadge." (Born in 1893, she wasn't that old.) However, Rin-Tin-Tin never did retire nor did he go back to Europe. Instead he made two serials. Old he was, but he kept working – who knows whether for fear or love? – until he died.

8
Rin-Tin-Tin's Last Years and the Career of His Son

In *The Lone Defender* (released in 1930 by Mascot Pictures), Rin-Tin-Tin's age shows in the forward set of his shoulders and his tired, shambling walk, so different from the crisp trot of his youth. Stand-ins take his place in scenes that require running and other athletic feats, though the dog who fights the wolf seems to be Rin-Tin-Tin himself. He performs many of his less strenuous tricks: putting a sympathetic paw on someone's knee, opening doors with his teeth and untying knots, stalking, jumping through a window, hiding on a closet shelf, climbing into a tree with conveniently low and horizontal branches.

Rin-Tin-Tin's valiant but sad performance in *The Lone Defender* presages the years to follow. From 1930 on, Rin-Tin-Tin's career and Duncan's fortunes went into decline, but the decline was slow. Rin-Tin-Tin's age, the Depression, and a change in movie-making all affected it.

After the Warner contract expired, Rin-Tin-Tin went to work for Mascot Pictures. It was a comedown. Even though *The Lone Defender* was a groundbreaking serial – a serial in which humans talked and the dog barked – it was still a serial, not a feature film, and Rin-Tin-Tin was earning less money. According to Jon Tuska in *The Vanishing Legion: A History of Mascot Pictures 1927-1935*, Nat Levine, founder of Mascot, offered Duncan $5000 on a term-of-the-picture contract, but Duncan "suppressed mention of this sum when he came to write his autobiography some years later." Tuska is right. In fact, Duncan suppressed more than the money – he never mentioned Mascot in his *Notes,* and James English in his *The Rin-Tin-Tin Story* suppressed the whole Mascot experience.

The Lone Defender might have cost $40,000 to make, and it might have been planned for adult as well as juvenile audiences, but it is clearly an unsophisticated potboiler; it consists of twelve short episodes, each introduced by Paul N. Robins, a pompous-voiced man in a suit. More than one critic (including, supposedly, the brother of June Marlowe, the female lead) called it the worst serial ever made. It features interminable repeating scenes of cowboys leaping up on their horses and galloping away, of men flailing ineffectually at each other in futile fights, of villains just by chance overhearing information important to finding the gold mine. A trap door leads to a tunnel. Messages are left in hollow trees. This is the stuff of adventure for children and, perhaps, credulous adults.

Yet in spite of the fact that the move to Mascot meant a decline in status for Duncan and Rin-Tin-Tin, it very likely *slowed* Rin-Tin-Tin's loss of popularity rather than hastened it. Even though he was on the screen less than he had been in his full-length pictures, he had top billing in his two serials. It was better than being a bit player in a feature film or acting in no films at all, as was the lot of many dog actors in the early 1930s.

Rin-Tin-Tin rode the increasing popularity of serials, which usually played on Friday and Saturday nights, designated as "family nights." In mid-June 1931, *Reel Journal* announced that the serial was a pioneer as "a family patronage builder . . . next to the western production." It went on to say that serials had had a resurgence of popularity everywhere in the country because their previous decline had caused a loss in the juvenile audience and because "the new type of serials" also appealed to adults. Mascot's Nat Levine reported that serials were playing in first-run theaters and as evidence said that Publix theaters were running his serials for "extended engagements" instead of just special Saturday matinees. "There is a moral in these facts," said Levine. "If such theatres as the Roxy and the Publix first run houses need serials, it is evident that no theatre, however large or small, can afford to omit them from its program." Of course, beyond the "moral" lay the fact that Levine had made a deal for Publix (owned by Paramount) to play Mascot serials. By 1936, *Los Angeles Times* writer John Scott was able to report that, in spite of censorship and technical problems with the use of sound, "the good old serial stands its ground" and was "increasing in popularity, particularly at matinees." Class A theaters in urban areas showed serials. Non-English speakers liked serials, in which action was more important than dialogue.

Nonetheless, some adults were tired of Rin-Tin-Tin. Certainly Bob Godley, a columnist for the *Wisconsin State Journal* in Madison, was when he wrote tongue in cheek in April 1930: "Personally we are fed up on Rinty. There was a time when we expressed our disgust (verbally) at a Rin Tin Tin picture at the

Orpheum and Mr. Harold Knudson stepped up and pitched us into the street, refunding the 35 cents as the box office sailed by. One supposes that the other 15 cents was kept to pay for the five acts of vodvil [sic] which we saw."

In 1930, the year he turned twelve, Rin-Tin-Tin led a very busy life: he made *The Lone Defender*, and he went on a tour that lasted nine months and took him and Duncan throughout the midwest to New York and Pennsylvania, and back home through Wisconsin. In March, when they were in Kansas City, appearing for a week at a theater, Duncan announced that, in June, he planned to marry Eva Linden of Los Angeles and take her on a honeymoon abroad. The two had met at Yosemite, perhaps during the filming of *Tiger Rose* in 1929. A long-planned tour to give Rin-Tin-Tin's impassioned European fans in all the "important cities" a look at their canine hero was, after all, going to be just a honeymoon for two humans. However, even the honeymoon did not happen as planned – Duncan and Linden did not marry until 1936.

In spite of the Depression and Rin-Tin-Tin's comedown to serials, with the accompanying reduction in income, Duncan was still a rich man. He was able to pay for a beach house in Malibu and "new studio home" for his sister Marjorie in North Hollywood, where, in January 1931, Rin-Tin-Tin helped to receive guests.

That February, a raging storm hit the California coast. Turned by powerful tides into a battering ram, a loose telephone pole slammed into the Duncan beach house and undermined it. The *Los Angeles Times* ran a photograph of Duncan and Rin-Tin-Tin looking at the wreck.

Duncan took Rin-Tin-Tin on tour again that year. In early April, traveling in an automobile especially equipped for the dog's comfort, the two stopped at New Castle, Pennsylvania, for dinner; they were en route from Toledo and on their way to Beaver Falls and Pittsburgh. A few days later, Rin-Tin-Tin was comforting a dog named Raggedy Ann at the Chicago North Side Animal shelter, "a sort of poor house for stray dogs and cats," according to the *San Antonio Light*. The head of a Chicago animal hospital, Dr. J. V. LaCroix, examined Rin-Tin-Tin and pronounced him in superb physical condition. In a newspaper article, Duncan commented that Rin-Tin-Tin was unusual in that he had worked very hard and suffered many hardships and inconveniences, yet was in excellent shape. He had a routine: fifteen minutes of romping, one meat meal at night (from two to eight pounds of canned horsemeat, depending on how hard he worked), biscuits in the morning.

In July, Rin-Tin-Tin appeared at the R.K.O Orpheum theater in Madison, Wisconsin, and Duncan interviewed him on the radio. "He dresses simply, doesn't even have a special collar, eats only the regular meals a well-kept canine gets, makes no secret of his age, 13 years [sic], and doesn't deny that he is married to Nanette, his companion German shepherd, and that he has 50 sons and daughters scattered around the country," said Madison's *Wisconsin State Journal*, which ran a photograph showing Rin-Tin-Tin dressed as a newspaper boy on the front page.

By October 1931, Rin-Tin-Tin was filming *The Lightning Warrior*, one of four twelve-part, all-talking serials Nat Levine planned for 1932. Duncan's (Rin-Tin-Tin's) contract with Mascot was to run two years more. By Christmas Eve, the first chapter of *The Lightning Warrior* was playing in a theater in Olean, New York. In February 1932, *New England Film News* reported that the serial was playing for a week in first-run theaters in big cities and that Herman Rifkin, the film's distributor, said it was "received with enthusiasm by the adults as well as the children." The plot is a twist on the Indian-white man theme, except that the Wolf Man, the "Indian" agitator trying to rouse the Indians to warfare, hides his face with his hat and his cloak, and turns out in the end to be a white man, not an Indian at all.

There is no question that Rin-Tin-Tin had stand-ins for at least the action sequences in *The Lightning Warrior*. One of the running dogs, for instance, has longer legs and is lighter in color. Doubles do the tough stunts: leaping onto a moving ore car from a wooden beam to land on the Wolf Man, then hanging perilously from the car, now overturned; jumping into the back of a fast-moving wagon after a failed attempt. Grizzled and stiff, Rin-Tin-Tin goes through the stunts he can still do himself: attacking villains, rounding up horses, jumping through low windows, and prophetically playing dead.

In late May 1932, Edwin Schallert of the *Los Angeles Times* talked of a comeback for Rin-Tin-Tin in the four pictures he was slated to make that year with his son, Rin-Tin-Tin Jr.: "Strongheart, Peter the Great, and various other famous canines have passed on, but Rin-Tin-Tin still goes on merrily at 14 years of age. [He was actually 13.] There was a time when he was the topnotch drawing card of Warner." Shortly after, Lee Shippey, another *Los Angeles Times* columnist, commenting on a comic strip featuring a dog, said, "Just as the movies are going back to Rin Tin Tin, realizing the amazing appeal of dogs, editors are interested by a feature with a really lovable dog in it."

The 1930s resurgence of dog movies, and it did exist, was a small repeat of the big peak 1920s, but the end of Rin-Tin-Tin's career occurred at the low point between the two. (See graph: "Dogs in U.S. Movies as a Percent of Total, 1920-1941," page 65.)

The Great Depression brought hard times for Duncan. On June 3, 1932, the First National Bank of Beverly Hills, where he and many other famous Hollywood people kept their money, closed its doors. The bank president explained that the bank had taken this action because a depositor had demanded $300,000 in one lump sum; he said that the plan was to reopen. Three days later, depositor Greta Garbo denied that she had lost $1,000,000 at the bank; she said that instead she had lost only a "few thousand dollars at the most." Jean Harlow's story was similar. However, Wallace Beery and other stars did lose considerable money. On June 14, 1932, the bank was placed in receivership. Though the *Los Angeles Times* announced in September that there was hope the bank would reopen, it didn't. Duncan was broke.

Two months later, the worst happened. On Wednesday, August 10, 1932, Rin-Tin-Tin died at his kennel on Club View Drive. His death made the front page of the *Los Angeles Times* the following day, though it played second to financial news and the marriage of John Gilbert and Virginia Bruce. The *Chicago Tribune* gave the event a short first-page story; a picture of him sitting at a typewriter answering fan mail appeared later in the paper. *The New York Times* announced his death on page 17. In many local papers it was front-page news. Of 270 newspapers scanned into Newspaper Archive at the time I researched it, ninety-six carried a story about his death between August 11 and August 18; of those, thirty-six put the story on the front page. Meanwhile, several carried ads for *The Lightning Warrior*. The *Los Angeles* Times included the death of Rin-Tin-Tin as one of the major events of 1932, along with a record snow, kidnapping of the Lindbergh baby, the death of a former golf champion by "radium in patent medicine," Al Capone's entrance into the federal penitentiary, and a flight by Amelia Earhart.

Like the stories of the rest of Rin-Tin-Tin's life, those of his death conflict. The United Press, which claimed that it was "as if a great human star had been stricken," reported that the dog was romping with Duncan, then, paralyzed, lay down, closed his eyes, and died before the veterinarian arrived. The Associated Press did not mention the romping but stated that he had eaten breakfast before he became paralyzed.

According to *"Hollywood Be Thy Name": The Warner Brothers Story*, Jack Warner said sentimentally (and perhaps inaccurately):

> Rinty's gallant heart was tired and old, the strength had long since ebbed from the massive shoulders and legs. He was barely able to crawl to his master's side, and Duncan knew at once that no power on earth could help. He phoned across the street to his neighbor, the lovely, shimmering Jean Harlow, and she came running. And she cradled the great furry head on her lap, and there he died.

The production file for *Now It's Showtime* (at the Margaret Herrick Library) tells a still different story:

> Rin Tin Tin died . . . collapsing in Duncan's arms during a romp on the lawn of their Beverly Hills home. A neighbor, seeing the magnificent animal prostrate, rushed to his side and wept over his body.
>
> She was Jean Harlow.

While Jack Warner's story could possibly be true, even though newspapers at the time of Rin-Tin-Tin's death said that Duncan "told no one," the production file story cannot. Jean Harlow lived in a house at 1353 Club View Drive, four doors down and on the other side of the street from Duncan, so she could not possibly have seen Rin-Tin-Tin in his yard.

Duncan buried Rin-Tin-Tin by a white rose bush in a bronze coffin with his squeaky doll and other toys. James English claimed that only Duncan and "a few personal friends" attended the ceremony, but *The New York Times* had it that "numerous picture celebrities [were] in attendance, including many who had co-starred with him." The *Chicago Tribune* announced that the rose bush was a favorite of Duncan's semi-invalid mother and that she was at the ceremony, along with three other friends. However, this story contains falsehoods: that Rin-Tin-Tin died on a Mascot Studio lot and that Duncan had never been married. But the *Tribune* was not alone in its flouting of fact. In 1954, the venerable *New York Times* said that Rin-Tin-Tin ended his life "in harness, dying on a set in 1933 while cameras were turning on his 'comeback' film."

Newspapers recounted his life and career – his birth in France, the notion that he saved Warner from bankruptcy, and his fame. They talked of his earning capacity, ranging from total earnings of $300,000 to vague estimates of "thousands of dollars" to "in the millions." The *Los Angeles Times* stated that he never made less than $30,000 a year and often as much as $65,000. In *Hollywood Be Thy Name*, the authors estimated Rin-Tin-Tin's earnings at $5 million – maybe they included money that accrued from Rin-Tin-Tin's movies after he died.

Several of Rin-Tin-Tin's obituaries celebrated his iconic status as a creature more moral than most humans – an implicit rebuke to the excesses of Hollywood stars. As the *McKean Democrat* (Smethport, Pennsylvania) put it: "The movies can illy afford to lose stars like Rin Tin Tin who did much to present decent entertainment. . .." Other newspapers praised him for not advertising cigarettes (not true, he was featured in Old Gold ads), not getting a divorce, staying away from wild parties, and being modest.

And Rin-Tin-Tin's success was a good deal his own doing. The *Charleston Gazette* (West Virginia) said: "Rinty's glory was not the glory of association with a famous man as his pet, as is the glory of White House dogs or some rich man's pet. But Rin Tin Tin earned his fame by work . . . that thousands of humans might be entertained." A story carried by several newspapers praised his honest humility in a narcissistic Hollywood :

> If there is a dog's paradise, Rin Tin Tin should be roving through it today towards a good beefsteak dinner. . . . Rin Tin Tin's was a dog's life but his career was one which set him apart, in the realm of make-believe which is the special province of Will Hays, as an actor who knew superbly how to be his age and recognized his humble canine limitations.

On August, 11, 1932, the day after Rin-Tin-Tin died, *New England Film News* printed a story stating that Mascot Productions had announced four Rin-Tin-Tin special features for 1932-1933. It was to be Rin-Tin-Tin's comeback, under a three-year contract. With unseemly haste, Mascot made another statement that appeared the same day in newspapers: Rin-Tin-Tin Jr. would replace Rin-Tin-Tin and gave "promise of equaling if not excelling his father as an actor." Louella Parsons, gossip queen of Hollywood, who made Rin-Tin-Tin's death the lead paragraph in her column, said that Duncan had been training Junior to take over. I think she was right. A story which appeared in more than one newspaper about two weeks after Rin-Tin-Tin died went into detail: "The young dog is already trained to follow in his sire's footsteps. Lean, lithe, with a fine head and intelligent eyes, Rinty, Jr. has had the same 'education' that his father was given by Duncan." The clincher: *Pride of the Legion*, in which Rin-Tin-Tin Jr. played a role (did he not have to be trained for it?), was released on October 18, 1932, only two months after Rin-Tin-Tin's death.

Rin-Tin-Tin Jr. mourning the death of his father (Courtesy Rin-Tin-Tin Collection, Riverside, California).

Duncan, perhaps saddened by Rin-Tin-Tin's death, lacked enthusiasm for Junior. In his book on Rin-Tin-Tin, James English, probably prompted by Duncan, pointed out Junior's flaws: too leggy to be properly athletic, looked more like his mother (a blond) than his father, lacked "drive," was too heavy at 110 pounds. Duncan and English also said that Junior was less than a year old and had been trained only in basic obedience. English talked about how Duncan had to train Junior for the talkies as if that was something new; actually, he had trained the father, much earlier. Besides, English claimed, Duncan was no longer interested in making movies and all that entailed, but instead wanted to move to a ranch and marry Eva Linden.

On August 22, 1932, the *Hayward Review* ran a photograph of Rin-Tin-Tin Jr., his chin on top of the cross over his father's grave, one foot on the crosspiece; the caption said that Junior was mourning the loss of his "super-intelligent sire by refusing to budge from the elder dog's grave."

The question was: could the son replace the father? Junior himself said in an interview with Mollie Merrick on August 13, 1932, "Another dog could have come in with a mere pleasing talent; I will have to show genius. My father was on the eve of a great comeback – this makes it the harder for me – the public was all prepared to see the great Rin-Tin-Tin himself."

He was right. He didn't stand a chance. And it wasn't just because he was in the shadow of his father. Junior's fame compared with his father's was, in a way, somewhat proportional to the times. In the 1930s, thirteen movies featured dogs in leading roles; three of those movies (about twenty-three percent) starred Rin-Tin-Tin Jr. On the other hand, in the 1920s forty-seven movies featured dogs in leading roles; Rin-Tin-Tin played the lead in sixteen of them (about thirty-four percent).

A statistical survey of movies with dogs in the cast (1920 to 1941) reveals that after a drop (to two movies) in 1932, cast lists again began to contain the names of dogs. (See graph, "Dogs in U.S. Movies as a Percent of Total, 1920-1941," on page 65.) The peak year, 1937, does not begin to equal the high point of the 1920s. Similarly, only a few 1930s movies featured a dog star with top billing, while far more 1920s movies did. In the 1930s, of the thirty dog actors, seventeen were German shepherds – Rin-Tin-Tin Jr. Kazan, Silver King, Tarzan, War Cry, Flash, Lightning, Zamba, Lobo, Captain, Silver Wolf, Smokey, Swift Lightning, Ace, Boots, Grey Shadow, and Zero. None of them was really famous except, perhaps, Rin-Tin-Tin Jr., and one could say that his fame rested on the reputation of his father. Incidentally, Rin-Tin-Tin Jr. was not the first second-generation dog actor. Silver King, who made two movies, one released in 1933 and the other in 1938, was supposedly the grandson of Strongheart and the son of Dynamite. Ironically, he was called a "successor to the lofty position once held by the famous dog star, Rin-Tin-Tin." Smokey and Grey Shadow were also were touted as descendants of Strongheart.

Other 1930s dog actors included terriers, a greyhound, a cocker spaniel, a Great Dane, a collie, and a Georgia pointer. True, the dogs that achieved starring roles were all male German shepherds, but the Western with the dog hero was giving way to other kinds of movies. The 1930s was the time of the family and pet dog film: Daisy in the Dagwood Bumpstead movies; Terry, the cairn terrier who played Toto in 1939's *The Wizard of Oz*; Asta (a.k.a. Skippy), the wire-haired fox terrier in *The Thin Man*).

The New York Times critic liked *Pride of the Legion* — and Junior, who was "not the least of the actors by any means." Otherwise, the movie did not receive much play in the newspapers.

In the three years from 1933 to 1936, Rin-Tin-Tin Jr. made five movies: a feature film, *The Test* (1935), and four Mascot serials — *Wolf Dog* (1933), *Law of the Wild* with Rex the horse (1934), *The Adventures of Rex and Rinty* also with Rex the horse (1935), and *Skull and Crown* (1935).

In March 1935, a deer crashed into Duncan's car on Ventura Boulevard. The *Los Angeles Times* ran a picture of the deer resting against the radiator as Junior nosed him and Duncan looked on. Never one to pass up an opportunity for publicity, Duncan, with Rin-Tin-Tin Jr., hosted a banquet of venison sandwiches made with the deer's 150 pounds of meat at the Salvation Army Shelter in Santa Monica.

Tough Guy (1936) was to be Rin-Tin-Tin Jr.'s big break, though fourteen-year-old Jackie Cooper and Joseph Calleia were billed above him. A *Los Angeles Times* writer praised him: "Of course, Rin-Tin-Tin, Jr., the canine hero, does everything except sums in arithmetic, and you feel he could accomplish those if necessary." *The New York Times* reviewer agreed: "The dog, incidentally, is Rin-Tin-Tin Jr., a recent graduate from the serials, and, if his performance in 'Tough Guy' is any criterion, well fitted to pad along the first-run trail in the footprints of his illustrious ancestor."

Rin-Tin-Tin's Last Years and Junior's Career

Tough Guy should have been Rin-Tin-Tin Jr.'s breakthough movie. It wasn't.

The year 1936 was relatively uneventful in terms of Junior's career, but very eventful for Duncan.

A February, 1936, a small *New York Times* ad for a "Rex and Rinty" movie shows the degree to which Junior's movies had become less important than those of his father. The type was tiny and the movie played second place to the feature, *Little Men.* Jeanette MacDonald and Nelson Eddy (*Rose Marie*), Charlie Chaplin (*Modern Times*), George Raft and Rosalind Russell (*It Had to Happen*), and Eddie Cantor (*Strike Me Pink*) scored the big, attention-getting ads. In that year, Reliable Pictures released two forgettable films starring Rin-Tin-Tin Jr.: *Caryl of the Mountains* and *Vengeance of Rannah*.

In December 1936, Duncan married Eva Linden. The ceremony took place at the Rangers Club in Yosemite. Duncan was identified as "trainer of the film dog Rin Tin Tin." (Rin-Tin-Tin Jr. was not mentioned.) After the wedding, the Duncans moved into a house on their ranch, Rancho Rin-Tin-Tin, at Riverside.

In the next three years, Junior had small roles in three more films: *The Silver Trail* (1937), *Fangs of the Wild* (1939), and *Death Goes North* (1939). Twentieth Century Fox's *Hollywood Cavalcade* (1939), Junior's last picture, might not have been as forgettable as they were, but Junior's part in it was. A revue about Hollywood from 1913 to 1927, it featured a huge list of actors, including Duncan himself. Edmund Schallert's rave review of the movie did not mention either Duncan or the dog.

Junior died in 1943, of pneumonia, but the press paid little attention. They were too intrigued with Rin-Tin-Tin III, who along with hundreds of German shepherds, was trained by Duncan for service in World War II.

Duncan died in 1960 at age sixty-seven. His death was covered on page 32 of *The New York Times*, page 12 of the *Los Angeles Times*, and page B4 of the *Chicago Daily Tribune*. Only eight local papers put the story of his death on the front page, though fifty-nine did cover it. Headlines identified him as Rin-Tin-Tin's trainer.

Sketch for "Famous Dog Actor Tells the Story of His Adventures," *Billings Gazette*, February 24, 1924, page 16

Filmography

Contents

The Man from Hell's River	176
My Dad	178
Where the North Begins	180
Shadows of the North	182
Find Your Man	184
The Lighthouse by the Sea	186
Tracked in the Snow Country	189
Below the Line	191
Clash of the Wolves	193
The Night Cry	195
A Hero of the Big Snows	197
While London Sleeps	199
Hills of Kentucky	201
Tracked by the Police	203
Jaws of Steel	205
A Dog of the Regiment	207
Race for Life	209
Rinty of the Desert	211
Land of the Silver Fox	213
Frozen River	215
The Million Dollar Collar	217
Tiger Rose	219
The Show of Shows	221
On the Border	223
The Man Hunter	225
Rough Waters	227
The Lone Defender	229
The Lightning Warrior	231

The Man From Hell's River (January 29, 1922)

Five reels

Cast:

Irving Cummings	Pierre de Barre
Eva Novak	Mabella
Wallace Beery	Gaspard the Wolf
Frank Whitson	Sergeant McKenna
Robert Klein	Lopente
William Herford	The Padre
Rin-Tin-Tin	Rin-Tin-Tin

Director: Irving Cummings
Writer: Irving Cummings
Photography: Abe Fried (Director)

Based on "The God of Her People," short story by James Oliver Curwood
Copyright: Irving Cummings Productions, March 16, 1922 (LU17647)
Silent. Black and white
Availability: Lost

Plot Summary:

Set in a French-Canadian trading post in the frozen North, the film was based on James Oliver Curwood's novel *The God of Her People*. It is a classic melodrama in which Rin-Tin-Tin saves the heroine, Mabella (daughter of a "squaw man," according to *Variety*), played by Eva Novak, from the evil Gaspard, a.k.a., the Wolf (Wallace Beery). Mabella's upright Mountie sweetheart Pierre (Irving Cummings) is away (of course) when Gaspard makes his move, trying to force her to marry him by threatening to have her father arrested for murder. Gaspard and Mabella have become engaged – against her will – when Pierre and Rin-Tin-Tin, playing Pierre's head sled dog, come back to the post. A priest reveals the truth to Pierre. Gaspard takes Mabella away, but Pierre chases them. The two men fight. At a crucial moment, Rin Rin Tin jumps on Gaspard, who then falls off a cliff.

Billing: Ads at first merely mentioned an "all-star cast," but within a month some were billing Rin-Tin-Tin as co-equal with Novak and Beery, though not always.

Reviews: *Motion Picture News* liked the movie:: "[I]t depends for its appeal – its strength upon its aboundant [sic] note of romance, its heart interest and the fact that it features a dog in Rin Tin [sic] who is entitled to share honors with Strongheart of 'Silent Call' fame." However, *Variety* did not list Rin-Tin-Tin in the cast list of five actors; the reviewer called the film "melodramatic," with "a splendid performance" by Cummings and an "excellent cast."

Availability: Lost.

Location: Yosemite National Park. According to promotion, it was the "first time winter scenes ha[d] been caught" at the park. The federal government gave permission for filming.

My Dad (July 23, 1922)

Six reels

Cast:

Johnnie Walker	Tom O'Day
Wilbur Higby	Barry O'Day
Mary Redmond	Mrs. O'Day
Ruth Clifford	Dawn
Les Bates	La Due
Harry von Meter	The Factor (Trading Post Manager)
Rin-Tin-Tin	Rin-Tin-Tin

Director: Cliff Smith
Producer: Cliff Smith
Writers: E. Richard Schayer (Scenario)
　　　　Walter Richard Hall (Story)
Photography: John Thompson (Director)

Copyright: R-C Pictures, March 13, 1922 (LP18054)
Distributor: Film Booking Offices of America
Silent. Black and white

Availability: Lost

Plot Summary:

The "dad" (Wilbur Higby), a passive sort, lives at a Northwest trading post, always fearing that its villainous manager (Harry von Meter) will turn him into the Mounted Police (who never actually show up in the movie) for a murder he thinks he committed when drunk. His "clean-cut" son, Tom (Johnnie Walker), loves Dawn (Ruth Clifford), the manager's stepdaughter, but of course the manager does not approve – in fact, wants her for himself – and uses his supposed knowledge of Tom's father's guilt to keep Tom in line. A conversation clues Tom in to the truth about the murder, and after some research, he finds out that the manager is the guilty one. Rin-Tin-Tin (already called Rinty) attacks two bad guys who threaten Tom with harm. A bear (the O'Day's pet) also has a role. All ends happily.

Billing: By September, 1922, Rin-Tin-Tin began to appear as a star in ads. For instance, an ad for *My Dad*, then showing at the Family Theatre in Davenport, featured the title in huge type, Johnny Walker's name (capitals and lower case) in very big type, and Rin-Tin-Tin's name a bit smaller but in all caps preceded by "and the famous dog star."

Reviews: In early September, though *My Dad* played on Broadway in a two-week run, *Variety*'s reviewer, "Fred," ridiculed its direction, pointing to a scene in a crowded trading store in which "the factor is whaling away at a door with a heavy chair, while his stepdaughter on the other side of the door is screaming at the top of her lungs, yet nobody in the store below pays any attention." A reviewer ("Reel Chatter") in the Fort Wayne *News Sentinel* made fun of a scene in which the hero carries his "somewhat heavy-looking lady love (her heftiness is increased by the luxurious fur wrap she is wearing) over the hill homeward" and characterized the villain, who engages in "unpleasant villainy – sex stuff," as nonetheless colorless. In the end, he applauded the black bear who "had so much more sense than the humans in the picture. While they ranted around about nothing much – he calmly ate – and ate – and ate." And Rin-Tin-Tin, the "adorable police dog, showed off his training as naturally as if it was a pleasure to oblige." He concluded with "Rin-Tin-Tin, the bear and the scenery are fine."

Where the North Begins (July 1, 1923)

Six reels

Cast:

Claire Adams	Felice McTavish
Walter McGrail	Gabrielle Dupré
Pat Hartigan	Shad Galloway
Myrtle Owen	Marie
Charles Stevens	The Fox
Fred Huntley	Scotty McTavish
Rin-Tin-Tin	The Dog

Director: Chester M. Franklin
Writers: Lee Duncan (Story)
    Fred Myton (Scenario, Story)
    Chester M. Franklin (Scenario)
    Millard Webb (Story)
    Raymond L. Schrock (Writer)

Copyright: Warner Brothers Pictures, July 7, 1923 (LP19256)
Silent. Black and white
Availability: On DVD.

Plot Summary:

    A crated German shepherd puppy falls off a dog sled while being transported to a trading post. A wolf pack raises him. It isn't until he is an adult that the puppy, now the Dog (Rin-Tin-Tin) again comes in contact with a human being – Gabrielle Dupré (Walter McGrail), a French-Canadian trapper who has been attacked and left for dead in the forest by the Fox (Charles Stevens), henchman of the evil Shad Galloway (Pat Hartigan), manager of the trading post. After the Dog fights off his fellow wolves, he joins forces with Dupré and trounces the Fox. Back at the trading post, Galloway makes unwanted advances to Felice McTavish (Claire Adams), Dupré's sweetheart. It is Galloway, of course, who is behind the Fox's attack on Dupré. Dupré and the Dog come back to the trading post. When the Dog is unjustly accused of killing a baby, Dupré whips him, whereupon, his heart broken, the Dog crawls off into the forest. However he comes back to save Felice when Galloway tries to carry her off on horseback. He traps Galloway on a cliff and causes him to fall off to his death. At the end of the picture the sweethearts are together, and the Dog and his wolf-wife come back to the cabin with a litter of adorable puppies.

Billing: Rin-Tin-Tin was clearly the star. The ad for the movie, playing at Los Angeles' Capitol theater, was typical: "The Greatest Dog Picture ever filmed. . .Featuring RIN-TIN-TIN [with no mention of the rest of the cast]."

Reviews: *Variety* said that *Where the North Begins* was:

a cracking good film for almost any audience. A film packed full of the old heroic stuff and having as its leading character a dog actor, 'Rin-Tin-Tin,' who bids fair to walk away from his competitor, 'Strongheart,' in this particular line. It has a good love story, plenty of snow atmosphere, the customary masculine-looking heroes and an excellent production in its favor. And what is even more important, it furnishes real entertainment of a certain kind.

Location: Feather River country, Lake Tahoe, Donner Lake, and Truckee in California; Reno, Nevada.

Shadows of the North (August 27, 1923)

Five reels

Cast:

William Desmond	Ben "Wolf" Darby
Virginia Brown Faire	Beatrice Neilson
Fred Kohler	Ray Brent
William Welsh	Jeffrey Neilson
Albert Hart	Hemingway
James O. Barrows	Ezra "Pancake" Darby
Rin-Tin-Tin	King

Director: Robert F. Hill
Producer: Cliff Smith
Writer: Paul Schofield (Scenario), based on Edison Marshall's novel *Skyline of Spruce*
Photography: John Thompson (Director)

Copyright: R-C Pictures, March 13, 1922 (LP18054)
Distributor: Film Booking Offices of America
Silent. Black and white
Availability: Lost

Plot Summary:

Shadows of the North, in which Rin-Tin-Tin plays King (the dog), was adapted from Edison Marshall's novel *Skyline of Spruce*, published in 1922. The characters will become familiar to Rin-Tin-Tin fans: a hero, "Wolf" Darby (William Desmond), bent on revenge, who focuses on the wrong man; Jeffrey Neilson (William Welsh); a dastardly villain; Ray Brent (Fred Kohler), who is the guilty party; a sweet heroine, Beatrice Neilson (Virginia Brown Faire); the faithful dog, King (Rin-Tin-Tin), who saves the day. Darby, a World War I veteran, comes home to find his father, a gold prospector, dead; claim jumpers have killed him. Suspicion falls on Beatrice's father. The father, of course, is not guilty, and King helps Wolf find the real killer. An exciting escape through the rapids in a canoe wraps the story up.

Billing: In October and early November, 1923, Desmond received star billing, with Rin-Tin-Tin mentioned second, in an ad for Saxe's Majestic in Oshkosh and in an ad in the *Naugatuck Daily News*. However, also in November, in an ad in the *Wisconsin Rapids Daily Tribune*, Rin-Tin-Tin was the only actor mentioned.

Reviews: A review in the *Los Angeles Times* said that the movie presented "real he-man entertainment. . . .It reminds of the good old days of thrilly thrillers" and added that "the shots of the dog, Rin-Tin-Tin, are rather attractive, although it is the same old stuff of his being vamped by the wolf."

Location: Feather River country, Northern California.

Find Your Man (September 1, 1924)

Seven reels

Cast:

June Marlowe	Carolina Blair
Rin-Tin-Tin	Buddy
Eric St. Clair	Paul Andrews
Charles Mailes	Gregory Mills
Pat Hartigan	Martin Dains
Fred Stanton	Sheriff
Lew Harvey	Half-breed
Charles Conklin	Lumberjack

Director: Malcolm St. Clair
Writer: Darryl Francis Zanuck (Scenario, Adaptation, Story)
Photography: Lee Garmes (Director)

Copyright: Warner Brothers Pictures, August 18, 1924 (LP20505)
Silent. Black and white
Availability: Lost.

Plot Summary:

The movie begins on a European battlefield in the First World War, with Buddy (Rin-Tin-Tin) as a Red Cross dog saving wounded soldiers. The hero, Paul Andrews (Eric St. Clair), brings him back to the United States, where a pair of villainous lumberjacks lure Andrews into a plot to float stolen logs down a river. Andrews doesn't know the logs were taken illegally, but the lumberjacks do. Andrews is arrested, both for stealing the logs and a murder, which he did not commit. Buddy helps Andrews escape from prison, then rescues him and his sweetheart, Carolina (June Marlowe), from drowning in the rapids.

Billing: Rin-Tin-Tin is the star. June Marlowe, "the girl with the soulful eyes," plays opposite him.

Filmography

Reviews: From *Variety*, "The picture looks to have every chance to get by on the strength of the dog, which is certainly both a beautiful and well-trained animal." From the *Los Angeles Times*: "An excellent show for your money, take it altogether, and, thank heaven, except for the really entertaining personal appearance of Rin-Tin-Tin, the canine Campinini, there is no vaudeville."

Location: Klamath Falls, Oregon

The Lighthouse by the Sea (December 1, 1924)

Seven reels

Cast:
William Collier Jr.	Albert Dorn
Louise Fazenda	Flora Gale
Charles Hill Mailes	Caleb Gale
Douglas Gerrard	Edward Cavanna
Matthew Betz	Joe Dagget
Rin-Tin-Tin	Rin-Tin-Tin

Director: Malcolm St. Clair
Assistant Directors:
    Clarence Bricker
    Clarence Kolster
Writer: Darryl F. Zanuck (Adaptation)
Victor Vance (Art titles)
Photography: Lynman Broening (Director)
Art Direction: Lewis Geib (Director)
    Esdras Hartley (Director)
Film Editor: Howard Bretherton
Electrical Effects: F.N. Murphy
Based on *The Lighthouse by the Sea*, a play by Owen Davis (copyright July 27, 1920)

Copyright: Warner Brothers Pictures, November 17, 1924 (LP20782)
Silent. Black and white
Availability: On DVD

Plot Summary:
    Caleb Gale (Charles Hill Mailes), an old lighthouse keeper, knows his job is in jeopardy because he is going blind. He and his daughter, Flora (Louise

Fazenda), succeed in keeping this fact from government men who visit the lighthouse to make sure the light will be working when they ambush rum-runners who seek darkness for their nefarious work. Flora goes into town to hire someone to assist them, which seems odd because before this she and her father had been perfectly capable, working together, of keeping the light burning. In town, she meets Joe Dagget (Matthew Betz), an uncouth rum-runner, who whispers such nasty remarks into her ear that she slaps him. She also meets a smooth operator, another rum-runner, Edward Cavanna (Douglas Gerrard), a remittance man, who sweet talks her. Meanwhile, ten minutes into the movie, a ship founders, and Albert Dorn (William Collier, Jr.) and his faithful dog (Rin-Tin-Tin) come ashore in a lifeboat. Flora saves Albert with the help of Rin-Tin-Tin. On a night a shipment is to come ashore, Dagget, wanting the sea to remain dark, ties up Albert and knocks out the lighthouse keeper. Rin-Tin-Tin is able to chew through Albert's ropes, but the bad guys capture and tie him up again. Rin-Tin-Tin brings a length of tow to Albert, who, using his feet and some conveniently placed matches, succeeds in setting it on fire. Rin-Tin-Tin dashes up the staircase with the burning flare to the light, ignites the kerosene, and the bad guys are caught in its brilliance. Then the old man awakes, unties Albert, and Albert and Rin-Tin-Tin race to the rum-runners' ship to rescue Flora. After much fighting, the revenue agents come, the rum-runners are vanquished, and Albert and Flora are in a clinch in the surf, anticipating the famous scene in *From Here to Eternity*.

Billing: In the end, Rin-Tin-Tin was the advertised star, though Louise Fazenda tried to unseat him.

Reviews: Mordaunt Hall, the reviewer for *The New York Times*, sets the tone for *The Lighthouse by the Sea*: the movie, is "rather lurid with accentuated heavy portions," but is "worth while seeing for the amazing actions of Rin-Tin-Tin." His review places Rin-Tin-Tin unquestionably as the star, a great favorite of audiences:

According to the enthusiasm in Piccadilly yesterday, most persons love dogs, especially those who perform heroic acts as Rin-Tin-Tin does in his latest vehicle, 'The Lighthouse by the Sea' . . . Rin-Tin-Tin is kept unusually busy, and his reaction to the direction makes his performance appear remarkable. He smells danger, appreciates a villain for his lack of worth, and knows that a hero must go through all sorts of misfortunes before the end of the picture comes.

The big city reviewers gave faint praise to the movie itself. "Fred," the reviewer for *Variety*, found *The Lighthouse by the Sea* "[l]ittle different from the usual run of the stories in which the police dog stars have been appearing."

Time said: "This present sample has a superbly absurd story about the blind ancient who keeps the light, his lovely daughter, her marcelled boy friend. Smugglers and kidnapping. Police Dog Rin-Tin-Tin does most of the rescuing, lights the beacon on the fatal night. For most people is an all-sufficing hero."

Location: Laguna Beach and Catalina Island.

Filmography

Tracked in the Snow Country (July 13, 1925)

Seven reels

Cast:

Rin-Tin-Tin	Rin-Tin-Tin
June Marlowe	Joan Hardy
David Butler	Terry Moulton
Mitchell Lewis	Jules Renault
Charles Sellon	Silent Hardy
Princess Lea	Wah-Wah

Director: Herman C. Raymaker
Writers: Herman C. Raymaker (Story and Continuity)
    Edward J. Meagher (Story and Continuity)
Photography: Ray June (Director)

Copyright: Warner Brothers Pictures, April 23, 1925 (LP21386)
Silent. Black and white
Availability: Lost

Plot Summary:

    Silent Hardy (Charles Sellon), his daughter Joan (June Marlowe), and Rin-Tin-Tin, whom they adopted as a wolf cub, live in the Northwoods, where Hardy has discovered a rich vein of gold and made a map of the location. He is murdered, and Rin-Tin-Tin, now grown, is suspect, because the old man has wolf teeth marks on him. Even Joan thinks he's guilty, as does her boyfriend, forest ranger Terry Moulton (David Butler). But Rin-Tin-Tin, who witnessed the murder when chained up, knows the guilty party is Jules Renault (Mitchell Lewis), a half-breed, who has designs on Joan. While trying to wrest the map from Joan, Renault was able to spot where the gold was, so he goes off to find it. Moulton takes a shot at Rin-Tin-Tin, who escapes to the wolves. Meanwhile, Renault has found the gold mine, but Rin-Tin-Tin has tracked him there, and – knife against teeth – they are engaged in ferocious battle on the lip of a well.

Renault says to Rin-Tin-Tin, "I'll kill you as I killed your master." Rin-Tin-Tin loses the battle and falls into the well, while Renault continues fighting, now against Terry, who, with Joan, has tracked him to the mine. Rin-Tin-Tin scrabbles his way out of the well and chases down Renault, who runs onto a frozen lake and falls through the ice. Each time Renault tries to get out of the freezing water, Rin-Tin-Tin forces him back down, until he finally drowns. Joan and Terry marry and have twins. Rin-Tin-Tin is part of their family with his own family of cubs.

Billing: Warner promoted their new star in ads by printing his name in big type, sometimes bigger than the title of the film, calling him "Police Dog Marvel" and ignoring the rest of the cast.

Reviews: *Variety*, which placed Rin-Tin-Tin's name first in the cast list, gave the movie a mixed review, while praising Rin-Tin-Tin's acting and the beauty of the snow scenes. The flaw, to *Variety*, was "focusing the spotlight on its animals, and its star in particular, to almost total exclusion of the men and women in the cast . . . who merely served as background for Rinty's talented capers and posing. . . . The result seems to be a certain amount of monotony." It compared Rin-Tin-Tin's "sufferings and adventures" to those "undergone in countless films by Bill Hart and others of the school of martyred, silent, western heroes."

P.K. Hendrix, of the Liberty Theatre, Wellsville, Kansas, gave the movie an enthusiastic review, twice as long as any others on the page in *The Reel Journal*'s "Box-Office Reviews.":

> Had good crowd in competition to church's play Friday night. Saturday night broke house record for me, having turned away from first show some one hundred people. Rin-Tin-Tin seems to be very popular with my people and had many comments on the picture. . . . [S]o far as I am concerned, as a critic, I would say was as perfect as any I have shown.

Time said, in its review of the movie, "Best of all the cinema dogs is Rin-Tin-Tin."

Filmography

Below the Line (September 26, 1925)

Seven reels

Cast:

Rin-Tin-Tin	Rin-Tin-Tin
John Harron	Donald Cass
June Marlowe	May Barton
Pat Hartigan	Jamber Niles
Victor Potel	"Cuckoo" Niles
Heine Conklin	Deputy Sheriff
Gilbert Clayton	Reverend Barton
Edith Yorke	Mrs. Cass
Taylor Duncan	Sheriff

Director: Herman C. Raymaker
    Assistant Director: Irving Asher
Writer: Charles A. Logue
Photography: John Mescall (Director)
    Ben Shipman

Copyright: Warner Brothers Pictures, August 8, 1925 (LP21757)
Silent. Black and white
Availability: Lost. Occasionally a foreign version will show up on YouTube

Plot Summary:

Rin-Tin-Tin, a fighting dog broken in spirit by his brutal training, is being sent south to join a pack of bloodhounds who trail criminals, when a mean baggage master throws his crate (with him in it) off the moving train. The crate tumbles down a hill into a river full of alligators. Young Donald Cass (John Harron) finds Rin-Tin-Tin, and he and his mother (Edith Yorke) treat him kindly, transforming him into a loyal, tame dog. Meanwhile the villain, Jamber Niles (Pat Hartigan), tries to rob a rich girl, then murders her. The sheriff, using as evidence a piece of cloth and a button taken from the dead girl's hand, goes on a search for him. Meanwhile Niles tries to steal church funds from Donald, and is choking him when Rin-Tin-Tin stops him by killing him. In another scene, bloodhounds, sent by "Cuckoo" Niles (Victor Potel), Jamber's mentally challenged brother, attack Donald and his sweetheart, May Barton (June Marlowe), who are lost in a crocodile-ridden swamp. In trying to escape the hounds, they end up trapped in a cave. Rin-Tin-Tin holds the hounds at bay, then chases them off. He climbs a tree in fighting "Cuckoo."

Billing: Rin-Tin-Tin was clearly the star. In ads, the other actors were left out or mentioned in small type. He was: "The wonder dog; nobler, smarter, more alert and beautiful than ever." If a picture accompanied the ad or story, he was the only individual in it – or the most important one.

Reviews: "[H]e rises to the heights of dumb-brute acting. . . . He is marvelous," enthused the *Los Angeles Times*, going on to say:

> The manner in which Rin-Tin-Tin holds the entire pack at bay, fights them to their complete defeat and thus saves his loved ones is the great climax of the melodrama. It is probably the most vivid thing of its kind ever seen on the screen – truly a superb piece of acting. It has its human parallel in Richard Barthelmess's fight with the hillbillies in 'Tol'able David.'" [Actor Barthlemess was famous for jumping from ice floe to ice floe to save a heroine (Lilian Gish) from going over a waterfall in *Way Back East* (1920). In *Tol'able David* he saves the U.S. Mail from a gang of thugs, the head thug of which delights in evil acts like crushing a cat with a rock, killing a dog with a board, and David's brother with a rock.]

According to *Variety*, "the story certainly has suspense and Rin-Tin-Tin does work. However, in his fight with the dogs the stuffed animals used in certain shots were all too noticeable."

Filmography

Clash of the Wolves (November 28, 1925)

Seven reels

Cast:

Rin-Tin-Tin	Lobo
Nanette (the dog)	Lobo's Mate
June Marlowe	May Barstowe
Charles Farrell	Dave Weston
Heinie Conklin	Alkali Bill
Will Walling	Sam Barstowe
Pat Hartigan	Wm. Borax Horton

Director: Noel M. Smith

Writer: Charles A. Logue (Scenario and Story)

Photography: Joe Walker (Director)

Film Editor: Clarence Kolster

Copyright: Warner Brothers Pictures, October 26, 1925 (LP21953)

Silent. Black and white

Availability: On DVD along with other silent movies

Plot Summary:

    A fierce forest fire forces a pack of wolves, led by Lobo (Rin-Tin-Tin), who is only half-wolf, down from the mountains. To survive, the wolves kill cattle, and the ranchers declare war on them. Fleeing from the ranchers, Lobo falls down a cliff and ends up with a thorn in his foot. In a scene reminiscent of the myth "Androcles and the Lion," prospector Dave Weston (Charles Farrell) picks Lobo up and carries him to his cabin, where he removes the thorn and gains Lobo's eternal friendship. Weston is in love with May Barstowe (June Marlowe), but her father, Sam (Will Walling), is against their alliance. When May, Alkali Bill (Heine Conklin), and Weston go into town, Bill creates a disguise for Lobo – a fake beard – so that he won't be recognized as a wolf. Meanwhile Borax Horton (Pat Hartigan), the chemist to whom Weston has taken a borax sample for testing, attacks Weston in a sandstorm and leaves him for dead. Lobo drags Weston into a cave, where Weston writes a message to May on a canteen and sends it with Lobo into town. Meanwhile, Horton files Weston's claim for himself. In town, Lobo drops the canteen and attacks Horton, but fails to win against him and has to retreat. May, not the brightest of girlfriends, finds the canteen but thinks it belongs to Horton. Horton sees the message and goes back to finish Weston off. Faithful Lobo finds and vanquishes him. Lobo is vindicated. Dave and May marry, and Lobo ends up living with them.

Billing: Rin-Tin-Tin is the star.

Reviews: "The story is immaterial, but it affords the dog a chance to be daring, human and immensely lovable, which is all that is necessary. The race to the rescue is thrilling and brands Rin-Tin-Tin as an up-and-coming hero," said the *Los Angeles Times*. The review of the movie in *The Chicago Daily Tribune* mentioned no cast member except Rin-Tin-Tin, who is "swift, shrewd and resourceful . . . brawny, brainy and kind as a friend of man, a darling as a pet and a clown when it occurs to one of the humans interested in his welfare to disguise him . . ." It concludes with: "So, though the plot is negligible, what do we care? Rin-Tin-Tin doesn't need any plot. All he needs is a master's voice – and he'll provide the action."

Filmography

The Night Cry (February 2, 1926)

Seven reels

Cast:

Rin-Tin-Tin	Rin-Tin-Tin
John Harron	John Martin
June Marlowe	Mrs. John Martin
Gayne Whitman	Miguel Hernández
Heine Conklin	Tony
Don Alvarado	Pedro
Mary Louise Miller	The Martin baby

Director: Herman C. Raymaker
    William McGann (Assistant Director)
    Al Zeidman (Assistant Director)
Writers: Ewart Adamson (Adaptation)
    Paul Klein (Story)
    Edward Meagher (Story)
Photography: Ed DuPar (Director)
    Walter Robinson (Additional Photography)
Film Editor: Clarence Kolster

Copyright: Warner Brothers Pictures, March 4, 1926 (LP22446)

Silent. Black-and-white

Availability: On DVD

Plot Summary: Rin-Tin-Tin plays a sheep dog accused unjustly of killing lambs. The real culprit is a condor, and, through much of the movie, Rin-Tin-Tin tries to hunt it down. The ranchers, angered at their losses, tell John Martin,

Rin-Tin-Tin's owner (John Harron), that he must kill Rin-Tin-Tin. However, Martin cannot bring himself to do it. In the culminating scene, the condor steals the Martin baby, toddler Mary Louise Miller (actually a doll), and carries her off to his mountain lair. Aided by Mrs. John Martin (June Marlowe) Rin-Tin-Tin, after breaking free from being tied up, rushes to the rescue. From on top of a rocky peak, the giant bird flaps his wings and hops up and down while Rin-Tin-Tin lunges at him and barks. Finally the two contenders (now represented by stuffed animals) fall off the cliff in a rotating embrace to crash on the ground below. Rin-Tin-Tin survives and is vindicated. (No one who made the movie cared, or maybe knew, that a condor exists mostly on carrion, and therefore was unlikely to be a killer. Nor did they care that the "night cry" for which the movie was named – the "weird cry" sounding somewhat like a scream that the condor was supposed to emit – didn't exist either. [Because it has no vocal cords, the condor can only grunt and hiss.])

Billing: Rin-Tin-Tin is the star.

Reviews: Mordaunt Hall, reporting in *The New York Times* on audience reaction at an afternoon showing at the Warners Theatre, commented: "There were groans when an eagle [sic] swooped down on a child and supposedly carried it away to the rocky heights, and the youngsters thought that neither Rin-Tin-Tin nor the woman would ever get free in time to rescue the little girl." *Picture Play* said, "Rin-Tin-Tin is more amazing than ever. I shouldn't be a bit surprised to hear that he was to try 'Dr. Jekyll and Mr. Hyde,' and it's going to be no time at all before he is photographed in a dressing gown smoking a pipe." *Time* panned the movie: "There has never yet been a dog film that had a sensible plot. This one is the usual string of improbabilities pieced together to give Rin-Tin-Tin a chance." *Film Daily* enthused:

> This is the dog picture of them all. Rinty better than ever in a picture that screams boxoffice from start to finish. . . .[N]ever has this dog's intelligence been tried to the extent that it is here. . . .built of meller hokum, but it's the best, most sure-fire hokum that has come to light in many a day. Story carries an unmistakable punch and unwinds amid an atmosphere of suspense and thrills that doesn't merely skim the surface.

Filmography

A Hero of the Big Snows (July 24, 1926)

Five reels

Cast:

Rin-Tin-Tin	Rin-Tin-Tin
Alice Calhoun	Mary Malloy
Don Alvarado	Ed Nolan
Leo Willis	Black Beasley
Mary Jane Milliken	The baby

Directors: Herman C. Raymaker (Director)
    Gene Anderson (Assistant Director)
Writer: Ewart Adamson (Scenario and Story)
Photography: Ed Du Par (Camera)
    Walter Robinson (Assistant Camera)

Copyright: Warner Brothers Pictures, October 7, 1926, Number: LP22902
Silent. Black and white
Availability: Lost

Plot Summary:

Ed Nolan (Don Alvarado) is something of a ne'er-do-well until he meets Rin-Tin-Tin, who is being abused by bad guy Black Beasley (Leo Willis) at a trading post in the Canadian woods. Rinty follows Ed home, but won't enter his shabby cabin, so Ed takes him to Mary Malloy (Alice Calhoun), his sometime girl friend, who considers Ed shiftless. Rinty brings them together, and Ed straightens up. A wolf bites Mary's little sister (Mary Jane Milliken) on the hand, and Rinty fights the wolf to save her. Mary suspects that Rinty is the culprit because he has blood on his paws. However, Rinty gets away before anyone can kill him. Meanwhile, the baby gets sick and Mary takes off in a blinding snowstorm with a dog team to find a doctor. A tree falls, the team bolts, and

Mary and baby are left stranded in the woods. Shooting with an empty gun, Mary tries to fight off a pack of wolves until Rinty, who has followed her, intervenes and saves them. Mary gives him a note to take to Ed, who brings a rescue party.

Billing: Though Rin-Tin-Tin had a new female co-star in Alice Calhoun, he still received top billing.

Reviews: Mae Timee in the *Chicago Daily Tribune* called the movie a pot boiler "with nothing to recommend it but the fine and sincere work of Rin-Tin-Tin and a good snowstorm." She found the acting "nice," the story "uninspiring," the situations "unlikely." She ended with "Here's wishing the beautiful brute better luck next time!" The theater manager of the Kansas City Pantages theater, reporting in *The Reel Journal*, was prosaic, noting that business was "good," audience reaction "very good," but that the only production highlight was "Rinty." He gave the movie seventy-five percent in "entertainment merits."

Filmography

While London Sleeps (November 27, 1926)

Six reels

Cast:

Rin-Tin-Tin	Rinty
Helene Costello	Dale Burke
Walter Merrill	Thomas Hallard
John Patrick	Foster
Otto Matieson	London Letter
George Kotsonaros	The Monk
DeWitt Jennings	Inspector Burke
Carl Stockdale	Stokes
Les Bates	Long Tom

Director: Howard P. Bretheton
    William Cannon (Assistant Director)
Writer: Walter Morosco (Scenario and Story)
Photography: Frank Kesson (Camera)
    Fred West (Assistant Camera)

Copyright: Warner Brothers Pictures, November 29, 1926 (LP23394)
Silent. Black and white
Availability: Lost

Plot Summary:

In this melodrama of crooks and "crookesses," criminal London Letter (Otto Matieson) controls a man-monster, The Monk (George Kotsonaros), who kills for him, and a wonderful dog, Rinty – as well as the Limehouse District of London. When Inspector Burke (DeWitt Jennings) comes close to catching his gang, Rinty stops him, and the gang kills its betrayer, Foster (John Patrick). Rinty loses a fight against another dog. Dale Burke (Helene Costello), the inspector's daughter, saves Rinty and he changes sides. Monk, directed by Letter, overpowers Dale's sweetheart (Walter Merrill), then kidnaps Dale and holds her hostage. Letter, after being wounded by Burke and his men, dies. Rinty vanquishes Monk in a spectacular battle.

Billing: Rin-Tin-Tin stars.

Reviews: "Rush," reviewing for *Variety*, was scathing: "Mystery about this one. On the face it must have been made several years ago at least, and then shelved as a weak sister." The woman actor wore clothes from three years before, the photography was bad, and the action "slow-motion." One scene in particular, when the ape-man sneaks into the heroine's bedroom to abduct her, aroused his contempt: "The thrill is canceled when anybody can see that the ape-man is being hoisted through the trees to the bedroom window by a cable hooked to the back of his coat." It was not only that the acting was bad: "The picture ought to have been left to rest on the shelves for the sake of the good name of the Warner Brothers." However, Rin-Tin-Tin was "the only convincing actor in the outfit, and gets more closeups in an hour than Gloria Swanson ever enjoyed." Paul Thompson in *Motion Picture News* agreed:. "I have not seen any picture in months that so vividly recalls the old melodramas of the ten-twenty-thirty-cent days. . . . EXPLOITATION ANGLES. The star's popularity. . . . DRAWING POWER. Good in cheaper houses."

Filmography

Hills of Kentucky (February 19, 1927)

Seven reels

Cast:

Rin-Tin-Tin	Grey Ghost
Jason Robards Sr.	Steve Harley
Dorothy Dwan	Janet
Tom Santschi	Ben Harley
Billy Kent Schaefer	Davey
Nanette	Herself

Director: Howard Bretherton
Assistant Director: Ted Stevens
Writers: Edward Clark (Scenario)
    Dorothy Yost (Story)
Cinematographer: Frank Kesson
Victor Vance (Art Titles)
Based on "The Untamed Heart," a story by Dorothy Yost

Silent. Black and white
Released in Germany in 1928, in Finland on April 30, 1928
Availability: Sometimes on tape (VCR)

Plot Summary:

    The Grey Ghost (Rin-Tin-Tin), leader of a pack of dogs abandoned by their owners in a time of famine, has a $500 price on his head. The pack has been living off the resources of a poor mountain hamlet in the Blue Ridge Mountains, which has little enough as it is. Just as the two main male characters – Ben Harley (Tom Santschi) and his half-brother Steve (Jason Robards) – are polar opposites (Cain and Abel), so the community is split between those who want education and those who disdain it. The schoolteacher, Janet (Dorothy

Dwan), is a catalyst for change. And so is her little crippled brother, Davey (Billy Kent Schaefer), who, unafraid, befriends the wounded Grey Ghost by giving him water and petting him – in an instant, the Grey Ghost goes from feral to tame. Meanwhile, Janet and Steve are falling in love, and Ben, who wants Janet for himself, hates it, so much so that he shoots Steve in a fight. Villagers who adhere to the dark side succeed in capturing Nanette, who has remained faithful to the Grey Ghost. The pack itself, having lost the Grey Ghost to human society, adopts another leader.

The heroic Grey Ghost manages to save Davey from the pack of dogs by fighting them off with sheer force, free Nanette by sagacious use of subterfuge, drown the villain in the river, and swim to the rescue of the heroine, who is tied to a raft speeding through the rapids towards the waterfall.

In the last scene, Steve and Janet are married and have a child. Grey Ghost and Nanette are living with them.

Billing: Rin-Tin-Tin had top billing.

Reviews: "Fred," reviewing for *Variety*, said *Hills of Kentucky* was "surefire with any audience, and with dog lovers it can't miss. " He added, "It's a 'best of show' bet, and if you know dog shows, you know what that means."

Filmography

Tracked by the Police (May 7, 1927)

Six reels

Cast:

Rin-Tin-Tin	Satan
Jason Robards Sr.	Bob Owen
Virginia Browne Faire	Marcella Bradley
Tom Santschi	"Sandy" Sturgeon
Nanette	Satan's girlfriend
Dave Morris	"Wyoming" Willie
Theodore Lorch	"Bull" Storm
Wilfred North	Tom Bradley
Ben Walker	Crook

Director: Ray Enright
Eddie Sowders (Assistant Director)
Writers: Gregory Rogers (Story)
   Darryl F. Zanuck and Johnnie Grey (Scenario)
Photography: Ed Du Par
Editor: Owen Marks

Copyright: Warner Brothers Pictures, April 30, 1927 (LP23900)
Availability: On DVD

Plot Summary:

Satan (Rin-Tin-Tin) saved the life of Bob Owen (Jason Robards Sr.) during World War I, and he goes on to rescue him again, along with his girlfriend Marcella (Virginia Brown Faire), daughter of Owen's boss, Tom Bradley (Wilfred North). In addition, by defeating bad guy Sandy Sturgeon (Tom Santschi), Satan saves the desert reclamation project that Owen is helping to build to bring water to the arid Arizona desert. It's not that easy: Sturgeon and his henchmen kidnap Marcella and Princess, Marcella's dog (Nanette), and lock up Owen. By various means, including climbing and descending a ladder, turning a lock mechanism to stop the water, and untying knots, Satan succeeds in rescuing them all, including Princess.

Billing: Rin-Tin-Tin stars.

Reviews: The reviewer for *The New York Times* marveled at Rin-Tin-Tin's achievements in the movie:

> Rin-tin-tin not only does heroic stunts, but he is made to act as if he reasoned out things. It seemed quite natural for this police dog to tug on a bolt until he succeeded in opening the door, and one is not surprised when Rin-tin-tin escapes through the back of a grandfather clock, but his exploits in determining the levers that close the locks seems [sic] like asking too much of any animal. However, through the reaction to instruction, Rinty, as the dog is known in this story, accomplishes the feat of stopping the turbulent waters. It is no wonder that the villain in this yarn always calls Rinty "that devil-dog."

Time agreed, saying that Rinty (the character) "not only saves the dam by a display of amazing engineering but also ducks all the bullets flying in his direction."

Location: Yuma, Arizona; the Laguna Dam and reclamation project across the Colorado River

Filmography

Jaws of Steel (September 10, 1927)

Six reels

Cast:

Rin-Tin-Tin	Rinty
Jason Robards Sr.	John Warren
Helen Ferguson	Mary Warren
Mary Louise Miller	Baby Warren
Jack Curtis	Thomas Grant Taylor
Robert Perry	The Sheriff
Buck Connors	Alkali Joe

Director: Ray Enright
Assistant Director: Joe Barry
Writers: Gregory Rogers (Story)
    Charles R. Condon and Darryl F. Zanuck (Scenario)
Photography: Barney McGill

Copyright: Warner Brothers Pictures, August 30, 1927 (LP24343)
Availability: Lost

Plot Summary:

Rinty (Rin-Tin-Tin) is a puppy traveling across the desert in a "rickety flivver" with his family, John Warren (Jason Robards Sr.), Warren's wife, Mary (Helen Ferguson), and their little girl, Baby Warren (Mary Louise Miller). The family has spent their savings on a house and gold claim in Calvao, a California desert town. Searching for the little girl's doll, Rinty becomes lost and grows up with a reputation of being a killer, a "wild, wolfish savage," a "fierce, bristling wolf-dog." He has a price on his head. Meanwhile, the Warrens find that Calvao is a ghost town, but they move into the house anyway. Though the locals hunt him, Rinty takes a chance and goes to visit Baby, whom he has always remembered. A crooked promoter, Taylor (Jack Curtis), makes a pass at Mary, but John saves her. Meanwhile, John and an old prospector, Alkali Joe (Buck Connors), have struck gold. Trying to steal the claim, Taylor kills Joe. Rinty attacks Taylor, but Taylor escapes. Rinty's bloody footprints ("clawlike marks") provide an erroneous clue that he is the killer. Rinty goes to the Warren house, where he watches over Baby, who is sick. This convinces Mary that he is indeed their long-lost dog. A posse chases Rin-Tin-Tin, and he is injured while trying to get away. He comes back, Baby gets well, he shows the humans who the real culprit is, and he himself is saved.

Billing: Though Rin-Tin-Tin had top billing, reviews and ads mentioned the "unusually strong human cast to support him" – especially Jason Robards, Helen Ferguson, and the child actress Mary Louise Miller.

Reviews: *Variety* noted that: "The dog star is still a knockout. That's all there is to this picture, but it's enough to carry it over successfully in the split weeks and daily changes." Otherwise the reviewer slammed the picture as too long and monotonous – "except when the dog is in action. Every movement of the animal is interesting. Even at play, and not doing tricks, he is a spellbinder. Some of his actions are almost human and as a trouper he ranks far above the regular run of two-legged actors appearing in films."

Filmography

A Dog of the Regiment (October 29, 1927)

Five reels

Cast:
Rin-Tin-Tin . . . . Rinty
Dorothy Gulliver . . . . Marie von Waldorf
Tom Gallery . . . . Richard Harrison
John Peters . . . . .Eric von Hager

Directors: D. Ross Lederman (Director)
 Joe Barry (Assistant Director)
Writer: Charles R, Condon (Scenario)
Based on a short story of the same name by Albert S. Howson
Photography: Ed Du Par (Director of Photography)
Film Editor: Clarence Kolster

Copyright: Warner Brothers Pictures, October 20, 1927, Number: LP24546
Silent. Black and white
Availability: Lost

Plot Summary:

Based on Rin-Tin-Tin's supposed World War I experience in France, the movie begins before the war starts. Rinty (Rin-Tin-Tin), is the pet of Marie von Waldorf (Dorothy Gulliver), a German girl. Both girl and dog fall in love with Dick Harrison (Tom Gallery), an American lawyer who is helping her settle an estate. Dick accuses her unscrupulous legal counsel and family friend, Eric von Hager (John Peters), of serving his own financial interests and of wanting Marie for himself.

When the war breaks out, Harrison becomes an aviator ace. Marie is a Red Cross nurse, Rinty a Red Cross dog, Von Hager a captain in the German army. Harrison is shot down behind German lines and trapped in his burning plane. Rinty saves Harrison's life, but the Germans capture him. When Von Hager forges a general's signature on an order of execution for Harrison, Rinty helps Harrison escape. Harrison steals a plane, and he and Rinty fly to the American side together. After the war, the two become reunited with Marie, and Rinty barks with happiness as the two human lovers embrace.

Billing: Rin-Tin-Tin had top billing.

Reviews: *Variety* gave the movie a short review, about one-third of a column long: "This dog picture is better than average, and should draw well among the younger element." If the review from *Variety* was lukewarm, distributors liked it: Mrs. Victor Cason of Osceola, Missouri, said it was "[o]ne of the very best it has been our good fortune to play. It's a Warner Bros. Classic, and a real one, too. When you have a chance, just sign the dotted line and feel contented. Warner Bros. will do the rest."

The *Los Angeles Times* reported:

> Rinty was responsible for a large turnout on the part of members of the younger generation. They overflowed the seats, perched upon parents' laps, and occasionally in tense moments, such as when Rinty, in the picture, dangled by his teeth from a rope over the side of an airplane, fell into the aisle. They were an unusually appreciative audience.

The 1927 *National Board of Review* magazine also saw it as a family movie: "For the family audience including children."

Filmography

A Race for Life (January 26, 1928)

Five reels

Cast:

Rin-Tin-Tin	Rinty
Virginia Browne Faire	Virginia Calhoun
Carroll Nye	Robert Hammond
Robert Gordon	Danny O'Shea
Jim Mason	Bruce Morgan
Pat Hartigan	Tramp

Directors: D. Ross Lederman (Director)
    Chauncy Pyle (Assistant Director)
Writers: Charles R, Condon (Story and Scenario)
    James A. Starr (Titles)
Photography: Ed Du Par (Director of Photography)
Film Editor: Charles Henkel Jr.

Copyright: Warner Brothers Pictures, January 18, 1928, Number: LP24891
Silent with sound sequence (also silent version). Black and white. Vitaphone music score
Availability: Lost

Plot Summary:

After hoboing on trains around the country, Rinty and his child pal, Danny O'Shea (Robert Gordon), end up at a race track. Danny has ambitions of becoming a jockey and quickly achieves them when he is chosen to ride the number one horse, Black Raider, in a sweepstakes race. However, the owner of the stable, Bruce Morgan (Jim Mason), wanting his own horse to win the race, makes an attempt to injure Black Raider, and when Rinty attacks him, Rinty is blinded – though temporarily. Danny rescues Rinty and hides him, but then he himself is kidnapped by the bad guys. In true Rin-Tin-Tin spirit, the dog escapes and frees Danny just in time so he can compete in the big race. Black Raider (and Danny) win the race by half a length, at least partly because Rin-Tin-Tin is urging them on by running behind them barking. There is a romantic subplot between Virginia Calhoun (Virginia Browne Faire) and Robert Hammond (Carroll Nye).

Billing: Rin-Tin-Tin is the star.

Reviews: *Variety* predicted that *A Race for Life* would enjoy limited popularity:

> Enjoyment of a picture such as this requires a naive and sentimental disposition plus a regard for dogs. Where and when dog pictures are exhibited in big cities it is invariably as one-half of a double-feature bill. . . . In the smaller communities, however, the dog opera can and does stand alone, unaided and unapologetic. For these stands, "A Race for Life" will probably be okay. There is enough heart tug of a sort to have the kids whistling at Saturday matinees.

A note in *Motion Picture Times* by John Kamuda, a small town theater owner in Massachusetts, confirmed *Variety*'s prediction: "A Race for Life, Rin-Tin-Tin.– A good dog story which drew the crowd as everybody likes this dog star."

Filmography

Rinty of the Desert (April 21, 1928)

Five reels

Cast:

Rin-Tin-Tin	Rinty
Audrey Ferris	June
Carroll Nye	Pat Casey
Paul Panzer	Mike Doyle
Otto Hoffman	Pop Marlow

Directors: D. Ross Lederman (Director)
    Henry Blanke (Assistant Director)
Writers: Harvey Gates (Scenario)
    Frank Steele (Story)
    James A. Starr (Titles)
Director of Photography: Frank Kesson

Copyright: Warner Brothers Pictures, October 4, 1928 (LP25148)
Silent. Black and white with sound sequence by Vitaphone
Availability: Lost

Plot Summary:

Rinty, an outcast lost as a puppy in the desert but grown into a "wolf-dog," hitchhikes his way into town on a truck. Pop Marlow (Otto Hoffman) and his lovely grand-daughter, June (Audrey Ferris), who keep a small dime museum, adopt him. Rinty in return adopts a litter of puppies and befriends Mary's sweetheart, policeman Pat Casey (Carroll Nye). All goes well until Pop fires his employee/partner, Mike Doyle (Paul Panzer), who has forced himself on Mary. Pop disappears, and Mary, suspecting foul play, asks Pat to use Rinty's detective powers to find him. Rinty trails Pop to a gang hangout where Pop has been imprisoned by Doyle's gang. The gang's vicious bulldog attacks Pat, but the light is bad, and Pat thinks Rinty is the attacker. He vows he will shoot him. However,

Rinty escapes, revenges himself on the bulldog, rescues Mary and Pat from a deep pit in snake territory, and is vindicated.

Billing: Rin-Tin-Tin was the star, though Ferris and Nye were mentioned in ads.

Reviews: *Variety*'s reviewer complained that *Rinty of the Desert* was similar to other movies in which Rin-Tin-Tin starred and had "most improbable situations." He added that it would "entertain [the] majority who like that stuff" and the "[p]icture could stand elimination of the rest of meaningless bedroom scenes and shots of country streets." Theater managers were more enthusiastic: Warren L. Weber of the Ellinwood theater in Ellinwood, Kansas, said, "Draws the kids and action fans in. Everybody likes this clever dog star." And Glenn M. Deeter of the Liberty theater in Norcatur, Kansas, liked it, too: "It's a real picture."

Filmography

Land of the Silver Fox (October 13, 1928)

Seven reels

Cast:

Rin-Tin-Tin	Rinty
Leila Hyams	Marie du Fronque
John Miljan	James Crawford
Carroll Nye	Carroll Blackton
Tom Santschi	Butch Nelson
Princess Neola	The Squaw
Nanette	Nanette the Dog

Director: Ray Enright
Writers: Howard Smith (Scenario and Dialogue)
    Charles R. Condon (Story)
Photography: Frank Kesson (Director)
Film Editor: Owen Marks

Copyright: Warner Brothers Pictures, September 10, 1928 (LP25704)
Sound (also silent). Black and white
Availability: Lost

Plot Summary:

The plot of this movie of the Northwest has echoes of *Where the North Begins*. When trapper hero Carroll Blackton (Carroll Nye) sees evil trading-camp manager James Crawford (John Miljan) hitting beaten-down hang-dog Rinty, he buys the dog with the furs he was going to sell to be able to marry Marie du Fronque (Leila Hymans), Crawford's French ward. As is usual in this genre, Crawford is in love with his ward and will do almost anything to keep her from marrying another. He entrusts a sled-load of furs to Blackton and hires Butch Nelson (Tom Santschi) to follow and kill him. Nelson succeeds in taking the furs from Blackton and is fighting him when Rinty intervenes with a fierce attack. The killer escapes, leaving Blackton for dead. Rinty saves him from a timber wolf. By the time Blackton makes it back to the post, Crawford is about to marry Marie, but before he can do anything about it, Mounties arrest him for stealing furs. Rinty again comes to the rescue and makes Nelson confess to the crime. Nanette shows up with seven puppies.

Billing: Rin-Tin-Tin is the star.

Reviews: *Variety* gave *Land of the Silver Fox* a decent but half-hearted review: "It can't miss with the kids in the neighborhoods where Rinty brings 'em in." The *Oakland Tribune* agreed about the audience, but was more enthusiastic about Rin-Tin-Tin:

> "Land of the Silver Fox" will be most interesting to the younger generation and their elders will also find much to applaud. This reviewer had never seen Rin-Tin-Tin before and thus had an opportunity to marvel at the manner in which this police dog takes direction. Second rate actors could learn plenty from him if they would.

The trade papers were lukewarm towards the movie. *Film Daily* reported that it had no "particular new [story] angles" and showed "a tendency toward obvious theatrics." However, "[e]specially in the titles, the production stacks up well with other dog pictures."

Location: Yosemite National Park.

Filmography

Frozen River (April 20, 1929)

Six reels

Cast

Rin-Tin-Tin	Lobo
Davey Lee	Billy
Raymond McKee	Jerry
Nina Quartero	Jane
Josef Swickard	Hazy
Frank Campeau	Potter
Lew Harvey	Pierre

Director: F. Harmon Weight
Writers:
    Anthony Coldeway (Scenario)
    Harry Behn (Adaptation)
    John F. Fowler (Story)
    James A. Starr (Dialogue)
Director of Photography: Nelson Laraby
Film Editor: Harold McLemon
Musical Score: Louis Silvers

Copyright: Warner Brothers Pictures, November 4, 1929, Number: LP 289
Silent with talking and barking sequence, musical score by Vitaphone
Availability: Lost

Plot Summary:

    The dog instincts of Lobo (Rin-Tin-Tin), a husky raised by wolves since he was a puppy, drive him to leave his pack and befriend human beings, but those he finds first so mistreat him that he turns outlaw. Known as Killer, he is alleged to have attacked men; a $100 reward is offered for his capture. In the woods, Lobo meets a little boy, Billy (Davey Lee), who, not knowing his reputation, approaches him fearlessly, with "laughing affection" that wins him over. Lobo grows fond of Billy and his family – his sister, Jane (Nina Quartero), and their grandfather, Hazy (Josef Swickard), a "crazy" old prospector who has hidden some gold in a cabin north of Frozen River. Jane's sweetheart, Jerry (Raymond McKee), an engineer, helps to tame Lobo. Meanwhile, a miner named Potter (Frank Campeau) and a French halfbreed, Pierre (Lew Harvey), plot to get the gold and the girl. They kidnap Billy and threaten to torture him unless Jane tells them where the gold is. Lobo, having enlisted Jerry, rushes to the rescue and attacks Pierre, who escapes to safety in the wilderness. Lobo finds Potter wrestling with Jerry on the edge of a cliff, pushes Potter over the cliff to his death, and then intercepts the dogsled in which little Billy rides alone hurtling towards the cliff.

Billing: Starred with Davey Lee (at least in the beginning).

Reviews: *Variety* panned *Frozen River*'s sound, concluding that the movie "should not be worth more in prices over the silent versions than the per cent of the dialog it contains." There was little dialogue (Davey Lee did not speak at all) and "badly synchronized barking," acting only to "slow down the story"; therefore it was "little better than Rinty's usual silents." Moreover the story was "jumpy" and mundane. And the acting? The female lead was so "camera conscious" that it showed "in every move." On the other hand, "Rinty does his usual as the beast who is savage until the right people come along." "Spatz," writing in *Movie Age*, summed it up:

> This is a typical dog picture bound to click with the many Rin-Tin-Tin admirers. . . . Nothing particularly new but a well selected cast and interesting episodes depicting the taming of Rin-Tin-Tin. It should gather the sheckles [sic] from the canine fans.

The manager of Milwaukee's Majestic reported: "Business: Fair. Summary: Good acting by Davey Lee and Rin-Tin-Tin with splendid scenery. Entertainment Merits: 80 per cent."

Filmography

The Million Dollar Collar (June 12, 1929)

Six reels

Cast:

Rin-Tin-Tin . . . . Rinty
Matty Kemp . . . . Bill Holmes
Evelyn Pierce . . . . .Mary French
Philo McCullough . . . . .Joe French
Tom Dugan . . . . Ed Mack
Allan Cavan . . . . The Chief
Grove Ligon . . . . .Scar

Director: D. Ross Lederman
Writers: Robert Lord (Scenario, Story, Dialog)
    James A. Starr (Titles)
Director of Photography: Nelson Laraby
Film Editor: William Holmes

Copyright: Warner Brothers Pictures, October 1, 1929, Number: LP1
Silent with music, talking and barking sequences. Black and white

Availability: Lost

Plot Summary:

    Without knowing it, the upright Rinty (Rin-Tin-Tin), separated from his owner, a seaman, plays a thief in this crook melodrama as the canine companion of a man who pretends to be a blind beggar but is neither. Gangsters steal a pearl (or diamond) necklace in a daring robbery in broad daylight in a big city, sew it inside Rin-Tin-Tin's collar, then effect an escape in a car, which hurtles over a cliff. The crash kills the man, but Rin-Tin-Tin, tied to the car, survives. Along comes a kind young man, Bill Holmes (Matty Kemp), who takes him home. When the thieves kidnap the good samaritan, Rin-Tin-Tin joins up with a soft-hearted female thief, Mary French (Evelyn Pierece), wanting to go straight. They hole up in a hotel in the mountains. As usual, Rin-Tin-Tin and his human confederates foil the gangsters' plans. In the end, he is reunited with his original owner.

Billing: Rin-Tin-Tin has top billing.

Reviews: Though the movie was not favorably revewed, the *Los Angeles Times* liked it: ". . . provides thrills for the kiddies and some grown-ups. . . . Rinty reveals the hiding place by scratching his neck and barking loudly. The barks are recorded." This short review was part of a longish article about the bill at the Pantages featuring a road show, "Mitzi's Revels of 1929," in which Hadji Ali, "Human Volcano," swallowed a gallon of water, "thirty hazelnuts and a pitcher of kerosene," which he "rids himself of. . .in a most novel manner"; a ventriloquist, and two "girls . . .in a piano and violin offering" with saxophone, and a juggler." The ending sentence was: "A Pathe talking and sound news completes the bill."

Filmography

Tiger Rose (December 21, 1929)

Six reels

Cast:

Monte Blue	Devlin
Lupe Velez	Rose
H.B. Warner	Dr. Cusick
Tully Marshall	Hector McCollins
Grant Withers	Bruce
Gaston Glass	Pierre
Bull Montana	Joe
Rin-Tin-Tin	Scotty
Slim Summerville	Heine
Louis Mercier	Frenchie
Gordon Magee	Hainey
Heine Conklin	
Gus	
Leslie Sketchley	Mounted Police Officer

Alphabetical list of rest of cast:

Emile Chautard	Undetermined Role (uncredited)
Cy Clegg	Undetermined Role (uncredited)
Fred MacMurray	Rancher (uncredited)
Georgia Mazetti	Undetermined Role (uncredited)
Chief Yowlachie	Undetermined Role (uncredited)

Director: George Fitzmaurice
Writers:
    Harvey Thew (Dialogue)
    Gordon Rigby (Scenario)
    De Leon Anthony (Titles)
Director of Photography: Tony Gaudio
Film Editor: Thomas Pratt

Sound Engineer: Harvey Cunningham

Copyright: Warner Brothers Pictures, Inc., December 3, 1929, Number: LP882
Vitaphone: released both in silent and sound versions
Availability: Lost.

Plot Summary:
Adapted from the hit play of the same name by Willard Mack and produced by David Belasco, *Tiger Rose* tells of Canadian country people who fight against modernization. The eponymous "half-caste" heroine, Rose (Lupe Velez) – beautiful, passionate, and wild – has cut a romantic swath through the territory, but has settled on a young engineer, Bruce (Grant Withers), who is there to help build a railroad. Nutty Dr. Cusick (H. B. Warner), who hates the railroad and over-protects Rose, overhears them plan to elope and attacks Bruce, intending to kill him. However, the doctor is the one who ends up dead. Devlin (Monte Blue), the Irish Northwest Mounted sergeant who also loves Rose, pursues the couple. Devlin finally lets the couple go because he loves Rose, telling the people back home that they had "gone over the rapids" and died.

Billing: Rin-Tin-Tin is mentioned in ads, but his name is in much smaller type than those of Monte Blue and Lupe Velez.

Reviews: *Motion Picture Times* said:

This old time stage meller has lost much in the screen transition. The continuity is very jumpy with too much coincidence giving the otherwise dramatic affair a farcical tendency. Lupe Velez, as the French half-caste, supposedly desired by many, leaves much to be desired by the customers. . . . It might slide over fairly well in the neighborhoods but rather doubtful entertainment for the downtown patrons.

A lukewarm *Variety* review called the movie "dated, this minor legend of Manitoba."

Filmography

The Show of Shows (December 28, 1929)

15 reels

Cast:

Frank Fay	Master of Ceremonies
William Courtenay	The Minister
H.B. Warner	The Victim
Hobart Bosworth	Executioner
John Barrymore Jr.	Richard III in *Henry VI, Part III*

The rest of cast list includes 90 individuals. Among them are: Rin-Tin-Tin, Richard Barthelmess, Noah Beery, Monte Blue, Heinie Conklin, Douglas Fairbanks Jr., Beatrice Lillie, Myrna Loy, Ben Turpin, and Loretta Young.

Director: John G. Adolfi
Writers:
    J. Keirn Brennan (Writer)
    Frank Fay (Writer)
    William Shakespeare (uncredited)
Producer: Darryl F. Zanuck
Cinematographer: Barney McGill
Sound Department: Harvey Cunningham (Sound Engineer)
Camera and Electrical Department: Paul Ivano (Director of Photography)
Miscellaneous Crew:
    Larry Ceballos (Dance Director)
    Jack Haskell (Dance Director)

Copyright: Warner Brothers Pictures, Inc.
Availability: DVD

Rin-Tin-Tin: The Movie Star

Plot Summary: This is a musical revue, with many stars, that cost over $800,000 to make. The beginning production number had "192 girls arranged 16 abreast and 12 rows deep." Warner contract players perform in a variety of skits and musical numbers. John Barrymore Jr. recites Richard III's soliloquy from *Henry VI*. There actually is no plot.

Billing: Rin-Tin-Tin is a bit player. He merely introduces "Chinese Fantasy."

Reviews: *Variety* bemoaned the movie's lack of wide film and wide screen, lack of color in some places, the long production numbers, lack of comedy. It did not mention Rin-Tin-Tin at all.

Filmography

On the Border (March 15, 1930)

Five reels

Cast:

Rin-Tin-Tin	Rinty
Armida	Pepita
John B. Litel	Dave
Philo McCullough	Farrell
Bruce Covington	Don José
Walter Miller	Border Patrol Commander
William Irving	Dusty

Director: William McGann
Writer: Lillie Hayward (Story, scenario, and dialogue)
Photography: William Rees
Sound: Dolph Thomas (Recording engineer)

Copyright: Warner Brothers Pictures, Inc., February 18, 1930 (LP1085)
Black and white, sound by Vitaphone
Availability: Lost

Plot Summary:

Considered to be Rin-Tin-Tin's "first talking picture," *On the Border* takes place on the Texas-Mexico border, where a gang is smuggling Chinese workers into the United States. Five smugglers mask their activities by transporting vegetables, as well as contraband men, in trucks, but Rin-Tin-Tin, who belongs to Don José (Bruce Covington), a poor but aristocratic rancher, sniffs them out. Farrell (Philo McCullough), the head gang member, wants Pepita (Armida), Don José's daughter, and plans to buy the ranch from its San Francisco owners to use as headquarters while he woos her. Dave (John B. Litel) and Dusty (William Irving), two border agents disguised as tramps, figure out what's going on. Pepita and Rin-Tin-Tin become attached to Dave, whom the gang kidnaps.

Rinty rescues him after a terrific fight in which sixty people are saved. Farrell tries to escape in a car, but Rin-Tin-Tin overpowers him. In the end, the smugglers are defeated and the lovers united, with Rinty between them.

Billing: Rin-Tin-Tin is the star.

Reviews: The *New York Times* panned *On the Border* as:

> a trite bit of cinematography featuring Rin-Tin-Tin, the dog star who runs away with all honors. . . .The story, of the smuggling-across-the-border variety, is as banal as it is audible. In sonorous array, and punctured with the bark of revolvers, after which a smuggler bites the dust, the yarn of a tramp who turned out to be Captain Dave on government duty along the border, emerges as tame film fare.

Variety panned it, too ("weak entertainment"), but gave a thumbs-up to Rin-Tin-Tin: "Dialog has seemingly not interfered the slightest with Rinty's work." According to *Motion Picture Times*, "'On the Border' is an entertaining drama with the famous dog again exhibiting its prowess. . . .[after mention of the rest of the cast]. However, the dog is the character who will draw the kids to see this picture."

Location: New Mexico.

Filmography

The Man Hunter (May 3, 1930)

Six reels

Cast:

Rin-Tin-Tin	Rinty
Charles Delaney	Jim Clayton
Nora Lane	Lady Jane Winston
John Loder	George Castle
Pat Hartigan	Crosby
Christiane Yves	Maid
Floyd Shackelford	Simba
Billy Bletcher	Buggs
John Kelly	Charlie
Joe Bordeaux	Dennis

Director: D. Ross Lederman
Writers: James A. Starr (Scenario and Dialogue)
    Lillie Hayward (Story)
Photography: James Van Trees (Director)
Sound: Cal Applegate (Sound Engineer)

Copyright: Warner Brothers Pictures, April 23, 1930 (LP1249)
Sound. Black and white
Availability: Lost

Plot Summary:

In the search for exotic locations, Warner ends up supposedly on Africa's Ivory Coast for *Man Hunter*. Lady Jane Winston (Nora Lane), heiress to a company in the rubber and ivory trade, has traveled there, led by suspicions that the company's manager, George Castle (John Loder), is doctoring the books in order to steal from the company. Rinty (Rin-Tin-Tin), who has sailed on the same ship as Lady Jane, jumps overboard and swims ashore, where he is befriended by beachcomber Jim Clayton (Charles Delaney), who used to work for Lady Jane's company. After Clayton and Rinty rescue Lady Jane from ferocious sharks, the three work together to trap Castle in wrong-doing. Clayton finds some of Castle's hidden ivory, but Castle's men seize him and lock him up. Rin-Tin-Tin carries a message about what has happened to Lady Jane, then helps Jim escape. But Castle isn't done yet. He kidnaps Lady Jane and foments an uprising of Africans against whites. Rin-Tin-Tin finds help at a British outpost, and all is well.

Billing: Rin-Tin-Tin is still the star.

Reviews: *Variety* said:

Clumsily thrown-together melodrama of a type Warners made years ago in their shoestring days. . . .perfunctory heroics that incite laughter rather than thrills spell minuses in practically all departments. Photography and sound recording, however, meritorious. . . .Plot is full of absurdities but essentially it's a case of silly dialog transferred to the screen under unimaginative direction.

Billboard agreed:

The story is the cut-and-dried type that Rinty has had for the past many years. It is left for him to catch the bad men and the director has done everything to show the dog up in the leading role. . . . The production should add to Rin-Tin-Tin's legion of admirers. The sound is okay and no dog lover in America should miss seeing this production.

The critic at *Motion Picture* News didn't like the sets: "Another current Warner release, 'Isle of Escape,' contains many of the same sets. A hotel and rum joint used is identically the same as the indoor stuff in the 'The Man Hunter.' Somebody on the Warner lots apparently thought a lot of the spot. Here's hoping they call it quits."

Rough Waters (June 7, 1930)

Six reels

Cast:

Rin-Tin-Tin	Rinty
Lane Chandler	Cal Morton
Jobyna Ralston	Mary
Edmund Breese	Captain Thomas
Walter Miller	Morris
William Irving	Bill
George Rigon	Fred
Richard Alexander	Little
Skeets Noyes	Davis

Director: John Daumery
Writers: James A. Starr (Adaptation and Story)
   Lillie Hayward (Story)
Photography: William Rees (Director)
Sound: Robert B. Lee (Recording Engineer)

Copyright: Warner Brothers Pictures, May 18, 1930 (LP1310)
Sound. Black and white.
Availability: Lost.

Plot Summary:

At Pacific Palisades on the California Coast, three gangsters – Morris (Walter Miller), Little (Richard Alexander), and Davis (Skeets Noyes) – steal a payroll of $100,000 from a vehicle wrecked by the side of the road. They kill its drivers. Masquerading as government agents, they push their way into a ramshackle fishing hut, the home of old seaman Captain Thomas (Edmund Breese), who is confined to a wheelchair, and his pretty daughter, Mary (Jobyna

Ralston). Mary and a motorcycle cop, Cal Morton (Lane Chandler), who owns a marvelous dog, Rinty (Rin-Tin-Tin), are in love. When Rinty comes as usual with the daily paper, Mary manages to send a note to Cal. Two mail agents, Bill and Fred (William Irving and George Rigon), are captured by the robbers, and on the beach, one of the robbers wounds Cal and Rinty, but that doesn't stop them from keeping the robbers from getting away in a boat. With Bill's help, they handcuff the robbers.

Billing: Rin-Tin-Tin was the star of *Rough Waters*, often with no other actor mentioned in ads, but the picture received less publicity than his earlier ones.

Reviews: *Variety* said: "Okay for the double feature programs. . . . Picture couldn't have cost too much to produce. . . . Nothing much to the shooting nor the fighting here. Recording is good and photography okay."

Filmography

The Lone Defender (1930, later released as a feature in 1934)

12-episode serial

Cast:

Rin-Tin-Tin	Rinty
Walter Miller	Ramon [a.k.a Marco Roberti]
June Marlowe	Dolores Valdez
Joseph Swickard	Juan Valdez
Buzz Barton	Buzz
Lee Shumway	Amos Harkey
Julia Bejarano	Maria, the duenna
Lafe McKee	Sheriff Billings
Arthur Morrison	Limpy
Frank Lanning	Burke
Robert Kortman	Jenkins
Victor Metzetti	Red
Otto Metzetti	Butch
Bob Irwin	Deputy Sheriff
Arthur Metzeth	Dutch
Billy McGowan	Henchman

Director: Richard Thorpe
Producer: Nat Levine
Writers: William P. Burt and Bennett Cohen (Story and Dialogue)
Photography: Ernest Miller
Film Editor: Fred Baine

Black and white, talking
Sound: Disney Recording System; Powers Cinephone Sound System
Availability: On DVD

Plot Summary:
Evil-doers hired by villain Amos Harkey (Lee Shumway) accost Rinty's (Rin-Tin-Tin's) owner, blind prospector Juan Valdez (Joseph Swickard), in a sandstorm so they can find out where his gold mine is. They murder Valdez but

fail in their mission. The map to the mine is engraved on the back of Valdez's watch, but they can't get hold of it because Rinty fights them off. Valdez's partner, Burke (Frank Lanning), escapes, but his mind is severely damaged by the experience. From then on, Rinty frequently attacks the killer, Jenkins (Robert Kortman) without anyone quite realizing why. He is befriended by Ramon (Walter Miller), a mysterious figure who wears a cone-shaped hat and bedecked Mexican clothes, and who speaks with a fake Spanish accent. (It turns out he is really a Justice Department agent named Roberti). The claim jumpers capture Rinty, thinking he will lead them to the mine, but Ramon and his young sidekick, Buzz (Buzz Barton), rescue Rinty. Meanwhile Rinty kills a wolf who has killed a valuable colt (which looks like a mule), but of course Rinty himself is accused of killing the colt. Again Ramon and Buzz save his life. Trying to get the watch, the villains sneak around Dolores's place, in and out of trap doors and tunnels, and somehow the powder house blows up. Harkey captures Burke and makes him lead the way to the mine, while separately Rinty leads Ramon, Dolores, and Buzz there. Rinty fights the wolf again and clears his name of colt-killing. While Harkey seemingly beat them to the claims office, in actuality he ripped out the page where Buzz had filed the claim earlier. Ramon has looked suspiciously like the Cactus Kid, who robs stagecoaches, but it turns out that Harkey is that bad guy.

Billing: Rin-Tin-Tin stars.

Reviews:
"The Lone Defender, Rin-Tin-Tin – A real good serial as good as any I have ever played. It will please." Earl Somerville, Park, Raymond, Minn.

Filmography

The Lightning Warrior (November 1931)

12-episode serial

Cast:

Rin-Tin-Tin	Rinty
Frankie Darro	Jimmy Carter
Hayden Stevenson	Carter
George Brent	Alan Scott
Pat O'Malley	Sheriff A.W. Brown
Georgia Hale	Dianne La Farge
Theodore Lorch	Pierre La Farge
Lafe McKee	John Haden
Frank Brownlee	Angus McDonald
Bob Kortman	Henchman Wells
Dick Dickinson	Henchman Adams
Yakima Canutt	Ken Davis (in Chapter 1), Deputy (in Chapter 8)
Frank Lanning	Indian George/Jim
Bertee Beaumont	Pioneer Woman
Helen Gibson	Pioneer Woman
Steve Clemente	Henchman (uncredited)
William Desmond	Townsman (uncredited)
Cliff Lyons	Henchman (uncredited)
Kermit Maynard	Deputy (uncredited)
George Morrell	Townsman (uncredited)
Bob Reeves	Henchman (uncredited)
Al Taylor	Deputy (uncredited)

Directors: Ben Kline
    Armand Schaefer
Producer: Nat Levine
Writers: Ford Beebe, Wyndham Gittens, Colbert Clark (Screen Play)
Original music: Lee Zahler (uncredited)

Editors: Wyndham Gittens
    Ray Snyder

Sound Department: George Lowerre (Sound Engineer)

Stunts:
    Yakima Canutt, stunt double for George Brent (uncredited)
    Helen Gibson, stunt double for Georgia Hale (uncredited)
    Kermit Maynard, stunts (uncredited)
    Bob Reeves, stunts (uncredited)
    Richard Talmadge, stunts (uncredited)

Music Department
    Lee Zahler (musical director)

Miscellaneous Crew
    Lee Duncan (dog trainer, uncredited)

Production Company: Mascot Pictures
Availability: On DVD.

Plot Summary:

The mysterious Wolf Man, swathed in a sinister black cloak, is fomenting an Indian uprising (to take place at the new moon) in order to wrest the land away from settlers. He sometimes howls. No one knows who he is, but many people in town are suspect. When an agent for the territory does learn who he is, someone kills the agent, and the agent's brother, Alan Scott (George Brent), comes to identify the killer and get him put on trial. Jimmy Carter (Frankie Darro), whose father died at the hands of the Wolf Man, becomes Scott's trusty assistant, along with Rinty (Rin-Tin-Tin), the brother's dog. Gold mines worked by a couple of settlers figure also in the plot.

Billing: Rin-Tin-Tin is the star.

Reviews:
None.

Timeline
The Lives of Rin-Tin-Tin and Lee Duncan

1893
October: Lee (Leland Lavoy) Duncan is born to G.G. (George Grant) and Elizabeth (Lizzie) Duncan in Hanford, California.

1896
October: Marjorie Duncan, Lee's sister, is born.

1897
January: G.G. deserts the family.

1898
March: Lizzie puts Lee and Marjorie in Oakland's Fred Finch Orphanage.

1900
July: Lizzie, Lee, and Marjorie Duncan are living in Visalia, California, with Lee's great-uncle William's daughter's family.

1902
February: Lizzie marries Oscar S. Sampson, farm laborer, in Visalia.

c. 1905-1906
Sampson moves (probably with Lizzie and the children) to Fallbrook, California, near Lizzie's maternal uncle.

1906
A daughter, Shirley or Charlotte, is born to the Sampsons.

1910
May: The Sampsons are living in Burbank, near Los Angeles. Oscar is a day laborer in a poultry yard. Lee may be working as a store clerk in Porterville.

1911-1912

L.L. Duncan is working for Shaver's Grocery in Glendale.

c. 1912

Lee starts working for the B.H. Dyas sporting goods store in Los Angeles; he sells guns and provides information about hunting and fishing to clients.

1916

Oscar, a laborer, and Lizzie Sampson are living on Angeleno Avenue in Burbank.

1917

November: Duncan enlists in the 135th Aero Squadron.

1918

July: Corporal Duncan arrives in France, after training in gunnery in the United States and England.

c. 1918-1919

Rin-Tin-Tin and his sister, Nanette, are born in France; Duncan adopts them.

1919

May: The 135th Aero Squadron arrives back in the United States. Duncan leaves Nanette, sick with distemper and soon to die of it, in Hempstead, Long Island, with German shepherd breeders Leo F. Wanner and his wife, P. T. Barnum's daughter. The Wanners give Lee another female German shepherd, whom he also names Nanette. Duncan, Rin-Tin-Tin, and the new Nanette take the train to California.

Summer: Lee goes back to work at Dyas.

October: Rin-Tin-Tin is featured in a *Los Angeles Times* story when he performs in German shepherd trials at a dog show in Los Angeles.

1920

January: the Sampsons are living in Lankershim, north of Los Angeles. Oscar is now a farm manager. Lee, a sporting goods salesman, is boarding in Los Angeles, and Marjorie is boarding with a family in Lankershim and giving music lessons.

A voter registration list shows Lee, a salesman, living not far from the Sampsons in Lankershim.

1921

Rin-Tin-Tin has a part in *The Man from Hell's River*.

1922

Winter or spring of 1922: Lee marries socialite horsewoman Charlotte Anderson.

January 29: Irving Cummings Productions releases *Man from Hell's River*.

Late February or early March: Rin-Tin-Tin does a winning jump at a dog show and breaks his leg shortly after.

July 23: R-C Pictures releases *My Dad*.

December: Rin-Tin-Tin makes another spectacular jump at a dog show. The jump is filmed by Charlie Jones and made into a short film.

1923

Rin-Tin-Tin fathers a litter of puppies. He has a starring role in *Where the North Begins*, filmed in northern California and Nevada, and Warner awards him a three-year contract. He also has a role in *Shadows of the North*.

July 1: Warner releases *Where the North Begins*.

August: Charlotte is living in Pleasanton.

Mid-August: Contrary to the notion that dog pictures wouldn't play well in big cities, *Where the North Begins* is so popular in Los Angeles that after a week's run at the Alhambra Theater in Los Angeles, the run is extended.

August 27: R-C Pictures releases *Shadows of the North*.

Fall: Duncan and Rin-Tin-Tin go on a three-month tour through the midwest and the east coast to accompany showings of *Where the North Begins*. Their act is "just little impromptu things I had taught Rinty to do before the camera," says Duncan.

October 10: *Chicago Daily Tribune*'s Mae Timee reviews Rin-Tin-Tin's appearance at the McVicker's Theater: "A wonderful animal, that, in the dogsonal appearances he makes at afternoon and evening performances, conducts himself with ease and brilliancy. . . I don't care much for the 'personal appearances' of stars, but Rin-Tin-Tin's bow to the world at large is GOOD!"

October: While Rin-Tin-Tin and Duncan are on the road, Charlotte is showing off the paces of her horse, The Nobleman, at a "frolic" on the Pleasanton Fair Grounds.

1924

According to voter registration records, Oscar S. Sampson, a laborer, is living in Los Angeles on Fulton Avenue. Charlotte is listed in the 1924 Alameda County voting records as Mrs. Charlotte Anderson Duncan of Pleasanton, Republican horsebreeder.

Duncan buys three lots on Club View Drive and builds a house and kennels on them.

Warner releases a Rin-Tin-Tin short, *Hello, Frisco*.

Early March, Rin-Tin-Tin appears in a short film and on stage at the Hillstreet Headliner in Los Angeles.

July: Charlotte, identified as Charlotte Anderson Duncan of Pleasanton, hosts a show for "racing enthusiasts" and exhibits The Nobleman and Firefly (a horse) at Charmeran, her horse ranch in Pleasanton.

August: Charlotte shows her horses at county fairs.

September 1: Warner releases *Find Your Man*, which was filmed at Klamath Falls, Oregon.

November: Charlotte is at a horse show in Portland, where she wins with The Nobleman.

December 1: Warner releases *The Lighthouse by the Sea*, which was filmed at Laguna Beach and Catalina Island, California.

1925

January: Charlotte starts training for the Oakland and Sacramento horse shows.

January: Warner is ostensibly ready to back a world tour for Duncan, Rin-Tin-Tin, and Rin-Tin-Tin's "wife," Nanette (no mention of Duncan's wife). "In fact these pictures (*Where the North Begins*, *Find Your Man*, and *Lighthouse by the Sea*) have met with such remarkable response abroad, that the exhibitors of England, France, Germany, Spain, Australia, and other countries have repeatedly written and cabled to Warner Bros. studios on the coast, requesting Rin-Tin-Tin's personal appearance at their theaters, to satisfy their patrons," says a small-town newspaper. They do not go.

March: Charlotte Anderson Duncan files for divorce.

May 4: Rin-Tin-Tin appears on stage at a Los Angeles movie theater.

July 13: Warner releases *Tracked in the Snow Country*.

September: Rin-Tin-Tin, along with Peter the Great, Cameo, Queen, and "other noted dogs of pictures, in addition to the pedigreed pets of the celebrities of filmland," goes to a party at Grauman's Egyptian theater for the second birthday of "Ilak giant Arctic wolfhound." Following the dog dinner, Rin-Tin-Tin is the "bone-master" for "after-dinner barking."

September 26: Warner releases *Below the Line*. Shortly after, the movie opens at the Electric Theatre in Chillicothe, Ohio, a town of less than 20,000 people, for a two-day engagement. According to the *Chillicothe Constitution*, it is "the premier showing in the United States." The audience is "large and appreciative."

October (early): Rin-Tin-Tin appears in person at the Jubilee Pageant at the Olympic Auditorium in Los Angeles with Herbert Rawlinson, a nautch dancer named Suzette, singer Leo White, and dancer Lillian Woods. He "bark[s] his resentment at the scandalous stories being printed about Southern California."

November 28: Warner releases *Clash of the Wolves*, which was filmed at Joshua Tree and Chatsworth, California.

December: *Below the Line* fills the Forum (a Los Angeles movie house) to capacity.

1926

Oscar Sampson is still on Fulton Avenue. He is now listed as a rancher in voter registration records.

February 27: Warner releases *The Night Cry*, which was filmed in Northern California.

Timeline

March: Rin-Tin-Tin and Duncan leave Los Angeles in a special railroad car for a personal-appearance tour. Cleveland is their first stop.

April (early): Duncan and Rin-Tin-Tin are in New York for a personal appearance at the opening of *The Night Cry* at Warner Theatre.

April 5-9: In the *New York Times* Warner Theater display ad for *The Night Cry*, Rin-Tin-Tin's name is as big as the name of the picture: "RIN-TIN-TIN 'Himself' First time in New York Wonder Dog of the Screen Appears at every show." Rin-Tin-Tin and Duncan do their act at "Every DeLuxe Performance."

May 16: Rin-Tin-Tin goes on the radio, at W-G-N, Chicago. Radio is not new to him as he often takes part at the Warner radio station with stars like Monte Blue, John Barrymore, and Lillian Rich. "He [is] the first of the innumerable movie celebrities that we have escorted into the radio station who didn't exhibit great trepidation or discomfiture at facing the microphone," says Quin A. Ryan, announcer for the station. After his leash and muzzle are taken off, "he step[s] gingerly around the studio, glad for the freedom and heavy carpets, and cocking a suspicious eye at the sounds that emanated from Uncle Walt's toy animals." The radio interview starts with a recounting of his life story, then Duncan leads him through his tricks. On the way out, Rin-Tin-Tin signs the guest book with a red ink paw print. The print joins signatures of other celebrities like Rudolph Valentino, Clarence Darrow, and Red Grange.

July 24: Warner releases *A Hero of the Big Snows*.

August: Duncan and Rin-Tin-Tin are in Syracuse, where Rin-Tin-Tin awards prizes for homeliest, smallest, and largest dog in a contest for children under fifteen at B.F. Keith's Theater. Rin-Tin-Tin is supposedly getting about ten thousand pieces of fan mail a week, mostly from children, who receive a photograph with an autographed paw print in return.

November 27: Warner releases *While London Sleeps*.

1927

February 19: Warner releases *Hills of Kentucky*.

May 7: Warner releases *Tracked by the Police*. Later *Tracked by the Police* is made into a serial novel, written by William B. Courtney and copyrighted by Warner, that runs in newspapers.

June 1: The interlocutory judgment on the Duncan divorce case is entered.

September 19: Warner releases *Jaws of Steel*.

October 29: Warner releases *A Dog of the Regiment*.

1928

Warner releases a Rin-Tin-Tin short (*Famous Warner Brothers Star*)

January 26: Warner releases *A Race for Life*.

March 24: Burglars break into Duncan's house, but don't awaken the sleeping Rin-Tin-Tin (probably in his adjoining kennel). They raid the icebox. Some newspapers report that they also took silverware.

April 21: Warner releases *Rinty of the Desert*. Writers of the press releases use the adjective "riproaringest!" to describe it.

June 4: The final judgment of the Duncan divorce comes through.

October 13: Warner releases *Land of the Silver Fox*, first Rin-Tin-Tin talkie and barkie. The movie is mostly silent, though Rin-Tin-Tin can be heard barking. The movie's ad in the *Washington Post* in December is dwarfed by ads for *Dream of Love* (Joan Crawford), *Uncle Tom's Cabin*, and *Revenge* (with Delores Del Rio).

Winter of 1928-1929: Duncan and Rin-Tin-Tin go on a personal-appearance tour.

1929
Duncan hires an architect to design a music school for his sister Marjorie, who is living in Glendale, and starts work building his beach house.

February 9: Duncan and Rin-Tin-Tin are in Hamilton, Ohio.

April 20: Warner releases *Frozen River*.

June 12: Warner releases *The Million Dollar Collar*, a talkie about "a bobbed-hair bandit and a gang of hard-boiled crooks." In advertisements, Rin-Tin-Tin's name appears in large caps.

December 6: Warner executive P.A. Chase writes a letter to Ralph E. Lewis, of the Los Angeles law firm Freston and Files, about cancelling Rin-Tin-Tin's contract because he thinks that a dog cannot compete against humans in a world of talking pictures.

December 21: Warner releases *Tiger Rose*.

December 28: Warners releases *The Show of Shows*.

1930
January 25: Rin-Tin-Tin and Duncan open at a theater in Cincinnati, the first stop on a five-week vaudeville tour. They visit a crippled children's home.

March: Duncan and Rin-Tin-Tin are on a vaudeville tour.

March 15: Warner releases *On the Border*, filmed in New Mexico.

April: Duncan's mother, Elizabeth Sampson, and Duncan's stepsister, Shirley, 24, are living with Duncan on Club View Drive in Beverly Hills. Their house is valued at $50,000; half belongs to Duncan, half belongs to his mother. Duncan is listed as a director and showman.

May 3: Warner releases *The Man Hunter*.

June 7: Warner releases *Rough Waters*.

June (late): Rin-Tin-Tin knocks over a "make-believe bandit" at a theater where he is appearing on Broadway. Duncan tells the press that he is planning to write a book about Rin-Tin-Tin.

July 4: Rin-Tin-Tin appears at a Warner Bros. theater in Appleton, Wisconsin, in a vaudeville show accompanying a showing of a Sophie Tucker movie, *Honky Tonk*.

July 11: Rin-Tin-Tin and Duncan, with Duncan's sister "Mary," eat dinner at Russ's Roadhouse in Bedford, Pennsylvania.

September: *The Lone Defender* (produced by Mascot Pictures) opens in theaters.

1931

January: Rin-Tin-Tin receives guests at Marjorie Duncan Baker's "new studio home" in North Hollywood, which his money built.

February: A storm destroys Duncan's beach house.

April: Duncan and Rin-Tin-Tin leave Los Angeles for a personal-appearance tour.

August: Rin-Tin-Tin makes an appearance at the Southwest Washington State Fair in Centralia, Washington.

November: Mascot Pictures releases *The Lightning Warrior*.

1932

June 3: The First National Bank of Beverly Hills, where Duncan keeps his money, shuts its doors. Duncan is broke.

August 10: Rin-Tin-Tin dies.

October 18: Mascot Pictures releases *Pride of the Legion*, in which Rin-Tin-Tin Jr., has a part.

1933

September 30: Mascot Pictures releases *Wolf Dog*, a 12-part serial with Rin-Tin-Tin Jr. playing second lead.

1934

September 5: Mascot Pictures releases another serial, *Law of the Wild*, in which Rin-Tin-Tin Jr. again achieves second billing – after Rex the Horse.

1935

March: A deer crashes into Duncan's car on Ventura Boulevard.

May 11: Mascot Pictures releases *The Test*, in which Rin-Tin-Tin Jr. has a part.

August 31: Mascot Pictures releases *The Adventures of Rex and Rinty*, in which Rin-Tin-Tin Jr., is again given second billing after Rex the horse.

December: Rin Tin Tin, Jr., is "on exhibit" at the Palm Springs Dog Show.

1936

January 5: Reliable Pictures releases *Skull and Crown*, a serial starring Rin-Tin-Tin Jr., filmed at Big Bear Lake, California.

January 24: Metro-Goldwyn-Mayer releases *Tough Guy*, a feature film starring Jackie Cooper. Rin-Tin-Tin Jr. plays Cooper's dog.

May: A story about Rin-Tin-Tin Jr. (similar to an earlier one about his father) appears in newspapers: he slept through a burglary.

December: Duncan marries Eva Linden.

1937
February 27: Reliable Pictures releases *The Silver Trail*. Rin-Tin-Tin Jr. is in the cast.

1938
May: Duncan and Rin-Tin-Tin Jr. put on an act in the "Hollywood Vaudeville Frolics," at the Las Palmas Theater.

June: Duncan and Rin-Tin-Tin Jr. go on the radio and put on a personal appearance in Oakland to raise money for the Oakland Community Chest.

October: Duncan and Rin-Tin-Tin Jr. make a personal appearance on the Pageant of Life, a radio program, to raise money for the San Mateo Community Chest.

1939
Metropolitan Pictures releases *Fangs of the Wild*. Rin-Tin-Tin Jr. is in the cast.

July 1: Kenneth J. Bishop Productions releases *Death Goes North*, filmed in British Columbia. Rin-Tin-Tin Jr. is in the cast.

October 13: Twentieth Century Fox releases *Hollywood Cavalcade*, Rin-Tin-Tin Jr.'s last picture.

Appendices

Appendix 1: Backgrounds of the Pilots, Observers, and Enlisted Men of the 135th Aero Squadron

This study is based on lists in squadron histories, one of which included addresses, matched with census records and draft registrations. The findings most likely to be accurate are for those men with names and addresses matching in two records – they appear in the list as perfect/probable matches. Some men appear in more than one category.

Rank	Pilots		Observers		Enlisted	
Total number	26		39		135	
Perfect/probable matches	Number	Percent	Number	Percent	Number	Percent
Total number of matches	18	69	14	36	35	26
college-educated	7	39	12	86	1	3
white collar/lawyer	3	17	2	14		
blue collar					15	43
military when entered 135th	3	17	5	36	2	6
military	8	44	3	21		
student			4	29		
manager	2	11	2	14		
farmer	2	11	1	7	7	20
salesman	5	28			5	14
pilot	1	6				
teacher			1	7	2	6
engineer			2	14	1	3
car/plane related jobs					16	46
Machinist/mechanic	1	6			12	34

Rank	Pilots		Observers		Enlisted	
Possible Matches	Number	Percent	Number	Percent	Number	Percent
Total number of matches	6	20	32	82	52	39
military					20	38
white collar: business/arts/lawyer, etc.			11	34	13	25
blue collar					36	69
manager			1	3	1	2
farmer	1	17			5	10
salesman	2	33	5	16	16	31
teacher			2	6		
engineer	3	50	3	9	4	8
car/plane related jobs			2	6	9	17
machinist/mechanic					17	33

Appendices

Appendix 2: Lee Duncan's Family Trees

(The trees do not include all family members.)

Duncan (Duncan's father's family)

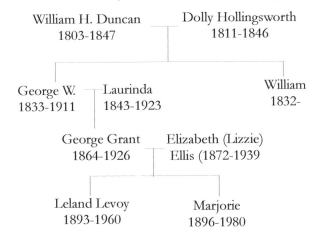

Ellis (Duncan's mother's family)

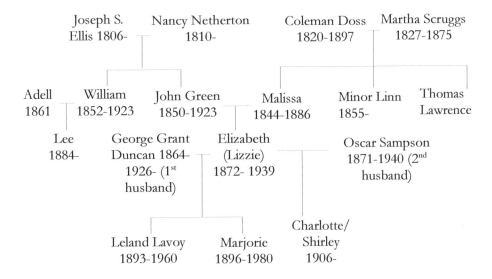

Rin-Tin-Tin and Nanette (Courtesy Rin-Tin-Tin Collection, Riverside, California)

Duncan and the Rin-Tin-Tins (Courtesy Rin-Tin-Tin Collection, Riverside, California).

Sources

Sources listed below do not include most newspaper articles and some magazine articles that were gleaned from http://www.newspaperarchive.com, APS Online, and Proquest Historical Newspapers. If you want a specific citation, please email me at aelwood@ucsd.edu, and I will send it to you.

Rin-Tin-Tin's Movies That Are Available
Where the North Begins (1923) (DVD, Grapevine Video).
The Lighthouse by the Sea (1924) (DVD, Grapevine Video).
Clash of the Wolves (1925) (DVD, part of a boxed set, *More Treasures from American Film Archives 1894-1931)* (Image Entertainment, 2004).
The Night Cry (1926) (DVD, Grapevine Video).
Hills of Kentucky (1927) (VHS, only available used, hard to find.)
Tracked by the Police (1927) (DVD, Grapevine Video).
The Show of Shows (1929((DVD, Warner Bros. Archives)
The Lone Defender (1930) (DVD, Alpha Home Entertainment).
The Lightning Warrior (1931). (DVD, Alpha Home Entertainment).

Preface

Movietone News (1932) http://www.youtube.com/watch?v=_8eECG4DgvE

Dale and Doug Fetherling (editors), *Carl Sandburg at the Movies: A Poet in the Silent Era 1920-1927* (Metuchen, New Jersey and London: The Scarecrow Press, 1985).

James Woodress, *Willa Cather: A Literary Life* (Lincoln, Nebraska: University of Nebraska Press, 1989).

Life, January 25, 1929 (for Goldwyn interview).

Letter from B.F. Yard, Box 7, Rin-Tin-Tin Collection, Riverside, California, Local History Resource Center.

Lee Duncan, *Mr Duncan's Notes*, unpublished manuscript, Box 8, Folders 31-33 (June 21, 1933), Rin Tin Tin Collection, Riverside, California, Local History Resource Center.

James W. English, *The Rin Tin Tin Story* (New York: Dodd, Mead & Company, 1949).

Charles Higham, *Warner Brothers* (New York: Charles Scribner's Sons, 1975).

Sandy Fritz, "Why Dogs Don't Enjoy Music," *Scientific American Mind*, October, 2008.

"The Movies, " Harry Evans, *Life*, July, 1932.

1 The Legend of the Pilot and the War Puppy

Lee Duncan's Story As He Told It

Lee Duncan, *Mr Duncan's Notes*, unpublished manuscript, Box 8, Folders 31-33 (June 21, 1933), Rin Tin Tin Collection, Riverside, California, Local History Resource Center.

James W. English, *The Rin Tin Tin Story* (New York: Dodd, Mead & Company, 1949).

The Story As Told by the Officers and Men of the 135th Aero Squadron

Lawrence L. Smart, *The Hawks that Guided the Guns* (Privately Printed, 1968).

Percival Gray Hart, *History of the 135th Aero Squadron: The 'Statue of Liberty' Observation Squadron in World War I* (Nashville: The Battery Press, 1990). Hart's book is based on his own experiences and those of several other officers who supplied him with reminiscences as well as diaries and letters from World War I.

Second Army Air Service Book (Nancy, France: Berger-Levrault, 1919, and Digital Bookshelf: Digital Version, 2001). The *Second Army Air Service Book* contains some primary sources – letters, for instance.

A Brief History of the 135th Aero Squadron (Observation) (Bordeaux: Imprimerie F. Pech & Cie, 1919).

Letter from Otto Sandman, September 21, 1960, Box 7, Folder 13-H, Rin Tin Tin Collection, Riverside, California, Local History Resource Center.

The History of the 90th Aero Squadron

Leland M. Carver, Gustaf A. Lindstrom, and A.T. Foster (compilers and writers), E. Harold Greist (editor), *The Nineteenth Aero Squadron: American Expeditionary Forces: A History of Its Activities During the World War, from Its Formation to Its Return to the United States* (Hinsdale, Illinois: E.H. Greist, 1920).

Other Soldiers' Letters and Diaries

William Schira, "The Personal Diary of William J. 'Bill' Schira in World War I," http://net.lib.byu.edu/~rdh7/wwi/memoir/Schira/Schira.htm.

Sources

Snoden L. Vance, Co. H, 61st Inf. A.E.F. France (which was at St. Mihiel), "Letters Home from the Great War," Transcribed from the *Pendleton Times*, http://www.rootsweb.com/~wvpendle/pendwwi.htm.

Paul B. Hendrickson. "The Letters, Diary, Postcards and Pictures of a World War I Soldier,"
http://www.jimgill.net/gill/wwipages/diary/pd181117.html.
Http://www.theaerodrome.com

General Histories of the Air Service in the Great War

Maurer Maurer (compiler/editor), *The U.S. Air Service in World War I*, Volume III. (Maxwell AFB Alabama: The Albert F. Simpson Historical Research Center; Washington, D.C.: Office of Air Force History, Headquarters, United States Air Force, 1979).

Linda R. Robertson, *The Dream of Civilized Warfare: World War I Flying Aces and the American Imagination* (Minneapolis: University of Minnesota Press, 2003).

James J. Cooke, *The U.S. Air Service in the Great War, 1917-1919* (Westport, Connecticut: Praeger, 1996).

Duncan's War Record

National Archives, Communication from National Archives and Records Administration, National Personnel Records Center, Military Personnel Records, National Archives form 13164 (Rec. 02-02), January 26, 2007, in answer to a request for Leland Lavoy Duncan's war record (World War I).

Duncan's draft registration card: Registration Location: *Los Angeles County, California*; Roll 1531198; Draft Board: 7.

"Honorable Discharge from The United States Army," Box 8, Folder 30, Rin Tin Tin Collection, Riverside, California, Local History Resource Center.

Duncan's Stay in the Orphanage

Orphanage, Box 1, Folder 9, A 719 599; Fred Finch, Box 3, 1930-1939, Correspondence B; Box 7, Folders 3, 9-11, Rin-Tin-Tin Collection, Riverside, California, Local History Resource Center.

Reginald Ray and Grace Dell Stuart, *A History of the Fred Finch Children's Home: Oldest Methodist Home for Children in California, 1891-1955* (Oakland, California: Fred Finch Children's Home, 1955).

Timothy A. Hacsi, *Second Home: Orphan Asylums and Poor Families in America* (Cambridge, Massachusetts; London, England, 1997).

Genealogical Records of the Duncan and Ellis Families

Federal census and voter registration records at http://www.ancestry.com.

Genealogical records at http://www.rootsweb.com.

Fallbrook Historical Society (California).

History of Tulare County

Memorial and Biographical History of the Counties of Fresno, Tulare and Kern, California Chicago, The Lewis Publishing Company, 1892. http://www.calarchives4u.com/history/tulare/1892-206.htm.

Jeff Edwards and the Tule River Historical Society, *100 Year History of the Tule River Mountain Country* (Fresno, California: Panorama West Books, 1986).

Eugene L. Menefee and Fred A. Dodge, *History of Tulare and Kings Counties, California History* (Los Angeles, California: Historical Record Company, 1913), http://www.calarchives4u.com/history/tulare/tul1913-ch7.htm.

War Dogs

"The Sagacity and Courage of Dogs: Instances of the Remarkable Intelligence and Unselfish Devotion of Man's Best Friend Among the Dumb Animals," *The National Geographic Magazine*, March 1919.

Rin-Tin-Tin and Duncan After the Great War

"Animal Stars in the Movies," *The Literary Digest*, June 20, 1925.

Life, October 20, 1958.

Time, April 14, 1930.

Letter of May 1, 1930, from the General Publicity Department, Warner Brothers, Re: Rin Tin Tin Flight to Rochester, Releases – Press, etc., Box 4, Rin Tin Tin Collection, Riverside, California, Local History Resource Center.

2 Duncan, The Not-So-Obscure

Lee Duncan's Story As He Told It

Lee Duncan, *Mr Duncan's Notes*, unpublished manuscript, Box 8, Folders 31-33 (June 21, 1933), Rin Tin Tin Collection, Riverside, California, Local History Resource Center.

James W. English, *The Rin Tin Tin Story* (New York: Dodd, Mead & Company, 1949).

Sources

Records for the Duncans, Ellises, and Charlotte Anderson
Federal census and voter registration records at http://www.ancestry.com.
Genealogical records at http://www.rootsweb.com.
Fallbrook Historical Society (California).
Glendale City Directory, courtesy of George Ellison, Special Collections, Glendale Public Library.

History of Tulare County
Jeff Edwards and the Tule River Historical Society, *100 Year History of the Tule River Mountain Country* (Fresno, California: Panorama West Books, 1986).
Memorial and Biographical History of the Counties of Fresno, Tulare and Kern, California (Chicago, The Lewis Publishing Company, 1892)
Eugene L. Menefee and Fred A. Dodge, *History of Tulare and Kings Counties, California* (Historic Record Company: Los Angeles, California, 1913).

Memoirs of Duncan and Ellis Relatives
George W. Duncan, "Memoirs," *Los Tulares*, Issue 130, March, 1981, unpaged; Issue 131, June 1981.
William Tilden Duncan, "Yokohl Valley, Past and Present," "Ben Mayfield as I Knew Him," "Hunter Jim," *Los Tulares*, Issue 122, March, 1979.
"Remembering the Past," manuscript contributed by the Fallbrook Historical Society to *Village News*, October 8, 1998. In the Ellis folder at the Fallbook Historical Society.

Kaibab
Dama Margaret Smith, *I Married a Ranger* (Stanford, California: Stanford University Press, 1930).

Dyas Sporting Goods Store
Dyas Map of California (Los Angeles: The Company, 1923?), in Special Collections at the University of California Library
Dyas Map of California (Los Angeles: The Company, 1928?), in Special Collections at the University of California Library.

Biography of Leach Cross
William Schutte, *Fighting Dentist: The Boxing Career of Dr. Leach Cross* (Fullerton, California: [s.n.], 1977).

Biographies of Eugene Pallette and Pauline Frederick

Alfred E. Twomey and Arthur F. McClure, *The Versatiles: A Study of Supporting Character Actors and Actresses in the American Motion Picture, 1930-1955* (South Brunswick and New York: A.S. Barnes and Company, 1969).

David Robinson, *Hollywood in the Twenties* (London: A. Zwemmer, Limited; New York: A.S. Barnes & Company, 1968).

Larry Langman, *American Film Cycles: The Silent Era* (Westport, Connecticut, London: Greenwood Press, 1998).

Muriel Elwood, *Pauline Frederick: On and Off the Stage* (Chicago: A. Kroch, 1940).

Duncan's Marriage to Charlotte Anderson

Los Angeles Superior Court, Case No. D-45, 273, Final Judgment of Divorce, June 4, 1928. This document mentions that the interlocutory judgment was entered on June 1, 1927.

The Llewellen Story

Jean Claude Schmitt, *The Holy Greyhound: Guinefort, healer of children since the thirteenth century* (Cambridge; New York: Cambridge University Press; Paris, Edition de la maison des sciences de l'homme, 1983).

Edmund Shorthouse, "Anger," *A Present for Youths and Young Men, Book I* (Privately printed: 1891). Digitized by the New York Public Library.

J. Earl Clauson, *The Dog's Book of Verse* (Boston: Small, Maynard, & Company, 1916).

Warner Bros.

Neal Gabler, *An Empire of Their Own: How the Jews Invented Hollywood* (New York: Crown Publishers, 1988) with Leo Rosten interview, Columbia University Oral History Collection, p. 2227.

Charles Higham, *Warner Brothers* (New York: Charles Scribner's Sons, 1975).

Jeanine Basinger, *Silent Stars* (New York: Alfred A. Knopf, 2000).

Sources

3 The Right Dog at the Right Time

Graphs
 Internet Movie Database, http://www.imdb.com.
 American Film Institute catalog at http://www.afi.com.
 Newspaper Archive, www.newspaperarchive.com.

Dogs in Stage Plays and Vaudeville
 Jack London, *Michael, Brother of Jerry*,
http://www.scribd.com/doc/1452/Michael-Brother-of-Jerry-By-Jack-London
 http://memory.loc.gov/.

General Works on Dog Breeds and the History of Dogs
 Mark Derr, *A Dog's History of America: How Our Best Friend Explored, Conquered, and Settled a Continent* (New York: North Point Press, 2004).
 Malcolm B. Willis, *The German Shepherd Dog: Its History, Development and Genetics* (New York: Arco Publishing Company, 1977).
 Farmer's Bulletin No. 1491, *Breeds of Dogs* (Washington, D.C.: U.S. Department of Agriculture, February, 1927).
 Walter E. Mason, *Dogs of All Nations* (San Francisco: H. Judd, 1915).
 Vinton P. Breese, "Dog Stars: The German Shepherd," *Country Life and the Sportsman*, August, 1938.
 "Other 5 – No Title" ("The Kennel Mart"), *Forest and Stream: A Journal of Outdoor Life, Travel, Nature Study, Shooting, Yachting, Fishing*, March, 1918.
 "Advertisement 20," *The Independent . . .Devoted to the Consideration of Politics, Social and Economic Tendencies, History, Literature, and the Arts*, January 5, 1918.
 Robert S. Lemmon, "Some Dogs for the Large Estate," *House and Garden*, January, 1925.

Dog Training
 Hans Tossutti, *Companion Dog Training: A Practical Manual on Systematic Obedience; Dog Training in Word and Picture* (New York: Orange Judd, 1942*)*

Child Raising in the 1920s
Viviana A. Zelizer, *Pricing the Priceless Child: The Changing Social Value of Children* (New York: Basic Books, 1985).

War Dogs and Police Dogs
Ernest Harold Baynes, "Mankind's Best Friend, Companion of His Solitude, Advance Guard on the Hunt, and Ally of the Trenches," *The National Geographic Magazine*, March 1919.

The Sagacity and Courage of Dogs: Instances of the Remarkable Intelligence and Unselfish Devotion of Man's Best Friend Among the Dumb Animals," *The National Geographic Magazine*, March 1919.

Louis Agassiz Fuertes and Ernest Harold Baynes, "Our Common Dogs," *The National Geographic Magazine*, March 1919.

Gustave Abel, "Dogs as Policemen," *The Independent. . .Devoted to the Consideration of Politics, Social and Economic Tendencies, History, Literature, and the Arts,* June 27, 1907.

World War I in Movies
Leslie Midkiff DeBauche, *Reel Patriotism: The Movies and World War I* (Madison, Wisconsin: University of Wisconsin Press, 1997).

Michael T. Isenberg, "The Great War Viewed from the Twenties: *The Big Parade,*" in Peter C. Rollins and John E. O'Connor (eds.), *Hollywood's World War I: Motion Picture Images* (Bowling Green, Ohio: Bowling Green State University Popular Press, 1997).

General Movie History
J.J. Phelan, *Motion Pictures As a Phase of Commercialized Amusement in Toledo, Ohio.* Social Survey Series III (Toledo: Little Book Press, 1919).

Richard Koszarski, *An Evening's Entertainment: The Age of the Silent Feature Picture: 1915-1928.* Volume 3 in Charles Harpole, General Editor, *History of the American Cinema* (New York: Charles Scribner's Sons, 1990).

Kenneth W. Payne, "Junior Movies: The Producer's Attempt to Meet a Juvenile Public," *McClure's Magazine,* September, 1925.

Janine Basinger, *Silent Stars* (Middletown, Connecticut: Wesleyan University Press, 2000).

Sources

Duncan's Divorce

Los Angeles Superior Court, Case No. D-45, 273, Final Judgment of Divorce, June 4, 1928. This document mentions that the interlocutory judgment was entered on June 1, 1927.

Rin-Tin-Tin As a Family Man

"Now Rin-Tin-Tin Let's [sic] the 'Boys' Do the Work," *The Reel Journal*, January 10, 1925.

"The Rin Tin Tins" [Illustration], *Motion Picture Magazine*, June 1927, Margaret Herrick Library.

Little Folks Story of Rin-Tin-Tin, (Racine, Wisconsin: Whitman Publishing Company, 1927).

Canine Movie Stars

Catherine Brody, "Dog Stars and Horse Heroes," *The Saturday Evening Post*, February 14, 1925.

Laurence Trimble, "Teaching a Dog to Act," *The New York Times*, May 18, 1924.

Laurence Trimble, "Motion Picture Dogs and Others," *The Saturday Evening Post*, February 2, 1929.

4 The Dog of War, The Dog of the West

Lee Duncan and Rin-Tin-Tin

Lee Duncan, *Mr Duncan's Notes*, unpublished manuscript, Box 8, Folders 31-33 (June 21, 1933), Rin Tin Tin Collection, Riverside, California, Local History Resource Center.

World War I

Michael T. Isenberg, "The Great War Viewed from the Twenties: *The Big Parade*," and James M. Welsh, "The Great War and the War Film as Genre: *Hearts of the World* and *What Price Glory?*" in Peter C. Rollins and John E. O'Connor (eds.), *Hollywood's World War I: Motion Picture Images* (Bowling Green, Ohio: Bowling Green State University Popular Press, 1997).

Leslie Midkiff DeBauche, "The United States Film Industry and World War I," in Michael Paris, *The First World War and Popular Cinema: 1914 to the Present* (New Brunswick, New Jersey, Rutgers University Press, 2000).

Leslie Midkiff DeBauche, *Reel Patriotism: The Movies and World War I* (Madison, Wisconsin: University of Wisconsin Press, 1997).

Rin-Tin-Tin and His Movies

"A Dog We Like: Rin-Tin-Tin is a versatile beast," *The Youth's Companion (1827-1929)*, February 1928.

"Dog of the Regiment," *Variety*, November 9, 1927, production file for *A Dog of the Regiment*, Margaret Herrick Library.

Quin Martin, "The Dog Star Shines 'In Person,'" *The Literary Digest*, May 1, 1926).

"Hell's River," *Motion Picture News*, April 15, 1922, from production file for "Hell's River," Margaret Herrick Library.

"While London Sleeps," *Variety*, December 22, 1926, from production files for *Whille London Sleeps*, Margaret Herrick Library.

Warner Bros.

Ted Sennett, *Warner Brothers Presents: The most exciting years – from The Jazz Singer to White Heat* (New Rochelle, New York: Arlington House, 1971).

Aristocracy of Dogs

Jack London, *Jerry of the Islands* (London: T. Werner Laurie Ltd., 1937 [1915]), accessed as ebook, search for "no common bush-dog, but a blooded."

Dogs and Wolves

Valerie M. Fogleman, "American Attitudes Towards Wolves: A History of Misperception," *Environmental Review*, (Spring, 1989).

Heidi G. Parker, Lisa V. Kim, Nathan B. Sutter, Scott Carlson, Travis D. Lorentzen, Tiffany B. Malek, Gary S. Johnson, Hawkins B. DeFrance, Elaine A. Ostrander, Leonid Kruglyak, "Genetic Structure of the Purebred Domestic Dog," *Science*, May 21, 2004.

Westerns

Scott Simmons, *The Invention of the Western Film: A Cultural History of the Genre's First Half-Century* (New York and Cambridge: Cambridge University Press, 2003).

Deborah A. Carmichael (ed.), *The Landscape of Hollywood Westerns:*

Sources

Ecocriticism in an American Film Genre (Salt Lake City: The University of Utah Press, 2006).

West As Frontier

Francis Parkman, *France and England in North America* (Boston: Little, Brown and company, 1890).

Theodore Roosevelt, *The Winning of the West* (New York : G.P. Putnam's Sons, 1894).

Frederick Jackson Turner, *Significance of the Frontier in American History* (Madison, Wisconsin: State Historical Society of Wisconsin, 1894).

5 The Limitations of a Dog Star

Lee Duncan's Observations

Lee Duncan, *Mr Duncan's Notes*, unpublished manuscript, Box 8, Folders 31-33 (June 21, 1933), Rin Tin Tin Collection, Riverside, California, Local History Resource Center.

James W. English, *The Rin Tin Tin Story* (New York: Dodd, Mead & Company, 1949).

Manhood

Michael Kimmel, *Manhood in America: A Cultural History* (New York: The Free Press, 1991).

Reviews in Trade Journals

Boxoffice

"Frank E. Savage, a Warner Showman Was an Amusing Industry Raconteur," December 23, 1963.

Motion Picture Times

Harry Burns, "Talk, Jus' Talk, about 'Talkies' in Hollywood," September 22, 1928.

"The Picture Guide, Thumbnail Reviews of Current Releases," March 11, 1930; March 18, 1930; April 1, 1930; April 8, 1930.

Motion Picture News

"Hell's River," April 15, 1922.

Paul Thompson, "While London Sleeps, Showing that Rin-Tin-Tin Does Not."

The Reel Journal
    "Warners to Make 40 for Season 1925-1926," May 2, 1925.
    "Still, Please," October 3, 1925.

Popular Magazine Articles about Rin-Tin-Tin
Time
    "The New Pictures," January 5, 1925.
The Literary Digest
    Quin Martin, "The Dog Star Shines 'In Person,'" May 1, 1926).

Dog Training
Max von Stephanitz, *The German Shepherd Dog in Word and Picture* (Jena, Germany: Anton Kämpfe, 1925; in German, 1905).
    Movietone News (1932):
http://www.youtube.com/watch?v=DD9C6DqQ2xY.

Western Movies
George N. Fenin and William K. Everson, *The Western: from silents to cinerama* (New York: Orion Press, 1962).
    David Lusted, *The Western* (Harlow, England: Pearson Longman, 2003).
    Jon Tuska, *Filming of the West* (London: Robert Hale Ltd, 1978).

Warner Bros.
Rudy Behlmer, *Inside Warner Bros.* (New York: Viking, 1987).

6 Rin-Tin-Tin, the Magic Actor

Movie Making
George N. Fenin and William K. Everson, *The Western: from silents to cinerama* (New York: Orion Press, 1962).
    Jack Warner, *My First Hundred Years in Hollywood* (New York: Random House, 1965).
    Richard Koszarski, *An Evening's Entertainment: The Age of the Silent Feature Picture 1915-1928* (New York: Charles Scribner's Sons, 1990),Volume 3 in

Sources

Charles Harpole, General Editor, *History of the American Cinema*.

Jon Tuska, *The Vanishing Legion: A History of Mascot Pictures 1927-1935* (Jefferson, North Carolina, and London: McFarland & Company, Publishers, 1982).

Dog Training

Reginald Arundel, *Police Dogs and Their Training* (London: Police Review Publishing Company, 1924).

Henry W. Diederich and H. Albert Johnson, *Police and Work Dogs in Europe* (Washington: United States Government Printing Office, 1909).

Albert Frederick Hochwalt, *The Working Dog and His Education. A Treatise on the Training of Pointers, Setters, Foxhounds, Beagles, Airedales, Spaniels, and Police Dogs.* (Cincinnati: Sportsmen's Review Publishing Company, 1921, 1925).

Theo. F. Jager, *Scout, Red Cross and Army Dogs: A Historical Sketch of Dogs in the Great War and a Training Guide for the Rank and File of the United States Army.* (Rochester, New York: Arrow Printing Company, Corp., 1917).

Fred Kollet, *Training the Shepherd Dog* (Chicago: Judy Publishing Company, 1924).

Robert S. Lemmon, *Training the Dog* (New York: McBride, Nast & Company, 1914).

Max von Stephanitz, *Schooling and Training the Shepherd Dog: Extracts from Von Stephanitz "Der Deutsche Schaferhund in Word und Bild"* (New York: Shepherd Dog Club of America, 1922).

Max von Stephanitz, *The German Shepherd Dog in Word and Picture* (Jena, Germany: Anton Kämpfe, 1925; in German, 1905). This was also available from *Forest and Stream; A Journal of Outdoor Life, Travel, Nature Study, Shooting, Yachting, Fishing* in 1923.

Anne B. Tracy (translator) *Training the Sanitary Service Dog* (Oldenberg: Deutsche Verein fur Sanitats Hunde, no date), Box 2, Rin Tin Tin Collection, Riverside, California, Local History Resource Center.

"Importing German Police Dogs," *Forest and Stream: A Journal of Outdoor Life, Travel, Nature Study, Shooting, Yachting, Fishing*, May 31, 1913.

Andrew R. Boone, Animal Movie Actors Trained by Strange Tricks, *Popular Science Monthly*, September, 1933.

Rin-Tin-Tin and His Movies

Find Your Man, *Variety*, October 8, 1924.

John B. Kennedy, Trailing the Dog Star, *Collier's, The National Weekly*, August 21, 1926.

Quin Martin, "The Dog Star Shines in 'Person,'" *The Literary Digest* 89, May 1, 1926.

"'The Man Hunter,' (Warner Bros. Vitaphone)," *The Billboard*, April 12, 1930. Production File, Margaret Herrick Library.

Paul Thompson, "While London Sleeps, Showing that Rin-Tin-Tin Does Not," *Motion Picture News*, undated.

7 Rin-Tin-Tin Carries Fire

Duncan and Rin-Tin-Tin

Lee Duncan, *Mr Duncan's Notes*, unpublished manuscript, Box 8, Folders 31-33 (June 21, 1933), Rin Tin Tin Collection, Riverside, California, Local History Resource Center.

James W. English, *The Rin Tin Tin Story* (New York: Dodd, Mead & Company, 1949).

Anthony Cassa, "Ernst [Lubitsch], John [Barrymore] and Rin Tin Tin. They were called Warner Bros. 'Unholy Three,'" *Hollywood Studio Magazine*, June 1981. Margaret Herrick Library.

John B. Kennedy, "Trailing the Dog Star," *Collier's, The National Weekly*, August 21, 1926.

Quin Martin, "The Dog Star Shines 'In Person,'" *The Literary Digest* 8, May 1, 1926.

Baroness Ravensdale, "The Hollywood Rhythm," from Baroness Ravensdale, *In Many Rhythms* (1953), in Christopher Silvester (editor), *The Grove Book of Hollywood* (New York: Grove Press, 1998).

"Lighthouse by the Sea," *Variety*, December 31, 1924.

"Rin-Tin-Tin Here, Famous Dog Makes Appearances," *Exhibitors' Forum*, April 28, 1930.

Culture of the 1920s

Lynn Dumenil, *The Modern Temper: American Culture and Society in the 1920s* (New York: Hill and Wang), 1995.

Sources

Dog Training Manuals (1907-1930)

Ed. F. Haberlein, *The Amateur Trainer: Force System without the Whip*. (McPherson, Kansas: Press of Ed. Haberlein, Jr., 1907).

Robert S. Lemmon, *Training the Dog* (New York: McBride, Nast & Company, 1914).

Theo. F. Jager, *Scout, Red Cross and Army Dogs: A Historical Sketch of Dogs in the Great War and a Training Guide for the Rank and File of the United States Army*. (Rochester, New York: Arrow Printing Company, Corp., 1917).

Albert Frederick Hochwalt, *The Working Dog and His Education. A Treatise on the Training of Pointers, Setters, Foxhounds, Beagles, Airedales, Spaniels, and Police Dogs* (Cincinnati: Sportsmen's Review Publishing Company, 1921).

Fred Kollet, *Training the Shepherd Dog* (Chicago: Judy Publishing Company, Publishers of Dog World, 1924).

Max von Stephanitz, *The German Shepherd Dog in Word and Picture* (Jena, Germany: Anton Kämpfe, 1925; in German, 1905).

Lieut.-Col E.H. Richardson, *Watch-Dogs: Their Training and Management* (Boston and New York: Houghton-Mifflin Company, 1925).

Anne B. Tracy (translator) *Training the Sanitary Service Dog* (Oldenberg: Deutsche Verein fur Sanitats Hunde, no date), Box 2, Rin Tin Tin Collection, Riverside, California, Local History Resource Center.

Robert Gersbach, *The Police Dog in Word and Picture*; *A Complete History of Police Dogs. . .; the trainer's hand-book, the breeder's guide, the officer's vade mecum* (Canandaigua, New York: T.F. Jager and A.E. Deming, 1910)

Reginald Arundel, *Police Dogs and Their Training*. (London: "Police review" Publishing Company, 1920s).

Henry W. Diederich and H. Albert Johnson, *Police and Work Dogs in Europe* (Washington: United States Government Printing Office, 1909).

"The Odyssey of a Devoted Dog" [interview with Albert Payson Terhune], *The Literary Digest*, December 25, 1920.

Child Training in the 1920s

"Are You Training Your Child to Be Happy?" Lesson Material in Child Management, Children's Bureau Publication No. 202 (Washington, D.C.: United States Government Printing Office, 1930)
http://www.mchlibrary.info/history/chbu/20851.PDF.

1920s and 1930s Movies

Charles Higham, *Warner Brothers* (New York: Charles Scribner's Sons, 1975).

Jon Tuska, *Filming of the West* (London: Robert Hale Ltd, 1978).

Jon Tuska, *The Vanishing Legion: A History of Mascot Pictures 1927-1935* (Jefferson, North Carolina, and London: McFarland & Company, Publishers, 1982).

Training Dogs for the Movies

"How Animals Are Turned into Stars for Movies," *Popular Mechanics Magazine, written so you can understand it,* June, 1924.

Andrew R. Boone, "Animal Movie Actors Trained by Strange Tricks," *Popular Science Monthly*, September, 1933.

Catherine Brody, "Dog Stars and Horse Heroes, *The Saturday Evening Post*, February 14, 1925.

"The Odyssey of a Devoted Dog" [interview with Albert Payson Terhune], *The Literary Digest*, December 25, 1920.

Helen Christine Bennett, "They Like the Life," *Collier's*, September 24, 1921.

Animal Cruelty

"Cruelty Charged in Training Trick Animals for Stage and Movies," *The Literary Digest*, September 25, 1920.

Diane L. Beers, *For the Prevention of Cruelty: The History and Legacy of Animal Rights Activism in the United States* (Athens, Ohio: Swallow Press/Ohio University Press, 2006).

Keith Thomas, *Man and the Natural World: Changing Attitudes in England, 1500-1800* (New York, Oxford: Oxford University Press, 1983).

"Ignorance," *Life (1883-1936)*, May 15, 1919.

"Example," *Life (1883-1936)*, May 13, 1920.

8 Rin-Tin-Tin's Last Years and Junior's Career

Jon Tuska, *The Vanishing Legion: A History of Mascot Pictures 1927-1935* (Jefferson, North Carolina, and London: McFarland & Company, Publishers, 1982).

Serial Plays, Perennial Action Films Now in the First Run Class," *The Reel Journal*, June 16, 1931.

Rin-Tin-Tin Here, Famous Dog Makes Appearances," *Exhibitors' Forum*, April 28, 1930.

"Four from Mascot," *Exhibitors' Forum*, May 19, 1931.

"Four for Rin-Tin-Tin," *New England Film News*, May 26, 1932.

"Mascot Bookings: Increase; Serials Playing Key Situations," *New England Film News*, February 11, 1932.

Cass Warner Sperling and Cork Miller with Jack Warner Jr., *Hollywood Be Thy Name" The Warner Brothers Story* (Lexington, Kentucky: The University Press of Kentucky, 1998).

"Rin Tin Tin, World's Most Famous Dog, Can Now Be Seen in 'It's Showtime,'" Production File for *It's Showtime*, Margaret Herrick Library.

"Four Rin-Tin-Tin Special Features," *New England Film News*, August 11, 1932.

"Pictures in the Making," *New England Film News*, September 29, 1932.

James English, *The Rin Tin Tin Story* (New York: Dodd, Mead and Company, 1949).

Filmography

The basic facts of the filmography came from two invaluable databases: www.imdb.com and www.afi.com. I wrote the plot summaries after watching the movies that were available, consulting those databases, and reading reviews from the 1920s and 1930s.

Timeline

The sources are relatively the same as the sources listed for the Preface, the first two chapters, and the last chapter.

Appendices

Appendix 1: Backgrounds of the Pilots, Observers, and Enlisted Men of the 135th Aero Squadron

Percival Gray Hart, *History of the 135th Aero Squadron: The 'Statue of Liberty' Observation Squadron in World War I* (Nashville: The Battery Press, 1990).

A Brief History of the 135th Aero Squadron (Observation) (Bordeaux: Imprimerie F. Pech & Cie, 1919).

Federal census and draft registration records at www.ancesty.com

Appendix 2: Lee Duncan's Family Trees

Federal census, voter registration, and draft records at http://www.ancestry.com.

Genealogical records at http://www.rootsweb.com.

Ellis file, Fallbrook Historical Society, Fallbrook, California.

About the Author

Ann Elwood and her dog, Louis, at the beach
(Photograph by Pat Keller of Lovepuppy).

Ann Elwood lives in Cardiff-by-the-Sea, California, with six cats, a desert tortoise, seven box turtles, and a German shepherd, Louis, who looks something like Rin Tin Tin in his soulfulness. At night she can hear the ocean when the tides are high.

When she was a child in New Jersey, her family had a shepherd dog, Mac, who died a tragic death, shot because someone thought his foaming-at-the-mouth fear of a thunderstorm meant he had rabies.

After college, she taught elementary school for a few miserable years, then moved to Camden, New Jersey and landed a job as a typist-clerk at the *Philadelpha Bulletin*. When her boss discovered she had difficulty typing up circulation figures with twelve carbons, she was fired and found another job writing copy for a paternalistic insurance company that offered a low salary and delicious free lunch. One of the typesetters had the magical ability to square up a stack of paper into a perfect cube.

Eventually she moved to a studio apartment on Irving Place in New York City, and, after a few months of writing copy for a textbook company, went on to freelance as a writer of anything anyone would pay her for. In 1967, she moved to Los Angeles, where she was advertising manager for a publishing company. Then the West Coast was a mecca for writers and adventurers. Within a couple of years, she visited a Malibu beach house, fell in love (long-distance) with Bob Dylan, met Thomas Pynchon (he wouldn't remember it), and saw *Hair*. In 1972, she returned to freelancing. The following year she moved to Cardiff and adopted her first dog as an adult – Puppy, a mixed breed who looked something like a fox. (To show you how inappropriate Puppy's name became, she'll tell you this: Puppy died at age 17.) She wrote articles for Irving Wallace and his son, David Wallichinsky (*People's Almanac* and *Book of Lists*), and did other wonderful things she won't mention here. With Carol Orsag Madigan, she wrote several non-fiction books.

A desire to delve more deeply into ideas finally drove her to graduate school in 1981. Her dissertation focused on an order of 17th and 18th century French nuns so she had to spend a happy year in France doing research. During that year, while not in the archives, she drank local wine with fellow historians and traveled the country with Puppy, who had far less trouble than she did communicating with the French.

Now, she teaches history part-time at California State University, San Marcos, spends time with Louis and the other animals, and writes the books she has always wanted to write but never had the time for.

i

Made in the USA
Lexington, KY
23 October 2011